NEGOTIATING ADULT–CHILD RELATIONSHIPS IN EARLY CHILDHOOD RESEARCH

Negotiating Adult–Child Relationships in Early Childhood Research presents a substantive critique of technicist and neoliberal approaches to ethics through an exploration of the complicated and often 'messy' situations faced in negotiating relationships in research with children. Despite growing acknowledgement of their centrality, relationships between adult researchers and very young participants have been neglected and under-theorised, and in response, this book offers a comprehensive conceptualisation of adult–child research relationships through examination of questions, including:

- How do power and inequity impact on adult–child research relationships?
- What does it mean for relationships when researchers 'intervene' in the field?
- How do bodies matter in research relationships?
- What does an emphasis on relationships with young children mean for the research process?

Drawing on data from their own research, the authors contend that relationships are part of a wider web of social relations and space–time configurations. They propose and develop a relational ethics of answerability and social justice, inspired by the work of Bakhtin and, in addition, explore the way material bodies come to matter, the ambiguity of consent in educator-research, and the risks and possibilities of research relationships. Chapters include innovative formulations of reciprocity, 'sensing practices', and political-ethical responsibility.

This book contributes to curerent debates about research with young children, offering an incisive and thorough exploration of the importance of relationships to the research process. Relevant for international audiences, this book is essential reading for early childhood students and educators, researchers, and lecturers with an interest in research with children.

Deborah Albon and **Rachel Rosen** are both Senior Lecturers in Early Childhood Studies at London Metropolitan University, UK.

NEGOTIATING ADULT–CHILD RELATIONSHIPS IN EARLY CHILDHOOD RESEARCH

Deborah Albon and Rachel Rosen

LONDON AND NEW YORK

First published 2014
by Routledge
2 Park Square, Milton Park, Abingdon, Oxon OX14 4RN

Simultaneously published in the USA and Canada
by Routledge
711 Third Avenue, New York, NY 10017

Routledge is an imprint of the Taylor & Francis Group, an informa business

© 2014 Deborah Albon and Rachel Rosen

The right of Deborah Albon and Rachel Rosen to be identified as authors of this work has been asserted by them in accordance with sections 77 and 78 of the Copyright, Designs and Patents Act 1988.

All rights reserved. No part of this book may be reprinted or reproduced or utilised in any form or by any electronic, mechanical, or other means, now known or hereafter invented, including photocopying and recording, or in any information storage or retrieval system, without permission in writing from the publishers.

Trademark notice: Product or corporate names may be trademarks or registered trademarks, and are used only for identification and explanation without intent to infringe.

British Library Cataloguing in Publication Data
A catalogue record for this book is available from the British Library

Library of Congress Cataloging in Publication Data
Albon, Deborah, author.
  Negotiating adult-child relationships in early childhood research/
authored by Deborah Albon and Rachel Rosen.
  pages cm
  Includes index.
  1. Child development—Research. 2. Early childhood education—
Research. 3. Children and adults. I. Rosen, Rachel, author. II. Title.
  HQ767.85.A43 2013
  305.23072—dc23   2013004102

ISBN: 978-0-415-63327-7 (hbk)
ISBN: 978-0-415-63331-4 (pbk)
ISBN: 978-0-203-09512-6 (ebk)

Typeset in Bembo and Stone Sans
by Florence Production Ltd, Stoodleigh, Devon, UK

Printed and bound in Great Britain by
TJ International Ltd, Padstow, Cornwall

CONTENTS

Acknowledgements		vi
1	Considering adult–child relationships in research	1
2	The spaces and places of research relationships	18
3	Children and adults, participants and researchers: What do we make of each other?	34
4	A web of relationships: Encounters between researchers, educators, and children	51
5	The educator as researcher: Implications for research relationships	67
6	Generating data, generating relationships: From observation to *sensing practices*	84
7	'Civilising' children, confronting inequalities: Navigating narratives of the 'good researcher'	101
8	Building common cause with children: Reciprocity in the research process	118
References		135
Index		151

ACKNOWLEDGEMENTS

We would like to thank the children, educators, families/carers, and early childhood students in Canada and England who have committed time, energy, and ideas to our research. Their contributions and indeed willingness to enter into research relationships with us have made this book possible.

In a book all about relationships, we would be remiss not to acknowledge our partners: Dave Albon and Britt Permien and thank them for not only 'putting up' with our complete immersion in the process of writing this book together, but for the care and inspiration they have offered us throughout. They have not been afraid to tell us when our ideas were 'way out there' and have kept our feet firmly planted on the ground. They have encouraged us to keep writing and have had unfailing faith in us – insisting that we had something important to offer. And, of course, they have made sure that we were fed, clothed, and well-rested in moments when we couldn't imagine being separated from our computers!

1

CONSIDERING ADULT–CHILD RELATIONSHIPS IN RESEARCH

'You be the momma dragon. We'll be the babies,' Zahrah said firmly to me on one of my early days of research, launching a series of dragon adventures involving us and five other children. After some time, the baby dragons began to cry: 'We're hungry!' Zahrah suggested: 'Let's go eat the children!' Despite the baby dragons' best efforts, the other children in the nursery wanted no part in being the fodder for the dragon's feast. Thinking quickly, Zahrah ran inside and got a doll: 'Here's a baby for us to eat. Let's cook it!'

She began to roast the 'baby' over a 'fire'. But Raeni – one of the other baby dragons – started to whimper, this time for 'real': 'No, that's my baby. Give her to me!' Zahrah was not to be swayed: 'We have to! Or else we'll be hungry!' I stood close by listening, uncertain how to respond in my 'researcher' role and desperately nervous about the way the observing educators would interpret this scene. The other baby dragons had no such concerns. They tucked into the meal, pulling at the 'baby' with their hands and devouring it ravenously. Waiting until they were satiated, Raeni grabbed the 'baby' and held it tightly in her arms for the rest of the afternoon.

When I mentioned this play to the educators later, one commented: 'That's my Raeni. She really cares about other people.'

(Rachel Rosen, Taboo play)

Children – and their educators – are required to wear a 'colour badge' (red, blue or green) identified with their 'snack group' in the nursery class. On previous occasions of observing, I found myself pulling my cardigan across my chest as the children checked whether everyone at the table was wearing the 'correct' colour badge. I was the only person – adult or child – who did not wear a badge.

Today I 'came clean' about my lack of a badge and my problem: a coloured badge would 'disqualify' me from observing at all the tables. On hearing my concern, the children immediately began thinking of ways around this situation. Ideas included having a special badge of a different colour or having three badges enabling me to change according to the group I would be observing. Notwithstanding their considerateness, all the children were *adamant* that a badge of some description was necessary.

(Deb Albon, Food events: Setting one)

While these two fieldnotes offer examples from very different studies – the former from Rachel's research into children's imaginative play about death and violence and the latter from Deb's research on food events in early childhood settings[1] – they raise a series of related critical questions for researchers of childhood. What issues must be considered when adult-researchers negotiate relationships with child-participants (for example generationing, power, institutional authority, and political-ethical concerns)? How do relationships with individuals or groups of people (such as children) interplay with relationships with others (such as educators)?[2] What does it mean for researchers to navigate relationships within the complex and dynamic social orders of early childhood settings? In what ways are research relationships embodied and affective and how does this impact on their negotiation? What does it mean for relationships when researchers 'intervene' in the field? And more generally, what does an emphasis on relationship mean for the research process?

Dialoguing about questions such as these is what led us to write this book. For, despite the growing body of work acknowledging the *centrality* of relationships in early childhood (for example, see Alanen and Mayall, 2001; Dahlberg and Moss, 2005) and the fundamental impact of research relationships on the quality of a research project (Burgess, 1989; Christensen and James, 2008; Coffey, 1999), relationships between adult-researchers and young participants have, as of yet, not been examined comprehensively in one volume.

This is not to say that such issues have been entirely ignored, however. Research studies and methodological texts either implicitly or explicitly highlight the importance of relations between researchers and participants in terms of quality of data and potential for analysis (e.g. Hammersley and Atkinson, 2007). Beyond the research process proper, Coffey (1999) suggests that research relationships are *key* factors shaping the way researchers and participants make sense of and remember research projects. But, the majority of this theorising – including within childhood studies literature – focuses on research relationships with adults or older children. In this book, we will be considering research relationships with *very* young children, including toddlers and infants.

Given the importance of relationships to research, a number of texts do take up *specific* aspects of adult-child research relationships in early childhood such as entry to a setting or peer groups, consent, and acceptance (e.g. Corsaro and Molinari, 2008); confidentiality (e.g. Dockett, Einarsdottir, and Perry, 2009); reciprocity and commitment (e.g. Warming, 2005); and status, positionality, and power (Connolly, 2008; Jipson and Jipson, 2005; Mayall, 2008). However, as we will argue in this book, relationship negotiation cannot be reduced to specific activities or de-contextualised processes. As the examples we began the chapter with suggest, adult–child research relationships are 'messy' and complex: What did Rachel communicate to the child-participants when she did not respond as Raeni began to cry? What were the impacts – on the child-participants, the educators, and Rachel herself – of her recital of the play moment to educators later? While Deb – as a high status adult in the setting – could have maintained her observational position without 'confessing' to the lack of a coloured badge, what were the implications of her decision to do otherwise? It is these 'grey areas' (Burgess, 1989: 61) of everyday research that necessitate difficult political-ethical decisions that have significant implications for participants, researchers, and research relationships. As such, this book aims to build on existing texts, seeking to address the gap in conceptualising relationships between adult-researchers and young children.

Limitations in the existing literature are indicative of a profound schism, one that exists between meanings – about adult–child relations – and the material world in which relational practices take place. As Bernstein (2000: 30) notes, when there is an indirect relationship between meaning and material phenomena, this creates a potential 'site for the unthinkable, the site of the impossible, and this site can clearly be both beneficial and dangerous at the same time'. Throughout this book, we will ask ourselves and the reader to keep hold of this understanding in order to consider what it might mean to conceptualise the negotiation of research relationships as simultaneously full of both contingent risk and great potential, existing as a 'crucial site of the *yet to be thought*' (Bernstein, 2000: 30).

Situating the project

This book arose from a series of conversations we had after meeting as lecturers in an Early Childhood Studies programme in London. In discussing the various research projects we have been involved in, we quickly realised that although our independent research had been about very different themes, we shared many common interests in the social studies of childhood and research with children. We were grappling with many similar questions about the ethical, political, and theoretical dilemmas involved in conducting research with young children. We found that bringing our different research projects into conversation with one another prompted new ways of examining such quandaries and we identified that the way in which we conceptualise and negotiate research relationships was at the heart of these dilemmas.

In this book, we continue and deepen this dialogue, drawing particularly on our doctoral research, the projects that 'generated' (Mason, 2002) the moments highlighted at the beginning of the chapter. The 'baby'-eating dragons were part of Rachel's research into children's imaginative play about themes of death and violence (hereafter referred to as 'Taboo play'). Rachel's research was inspired by her experiences as an early childhood educator and lecturer in which she encountered numerous debates among families, educators, students, and children about the place of death and violence play in early childhood settings. This has been a contentious issue in early years practice and research (Holland, 2003), at very least in the contemporary period in the English-speaking 'First World/North'.[3] Drawing on Mary Douglas' (2002) anthropological work, Rachel argues that such play is often viewed as 'matter out of place' or 'taboo' in the world of early childhood with its emphasis on 'civilising', control and 'human capital' development (Dahlberg, Moss, and Pence, 2007). However, this type of play has rarely been studied from children's perspectives – a gap Rachel's ethnographic study sought to address. Her research investigated the features of death and violence play in the setting – such as the symbols, material resources, ideologies, modalities, geographies, and temporality involved in the play; symbolic (mis)identification (Althusser, 1971; Žižek, 2000) with characters and themes through the embodied nature of the play; and how value – moral and economic – becomes inscribed on bodies (cf. Skeggs, 2004) as children interpret, reframe, resist, and/or transform inequities in this play.

Rachel's doctoral research began in 2010 and data generation carried on until 2012, with data analysis and writing continuing concurrently with publication of this book. Her research involved spending one day a week in an early childhood setting in West London. As the dragon story suggests, Rachel participated as a co-player with children, to a degree following Corsaro's (1985) ethnographic work within children's peer cultures and Edmiston's (2008) research with his son. Given the controversial status of this play, as well as generational and other inequities, Rachel's faced numerous dilemmas in negotiating relationships with both children and adults in the setting. In the case of the dragon story, Rachel became increasingly apprehensive about the practice of sharing stories with educators about children's play, feeling it violated her ethical obligations of confidentiality to the child-participants, as well as contributed to narrow categorisations of children – for example as 'caring' or not – and surveillance of their practices, issues that we take up in detail in Chapter 6. Rachel's ethnography also involved informal ethnographic interviews throughout the project and more formal semi-structured, activity-based interviews; for example, revisiting videotaped play episodes.

While Rachel's research focused on informal spaces and often 'hidden' aspects of children's play in early childhood settings, Deb's research (hereafter referred to as 'Food events')[4] set out to explore an aspect of early childhood practice that has been subject to a 'dizzying whirl of initiatives' (Valentine, 2005: 209): food and eating. Deb's focus, however, was not on nutrition and the future health of children – a view of the child as 'futurity' (Jenks, 1996) and as especially malleable in relation to health interventions (Pilcher, 2007). Deb's concern was to stress a less prominent narrative at the current time: the social and cultural relationship educators and children in early childhood settings have with food (cf. Caplan, 1997;

Lupton, 1996). This area is significant as food events are a prime vehicle for the 'transmission and "imbibing" of social and cultural knowledge' (Golden, 2005: 182), and are potential sites of conflict in which power relations between adults and children are constructed and played out (Grieshaber, 2004). Food events also provide a 'rhythm' to the day (Viruru, 2001), notably in full-day care, as well as being markers of special occasions. Despite this, food events are occasions that are so commonplace they are in danger of falling beneath the radar of educators. Thus, Deb drew, in part, on post-structuralist theorising in order to trouble taken-for-granted 'truths' about this aspect of early childhood practice (cf. Tobin, 1997a).

Between 2006 and 2010, Deb spent one day a week in one of four early childhood settings in southeast England as a participant observer in food events such as formally organised celebrations and more commonplace meal and snack times – apparent in the story of the 'colour badges' that began this chapter. She also observed and participated in children's imaginative play about food themes to gain an insight into food and drink practices, given that play is a 'cultural reality' not a *separate* sphere of childhood unrelated to 'real' life (Edmiston, 2008: 6) and that, through play, children learn to 'do' culture as well as *create* culture as social actors (James, Jenks, and Prout, 1998). Deb engaged in extensive dialoguing with educators throughout the study as well as carrying out more formal interviews towards the end of her time in each setting.

Deb's thesis emphasised, through the lens of food events, how early childhood practices are co-constructed between children and educators through the negotiation of 'rules' in relation to food events as well as playful resistance to these 'rules', which Deb likened to Bakhtinian (1984b: 252) notions of the carnivalesque and the parodying of all that is 'finished and polished'. Deb's conclusion stresses the importance of spontaneity and playfulness in early childhood practice – sometimes lacking in relation to food events – arguing that early childhood education and care (ECEC) is in danger of becoming overly future centred and joyless if it does not attend to being 'in the moment' with children (Albon, 2010). These concerns were mirrored in her reflections on the research process: for instance, how should we negotiate consent *in particular moments* in ways that acknowledge children as social actors and in ways that strive to address generational inequities, as the 'colour badges' example highlights at the beginning of the chapter?

While each of these studies investigated quite different phenomena, they share some significant commonalities that impact on the discussions and conclusions we offer in this book. A first obvious parallel is that both studies involved young children (under five years old) as active participants – an under-theorised group in terms of research relationships as we have noted. These studies were both undertaken in early childhood settings, making issues such as communication with children who do not necessarily share a common verbal language; care; and education of central importance in terms of conceptualising relationships. Further, the studies were both conducted in England and, without negating the specificities of each setting, they shared certain similarities as a result of increasingly centralist tendencies in English early years policy and curriculum. The increasingly global impact of 'First World/North' conceptions of childhood and approaches to early childhood education notwithstanding (Penn, 2011c), these research sites, however, are not offered as representative examples of *all* early childhood research contexts globally or even nationally.

Both projects also involved our ongoing embeddedness in early childhood settings. That *all* research involves relationships of some sort and – as we will argue throughout this book – time neither guarantees nor is an essential aspect of relationships, long-term involvement does make questions of relationship negotiation particularly salient and certainly difficult to avoid. A final note is that in both of these pieces of research, we were 'outsider' researchers conducting research in settings in which we had not previously spent time. While we will not leave the outsider/insider dichotomy unaddressed in this book, in Chapter 5 we will introduce two 'insider' studies that we were involved with as a way to explore the specific issues involved in negotiating relationships in educator-research.

Throughout the book, we will use critical moments from our research data to problematise dominant assumptions about research ethics and relationships and consider the implications for researchers. We use the term 'critical moments' to indicate two contradictory types of data. First, critical moments refer to incidents in research that disturb or jar the taken-for-granted; these are the moments that refuse to be forgotten. Second, we refer to those moments that are notable for quite opposite reasons: they are so mundane that we may miss their presence altogether. It is only by looking askew at these everyday moments that we can interrogate their entrenched assumptions, enabling consideration of the ways these practices are 'normalised' in the social order. It is important to note that we are *not* claiming that these critical moments are necessarily 'representative' of our research sites or will be reflective of other research settings or projects. The uniqueness of any research topic and field will complicate research relationships in diverse ways. However, we hope the discussion of these incidents will raise political and ethical dilemmas that are 'recognisable' (Youdell, 2006: 29) and, more importantly, inspire reflexivity even in diverse research contexts.

One final note in terms of situating this project is that, for both of us, being early childhood educators has had a profound impact on our interest in conducting research with children as well as the ways in which we think about negotiating research relationships. Deb began working with young children after training as a nursery nurse in 1981–1983 in Clifton, Bristol, in the UK. She worked as a maternity nanny in central London and then a nursery nurse in a school in the Inner London Education Authority and Wandsworth, London. She later trained as a teacher at the Roehampton Institute, having completed a degree as a mature student in the early 1990s and worked as a nursery teacher; foundation stage coordinator; and early years manager for a number of years – primarily in the London borough of Hounslow. Rachel's experience of working with young children in Canada has provided an interesting counterpoint in our discussions given both the similarities – such as the widespread introduction of neoliberal policies and approaches to early childhood – as well as differences between the Canadian and English early childhood systems. Rachel began as an untrained educator in after-school programmes for primary school children in 1993, moving into early childhood in 1995. She returned to higher education and trained as an early childhood educator. In 2002 she began working at a preschool in Burnaby, Canada, which won the Prime Minister's Award for Excellence in 2009. As a result of our practice, student mentorship, and interest in post-secondary education, we both began lecturing in early childhood higher education programmes in the 2000s: Deb in the UK and Rachel in Canada.

We have provided only the briefest of descriptions of ourselves and our research projects in this opening chapter, choosing instead to revisit contextual and situating factors throughout the book. In part, this reflects a theoretical commitment to an *embedded reflexivity*, rather than a surface listing of 'factsheet' characteristics that are never referred to again (Coffey, 1999). Rather than a form of 'narcissistic' and inward looking reflexivity, which causes us to lose sight of the broader social world (e.g. see discussion in Coffey, 2002), we aim towards a reflexivity involving attention to social relations of power, reciprocity, and responsibility (Skeggs, 2002). As such, readers will come to know us over the course of the book as we strive to remain reflexive about our 'positioned-practices' (Collier, 1994) and the political and ethical issues involved in research relationships.

From the technicist to the relational

Our discussion thus far has suggested the importance of considering relationships in research with young children and points to the ambiguity and im/possibilities involved in these negotiations. For example, the narrative of the baby-eating dragons provokes some fundamental questions about an adult-researcher's responses in such critical moments. As a researcher, was Rachel responsible only for the generation of 'quality' data, including observing how the children negotiated this moment themselves? Or did she have a responsibility to Raeni, a child who was 'really' upset by the imaginative play; the children and their narrative exploration more generally; or the educators in the setting who are tasked with keeping children safe, secure, and well – educators who had entrusted her to observe and join children in play within their setting?

In response to such complexities in the social world, dominant forms of (neo)liberal thought offer technicist approaches to people, relationships, and ethics. Such instrumentalism essentially reduces relationships between people to contractual relations between autonomous, rational individuals motivated by self-interest (Sevenhuijsen, 1998a). As with neoliberal practices more generally, attention to research relationships becomes focused on ensuring desired outcomes through attempts to answer the question of 'what works?' (Dahlberg and Moss, 2005). In research, for example, consideration is given to what practices will ensure 'access' to key research 'informants'. This is based on assumptions that answers to the question of 'what works?' are not only possible and universally appropriate but the effects of actions based on such prescriptions are foreseeable and repeatable.

Further, technicist approaches reduce ethics to a 'set of principles which are universalizable, impartial, concerned with describing what is right' (Tronto, 1993: 27). Here, ethics becomes a question of how closely and efficiently an individual follows a set of 'abstract and formal' (Tronto, 1993: 27) norms or rules. As Dennis (2009) notes, these universalist Kantian-influenced imperatives map directly on to the majority of ethical discussions in research texts, where ethics becomes a series of technical practices – such as achieving informed consent – in order to avoid risk or minimise harm. Yet, she notes that in more 'naturalistic' research, 'researchers will face complicated dilemmas not dissimilar from those faced in everyday life' (Dennis, 2009: 132); in these moments, such general and technical approaches to ethics are not only inadequate but may even be contradictory.

While we are in no way suggesting that ethical codes of conduct from professional and academic bodies and ethics approval boards from universities are unnecessary or to be abandoned, they are *fundamentally insufficient* in the complex, day-to-day negotiation of research relationships. Moreover, the intense pressures on researchers – through research training programmes, ethics' review boards and funding bodies, for example – to demonstrate that they have met technical obligations can overshadow the complex political and ethical concerns from which these more pragmatic practices arise.

As a result, in this book we will be advancing a fundamentally different notion: that of answerability and relational ethics. Here we will undertake a 'bricolage' of sorts, engaging different perspectives and theoretical traditions in productive dialogue with each other (Kincheloe, 2001). In particular, we will be drawing on work in the social studies of childhood (an interdisciplinary field in itself); embodiment and the senses; and feminist and other literature in the field of social justice and 'critical' theorising. The work of the Bakhtinian circle[5] – in relation to dialogics, the body, the carnivalesque, and answerability – also features centrally in this bricolage. In this move away from 'disciplinary parochialism' (Sayer, 2000: 7) and reductionism, we are not, however, advocating a form of relativism in relation to politics, ethics, and research relationships. Instead, we will be developing six key themes throughout the book that, we contend, have important implications for negotiating research relationships with young children.

First, we will advance a notion of research relationships as processes that occur in the spaces in-between bodies. This stands in contrast to views of relationships as 'things' or 'objects' created in the meeting between self-contained and autonomous individuals. In this dominant model of relationships, the view is that as people come to know one another, they gradually share fixed pieces of themselves with the other thereby developing a greater degree of intimacy. Emotions, ideas, and characteristics are considered to rest within the individuals who engage in these interactions. However, Bakhtin (1984a: 287) offers a striking critique of this Cartesian view of the self and relationships:

> I am conscious of myself and become myself only while revealing myself for another, through another, and with the help of another. The most important acts constituting self-consciousness are determined by a relationship toward another consciousness (toward a thou).

Arguing that selfhood has no 'internal sovereign territory' but is 'wholly and always on the boundary', Bakhtin (1984a: 287) contends that consciousness is a fundamentally social process. The implication of such an argument is that self–other relations are fundamentally ones of interdependence (Sevenhuijsen, 1998b).

Further, for Bakhtin, we need the other to see beyond our own consciousness. The other brings to a self what a self cannot: 'Let him rather remain outside of me, for that position he can see and know what I myself do not see and do not know from my own place, and he can essentially enrich the event of my own life' (Bakhtin, 1990: 87). In this sense, the self is constructed through the process of negotiating relationships with others rather than bringing, and potentially revealing, a completely formed self to the relationship. Bakhtin (1993) refers to this as 'Being-as-event', a never finalised self that is constituted through lived experiences with others. The self and the other rely on their relationship for their own becoming (Baxter and Montgomery, 1996).

Thus far, the discussion has focused on what appears as a singular relation between self and other. However, a second theme that will occupy us in this book is that any research relationship takes place within a fundamentally social space and is never merely dyadic. This argument is twofold: selves exist within a web of relationships and within the broader social relations of a given community or society. To begin, we note that any relationship between two people always interfaces with other interpersonal relationships. From an everyday perspective, when a researcher observes, participates with, or interviews a participant, others are present in some way, and this brings different values and modes of interaction into collision – as the baby-eating dragon narrative attests. Further, the social ecology shifts as a result of the presence of different people. For example, when Deb disclosed her lack of a coloured badge, this opened practices – which had previously seemed an accepted feature of the social order – to contestation. Similarly the presence of different children in a setting can fundamentally alter the relationships between researchers and children and children with each other. It was this web of relationships, and the effect such relationships have on one another, that Rachel was particularly attentive to as she considered the implications of her possible responses to Zahrah and Raeni's debate over the 'baby's' fate.

An additional point to make here is that relationships do not originate from within individuals in a contextual vacuum. It is here that the Bakhtinian notion of the dialogic becomes important. The Bakhtinian circle conceives of being and relationships as essentially constituted through practices ('acts') and an endless 'chain of speech communion' (Bakhtin, 1986: 84). Importantly here, Vološinov/Bakhtin (1976: 79) argues that:

> Not a single instance of verbal utterance can be reckoned exclusively to its utterer's account. Every utterance is the product of the interaction between speakers and the product of the broader context of the whole complex social situation in which the utterance emerges.

What Vološinov/Bakhtin is pointing to here is that the words we use, and the meanings 'joined' to those words, are always full of direct or indirect citations from the immediate conversation or more distant interactions as well as the audience to whom we address them. In turn, these utterances are informed by the material conditions of life and our place within the social order. While the notion of dialogue is sometimes critiqued for its 'overly-benign' presentation – which serves to render inequality and domination invisible within relationships – Morris (1994: 9) argues that 'the play of power and hierarchy are taken into account' when the Bakhtinian circle's texts are read as a whole, and this is certainly the notion of the dialogic that we will put forward.

The third theme that will wind through the book is that research relationships are not teleological, culminating in a 'finalised' endpoint of intimacy. However, in research texts, they are often presented in a linear manner beginning with entry and acceptance in the field, continuing through maintenance of relationships, and dissolving the relationship as the research is completed. Yet this belies the fluid and shifting nature of relationships which do not proceed with ever increasing intimacy towards an idealised point, such as between 'key informant' and researcher, until research ends. Instead, we would argue with Bakhtin that relationships are in a constant state of becoming and change. Relationships, like the self, are indeed 'unfinalisable'. Research relationships can proceed in myriad directions on different days with a variety of contextual factors, including what else is happening and who else is present, influencing the nature of particular interactions. This diversity, we argue, enhances the research process. Considering what is traditionally presented as the end point of a research relationship – dissolution at the end of a research project – may help to clarify this point. While a researcher may not interact with participants in the same manner after generating data, this does not mean that no relationship exists. Through the writing up and presenting of data, s/he is still engaged dialogically with participants, for example often anticipating how they may respond to interpretations and analysis. Further, interactions with participants often carry on after data generation and time in the 'field' (Coffey, 1999; Corsaro, 1985; Ellis, 2007); as such, relationship negotiations may continue beyond the research process 'proper'.

A fourth theme we will develop in this book is that research relationships are deeply 'emplaced', a term which highlights the inter-relationship between mind, body and place (Howes, 2005b), as it is through our body that we inhabit the research field. To this end, Coffey (1999: 59–60) points out:

> Fieldwork is necessarily an embodied activity. Our body and the bodies of others are central to the practical accomplishment of fieldwork. We locate

our physical being alongside those of others, as we negotiate the spatial context of the field. We concern ourselves with the positioning, visibility and performance of our own embodied self as we undertake participant observation . . . It has become usual to recognise that the body bears upon the experience of fieldwork, although arguably this recognition has to date been at a rather superficial level.

Implied here is the notion that embodiment is not an isolated experience. Indeed, *relationships* with participants are thoroughly embodied as researchers interact with participants in a multi-sensorial manner, feeling and coming to know through the interaction of the bodies we 'are' – 'the fleshy situatedness of our modes of living' (Mol and Law, 2004: 44).

Research relationships are also impacted by the bodies we 'have' (Mol and Law, 2004), the object-body that is subject to workings of labour, power, inequities, and education. In early childhood settings, for example, there are extensive 'body rules' about acceptable corporeality (Leavitt and Power, 1997) including how bodies should move and when; how bodies should sound; and where bodies should be placed – as the story of the coloured badges that began the chapter exemplified. Extensive body work is necessary in order to shape and shift bodies according to these rules.

This is where Mol and Law (2004) argue that bodies are more than what we 'are' or 'have', they are what we '*do*', a dynamic notion of the agentic body. Here we – children and adults alike – 'enact' our bodies in efforts to present ourselves in particular ways, sometimes to transgress and sometimes in line with body rules. For example, Deb's physical manipulations of her body due to the coloured-badge dilemma reflected an effort to fit her body into the social and institutional rules of the setting. Throughout this book then, we will consider how the body does matter a great deal in fieldwork relationships with young children. Here we will consider how bodies feel, interact, and *change* through the negotiation of research relationships, a process that is both constrained and made possible biologically and socially (Shilling, 2003).

This sense of the body as ever changing is significant as 'the child' is often perceived as a human being, particularly *malleable* and susceptible to environmental influences when compared to 'adults'. And it is this status of 'entity in the making' (Castañeda, 2003: 3) that forms the backdrop for sustained efforts to 'civilise' children. Elias (1978) uses the term 'civilising' to refer to the process whereby children learn and internalise their communities' expectations for social behaviour, emotional regulation and body management – such as the 'body rules' discussed earlier. This 'civilising process' has the consequence of demarcating people as either 'civilised' or 'uncivilised', such as the 'proper adult' (James et al., 1998) in comparison to the 'uncivilised' child, through normalisation of socially constructed behavioural expectations. Those who do not comply with hegemonic views of 'civilised' behaviour are often relegated to a lesser status and even disciplinary measures. It is this 'excessive' emphasis on the 'management' of children's bodies and selves that lead Leavitt and Power (1997: 44) to make the charge that in early years settings educators tend to '*over*civilize' young children. They note, for example, the way that children's eating, sleeping, and toileting are structured by externally imposed schedules, and that children who violate externally imposed regulations are subject to punishment and labelling, for example as having 'special educational needs'.

A fifth theme that informs this book is that adult–child relations are profoundly 'generationed', as well as raced, classed, and gendered. Generationing refers to the process:

> Whereby people come to be known as children, and whereby children and childhood acquire certain characteristics, linked to local contexts, and changing as the factors brought to bear change.
>
> *(Mayall, 2002: 27)*

Implied here is a sense that childhood is a *relational* term, relative to conceptions, experiences, and institutions of adulthood. Childhood implies what is *not adult*; when constructions of childhood change, constructions of adulthood change due to the internal relations between the two (Alanen, 2001). On this basis, rather than viewing childhood as determined solely by external characteristics, such as age, childhood is understood to be reproduced and transformed through the positioned practices of people in their everyday lives.

While generationing suggests a way of understanding how the lived experience of childhood and conceptions of childhood do not remain static over time and place, this does not diminish the sense in which childhood is a relatively permanent structural category (Qvortrup, 1999). Understandings of childhood, the concomitant treatment of real children, and group membership will change – at very least as people pass into adulthood – but childhood as a structural feature of society remains and has major implications for the 'activities, opportunities, experiences, and identities' of its members (Alanen, 2001: 14). Mayall's (2002: 40) stark note in relation to childhood – that 'the power to define it lies with adults' – is suggestive of the way that adult-researchers' conceptions of childhood inform not only research questions and analysis but relationships with child-participants. This is crucial given the way dominant modern conceptions constitute childhood as a time of lack or deficiency in comparison to adulthood, a time of 'human becoming' rather than 'human being' (Qvortrup, 1994). The ideal (Enlightenment) adult is viewed as one who is rational, autonomous, and responsible for her own actions, characteristics that children are seen to lack – both quantitatively and qualitatively (Archard, 2004).

In early childhood settings, developmental psychology – drawing largely on the work of Piaget – has played a key role in maintaining such distinctions, laying out as it does universal, prescribed stages of growth that 'progress' from sensory action to logical thought. Such naturalised and categorical views of growth consign childhood to be a time of intensive observation, monitoring, and evaluation of children against a normative framework (James et al., 1998). In looking back at the critical moment that began the chapter, while Raeni's protection of the 'baby' from the dragon fit with 'romanticised' (Ailwood, 2003) pedagogies of play that conflate it with innocence (Grieshaber and McArdle, 2010) and 'progress' (Sutton-Smith, 1997), the other children's more transgressive narrative threatened such instrumental views. It was knowledge of these dominant ways of thinking about childhood and play that served as a backdrop for Rachel's anxieties in the moment.

The impact of structural features of childhood on the lives of real children notwithstanding, we strongly support the growing body of work in childhood studies that, building on the pivotal work of James et al. (1998), suggests that children are *social actors* as well as individual and collective agents of change, not mere passive vessels of biological or socio-political imperatives. It is this sense of children as active participants in their social worlds – including in research conducted in their early childhood settings – that we attempt to bring to our discussion in this book, including the notion that it is not only 'adult imaginaries' (Taylor, 2011) but children's conceptions of childhood and adulthood that inform research relationships (Rosen, 2010).

To this point, the discussion has fallen primarily along generational fault lines. But not all adults are equal and rather than setting up a simplistic and oppositional relationship between adults and children it is necessary to consider the way in which generationing intersects with processes of gendering and racialisation in and between classed societies. While we heed Qvortrup's (2010) warning about the detrimental political effects of fracturing identities, where diversity and difference are raised to the level of principle as opposed to principles of social and economic justice, we argue that examination of the different articulations of generationing, class, racialisation, and gendering – as well as their intersections (e.g. see Bilge, 2010) – are necessary in understanding childhood(s) and the negotiation of research relationships. By way of example, in the story of the coloured badges that opened the chapter, Deb could have used her adult (and researcher) status to bypass rules about the wearing of coloured badges and still generated data for her research. Although she did so at first, she became increasing uncomfortable with that decision, feeling that it reinforced generational inequities that she was critiquing in her research. The ensuing discussion between Deb and the children was an attempt to challenge the positioning of adults as able to set and evade rules in contrast to children. However, it took the form of a 'rational', verbal discussion, which, as Vandenbroeck and Bouverne-De Bie (2006) point out, favours white, middle-class educational practices.

The sixth and final theme that we will develop throughout this book is a concept of relational ethics, drawing on the Bakhtinian circle's work on aesthetic activity and the answerable act. As noted already, Bakhtin (1993) suggests that life is constituted by an ongoing series of acts – the 'once-occurrent event of Being' – that encompasses both real deeds and 'thought-deeds'. Bakhtin (1993) was concerned to debunk a series of Cartesian dualities, including the way in which Enlightenment thinkers had separated the meaning of such acts from the actual experience of the act through, for example, universalist generalisations and formal ethics. He argued that such acts of abstraction mean 'we are now controlled by its autonomous laws or, to be exact, we are simply no longer present in it as individually and answerably active human beings' (Bakhtin, 1993: 7). Such separations, according to Bakhtin (1993: 9), essentially remove people from their everyday experiences and condense them into 'indifferent and, fundamentally, accomplished and finished theoretical Being[s]', resulting in an abdication of responsibility to others.

In contrast, Bakhtin sought to theorise, and indeed advocated for, the 'answerably performed act' taking place in a specific, temporal-historic moment. Here, life is anything but finalised, instead it is 'answerable, risk-fraught, and open becoming through performed actions' (Bakhtin, 1993: 9). As a result, Gardiner (2000: 44) argues that, for Bakhtin, 'the everyday therefore constitutes the central ground upon which our judgements and actions, particularly those of a moral or normative character, are exercised.' Such a view of everyday events has fundamental implications for the negotiation of research relationships as it indicates that it is in the moment-by-moment acts of negotiating relationships that we have the possibility of being answerable to research participants – hence our use of the term 'relational ethics'.

The answerable act, then, is one which brings meaning and value to others in the world. This happens for Bakhtin through a process of 'consummating' what the Enlightenment has sought to separate: the meaning of an act and the experience of it, 'sense and the fact, the universal and the individual, the real and the ideal' (Bakhtin, 1993: 29). Through this process we connect the fluidity of the 'small scrap of space and time' that we occupy with the 'large spatial and temporal whole' (Bakhtin, 1993: 51). He argues that it is our ability to see parts of the other that s/he cannot (such as her bodily borders, birth, death, and spatial-temporal environment) that allows us to – in our answerable, aesthetic activity – make the other whole: 'The excess of my seeing must "fill in" the horizon of the other human being who is being contemplated, must render his horizon complete, without at the same time forfeiting his distinctiveness' (Bakhtin, 1990: 25). This is a process of 'sympathetic co-experiencing' in which the self, 'co-experiences' with her/him in a new place made possible by the self's 'transgredience' and then returns to one's own self to 'consummate' the other or make the other whole.

Rather than viewing the process as a colonising gaze set on fixing meaning on the other (Alldred, 1998) or in some way 'renouncing the irreducibility of self and other through . . . seeking out knowledge about the other' (cf. Todd, 2004: 346), answerability provokes change in both the self and other. It refers to a dynamic and transformative process. Further, Bakhtin is insistent throughout his work that consummation is always tentative, never complete or finalised. To this end, in describing their use of a 'Bakhtinian interpretive approach' in research, Tobin and Kurban (2009: 28) eloquently comment: 'To answer means to listen carefully and then reply, as best we can, even when we fear we have not fully understood what was said to us and even when we know that our reply is inadequate.'

It is important to note that – rather than emphasising introspection – there is an insistence in answerability that we turn our gaze outwards at others in the social and physical world we inhabit (Gardiner, 2000). Here, it is not just consideration of the potential of an act but the *act itself* and its impacts which are important: 'The answerable act or deed alone surmounts anything hypothetical, for the answerable act is, after all, the actualization of a decision – inescapably, irremediably, and irrevocably' (Bakhtin, 1993: 28) and a 'going out once and for all from within possibility as such into what is once-occurrent' (Bakhtin, 1993: 29). In much the same vein, Alcoff (2009) suggests that merely deconstructing critical moments in research can render a researcher immobilised, falling into a 'retreat' position that is individualistic and politically untenable. She argues – specifically in relation to the question of 'speaking for others' in research – that it cannot be condemned a priori. Committing to an act and analysing the impact of this act are inseparable and fundamental aspects of being answerable.

With the evocative phrase 'non-alibi in Being', Bakhtin (1993: 40) implies that each person has a particular and unique responsibility: 'That which can be done by me can never be done by anyone else.' This is both a risky and transformative position, but one that is compelling in its insistence on 'the act'. As a result, we adhere to the suggestion that 'normativity and judgement are necessary and that we make judgements in our everyday practices' (Sevenhuijsen, 1998a: 29). This is significant as Sevenhuijsen (1998a: 29) is critical of postmodern approaches to ethics that marginalise the importance of taking 'binding decisions and the bearing of responsibility for these'. If early childhood research is to be framed within what we are terming as 'relational ethics' then it is important that we are able to 'judge with care', as Sevenhuijsen (1998a) promotes. Such care is not just about those closest to us or those research participants with whom we most immediately interact – a form of parochialism and even elitism (Tronto, 1989). Instead, the relational ethic of answerability that we advocate throughout this book fundamentally involves a commitment to social justice and challenging relations of domination and exploitation. For, despite advances in formal political equality, the 'gritty materialities' (Apple, 2006: 468) of social and economic inequity persist. A relational ethics involves being answerable not just to individuals but to marginalised collectivities and perhaps even more pointedly 'answerable to the *question of justice*' (Readings, 1996: 154).

A guide to the book

In this first chapter, we have 'set the stage', underlining the place of this book within the burgeoning body of childhood studies research and methodological literature. We have argued that social research is not amenable to technicist assumptions about people, relationships, and ethics. Instead, we have advanced a relational ethics of interdependence and answerability based on an understanding that adult–child research relationships are negotiated within complex realities and are fundamentally embodied, unfinalisable, and informed by social relations of inequality.

In Chapter 2, we will develop these themes by considering the spaces and places of early childhood research. We introduce the sites of our research projects, in particular underscoring the impact of neoliberalism with its regulatory and market-based 'logic' which creates particular understandings of children and the way they should be educated and cared for. We argue this has significant impacts on research relationships within early childhood settings.

The book moves on in Chapter 3 to look more specifically at the sense that child-participants and adult-researchers make of each other. We consider the variety of 'roles' available to adult-researchers, providing a critique of the 'least adult' position and putting forward the more preferable 'least-educator' role. Ultimately, however, we argue that holding steadfastly to a predefined role closes down possibilities for dialogic relationships to form. The chapter then moves on to consider some specific instances of the way *bodies matter* in negotiating relationships and the need for an embodied reflexivity.

Building on our argument that interactions in research take place within a web of relationships, in Chapter 4, we discuss the impact of research relationships with adults – specifically educators in early childhood settings – on relationship negotiations with children, as well as the implications of researcher–child relationships for these adults. While Chapter 4 considers relationship negotiation when researchers come from 'outside' a setting, Chapter 5 takes up the specific issues involved in negotiating relationships with children in educator-research. However, both chapters work together to problematise the dichotomised notions of 'insider/ outsider' research. In focusing on educator-research, Chapter 5 introduces two new research projects undertaken when we were both educators that highlight the complexities of navigating consent in 'insider' research.

Chapter 6 refocuses on data from our doctoral research projects to consider how researchers and participants come to 'know' in early childhood research. This chapter examines the tensions of observational methods in particular, given the ubiquity of such practices in early childhood settings, and argues that we cannot reify observation, either by negating the social relations under which such practices produce knowledge or by condemning it as inherently invasive. In contrast, we offer the notion of 'sensing practices' as a way of conceptualising the contextual and multi-sensorial negotiation of relationships. We argue for an 'interested-effective attitude' (Bakhtin, 1993: 32) in seeking to bring meaning to each other in the research process.

Chapter 7 moves on to explore some of the more contentious moments in negotiating research relationships: acts of injustice and the physically 'risky' situations child-participants may engage in. Here, notions of researcher 'neutrality' are critiqued and the impact of researcher 'intervention' is considered. We argue that intervention is both an inherent result of a researcher's presence in the field and a question for ethical and political consideration in relation to individual participants as well as marginalised collectivities.

Chapter 8, the final chapter, sums up our key arguments in the book through consideration of reciprocity in research relationships with children. Here, we seek to complicate the plethora of 'participatory methods' that have been advocated as a way to engage with children's perspectives, arguing that the goals of reciprocity are best served by an attitude of 'being with' children. We further contend that building 'common cause' (Warming, 2005) with children transcends the research process proper.

A final note is that this book is not organised as a linear exploration of the research cycle – not least because this would be a distortion of the iterative nature of research – but instead provides an exploration of critical issues in the ongoing negotiation of research relationships. Readers may wish to focus on particular chapters that speak more directly to their research topic(s) and practice. However, arguments in the book build on one another and, therefore, the chapters are best read sequentially. In part, this organisation is a reflection of the dialogic journey that we have taken as we have written this book. In the spirit of Bakhtin's (1990) constant commitment to finding 'loopholes' – an acknowledgement of the unfinalisability and fallibility of knowledge – we hope the themes and issues in this book will inspire and provoke responses from readers as much as they have for us.

Notes

1. We use 'early childhood settings' to refer to the various institutions (public or private, full-day, part-day or sessional, for profit or not-for-profit etc.) that provide care and education for children aged 0–5 years old.
2. We use the term 'educator' to refer to those adults in early childhood settings charged with the care and education of young children. This term, therefore, may include teachers, practitioners, assistants, heads of centre etc. Without wanting to minimise the significant differences between these groups, for the purposes of this book they are less salient.
3. Following Mohanty (2003), a feminist post-colonial scholar, we have chosen to use the terms 'First World/North' and 'Third World/South'. The terms 'North' and 'South' can be understood as metaphorical rather than strictly geographical distinctions between rich, dominant nations, regions or communities and those that are poorer and on the peripheries of flows of capital. Mohanty (2003) posits the importance of retaining the terms First/Third World given their insistently political reference to colonialism and capitalism. We recognise that these terms, like any other, are problematic not least because of the changing geopolitical landscape in the post-Cold War period, and they suggest a level of homogeneity among people in each grouping. As a result, we use the terms with a note of caution.
4. The use of the term 'food event', derived from the work of Douglas and Nicod (1974), was used throughout the study as it refers to occasions on which food is eaten regardless of whether these activities constitute a 'structured' event such as a mealtime.
5. The Bakhtinian circle was a group of philosophers, scientists, and artists who gravitated around Mikhail Bakhtin (1895–1975) in the years following the Russian Revolution. In 1973 claims were made that the texts published under the names of two other members of the circle were the sole work of Bakhtin. We have chosen to cite the contested texts with a split reference (for example, Vološinov/Bakhtin). This acknowledges the disputed authorship of the texts at the same time as reflecting the chosen pen name of the author(s) and their dialogic working relationship.

2
THE SPACES AND PLACES OF RESEARCH RELATIONSHIPS

In the previous chapter, we outlined how Bakhtinian ideas (notably Bakhtin, 1981; 1990; 1993) have been influential in our thinking about a relational ethics owing to their move away from technicism and abstraction to an ethics in which the universalistic and the particularistic come together in a complex web of relationships. Bakhtin (1993: 59) argues for the '*this*ness' of '*this* human being, *these* human beings and their world with all its actual moments'. And, following the ideas of Bakhtin (1990; 1993), it is the concreteness or '*this*ness' of our respective research projects that we aim to convey throughout this book while maintaining the constancy of our commitment to issues of social justice in early childhood education and care (ECEC).

In exploring the idea of '*this*ness', Bakhtin (1981) uses the term 'chronotope' – or 'time/space' – to denote the interconnectedness of temporal and spatial relationships. He argues that 'time, as it were, thickens, takes on flesh, becomes artistically visible: likewise, space becomes charged and responsive to the movements of time, plot and history' (Bakhtin, 1981: 84). One of the difficulties with Bakhtin, however, is that in outlining the uniqueness of individual events in time/space – described as the 'once-occurrent-event-of-being' (Bakhtin, 1993) – he provides few concrete examples. Of course, he does not set out to do this.

In essence, then, our task in this chapter is to embed our own research settings in their particular cultural-historic and economic 'chronotopes' as well as to 'spatialise' (Holloway and Valentine, 2000: 770) the settings on a more local level. Here we seek to address a question provoked by the notion of the chronotope: How do spatial and temporal configurations affect the web of relationships between adult-researchers and child-participants?

Throughout this chapter, we will argue that any focus on adult–child relationships in early childhood research needs to conceptualise relationships *beyond* the level of the researcher–participant dyad. The wider context within which these relationships are located is significant. Like Holloway and Valentine (2000), we believe that the global and the local are inextricably linked spaces rather than binary opposites. They suggest:

> Children's worlds of meaning are at one and the same time global and local, made through 'local' cultures which are in part shaped by their interconnectedness with the wider world.
>
> *(Holloway and Valentine, 2000: 769)*

The space that is central to the discussion in this book is the early childhood setting, particularly in the English context, given that this is where the principal research projects discussed in this book have taken place. We recognise that England is not entirely representative of the 'First World/North' and certainly research in the 'Third World/South' will raise myriad different problematics in negotiating research relations, not the least because of high levels of poverty and unemployment and the ongoing impact of war and colonialism. However, particular discourses about early childhood – as well as the practices that they support – are globally pervasive as a result, for example, of World Bank directives and consultancy in relation to early years projects (Penn, 2005) and the increase in policy 'transfer' (Namissan and Ball, 2010) under neoliberalism. While spaces such as early childhood settings are often deemed to be 'bounded' in a similar way to the home space, following Holloway and Valentine (2000), our intention is to elaborate on the *porosity* of early childhood settings as spaces where the global and local configure in particularly interesting ways, lending 'recognisability' (Youdell, 2006) across different contexts.

The early childhood setting as a research context

Early childhood research has been undertaken in a variety of different spaces such as children's own homes (e.g. Edmiston, 2008; Dunn, 1988); playgrounds (e.g. Opie and Opie, 1959); hospitals (e.g. Alderson, 1993); between home and school (e.g. Alldred, David, and Edwards, 2002); and, indeed, more broadly on children's lives as lived in particular communities (e.g. the longer-term anthropological work of Mead, 1930). Each of these contexts frames the kinds of relationship that are possible and, in turn, affect the negotiation of relationships between adult-researchers and young children. In this book, we will focus on the kinds of relationship that are made possible within the 'chronotope' of early childhood settings more broadly and our own research settings specifically.

Our research projects were carried out in early childhood settings across London/southeast England. Deb's research looking at food events was carried out in four different early childhood settings from 2006–2009 and she visited each for a day a week for about two terms each. Setting one is a purpose-built, publicly funded nursery class (children aged 3–5 years) attached to a primary school, which is open on a sessional basis. Unlike the educators (primarily white and monolingual in English), the children come from diverse linguistic, ethnic, and religious communities, and most are in receipt of Income Support and other associated benefits paid to families/carers not in regular paid employment. Setting two is a privately owned, fee-paying nursery (children aged 2–5 years) operating in a church hall and offering full-day care. The educators and children come from diverse ethnic, linguistic, and religious communities – a large proportion of the families/carers are middle-class, medical professionals such as doctors and dentists working in the local hospitals. Setting three is a community nursery (children aged 2–5 years) open on a sessional basis, operating in a community hall. The majority of educators and children are white British, apart from a small group of children from South Korea (but residing in the UK), and are a mix of working-class and middle-class families. Setting four is a privately owned, fee-paying nursery and school (part of a chain run on Montessori principles; children aged 6 months–7 years) operating in a church building and offering full-day care. The families are primarily white British and affluent – many parents are journalists, whereas the educators are primarily of Bangladeshi origin. Rachel's research was carried out in a maintained, not-for-profit children's centre, which she visited weekly from 2010–2012 (for one and a half years). Children in the setting range from 2–4 years old and, along with educators, come from diverse linguistic, religious, and ethnic communities, although most are from working-class families.

In order to provide an entry point into the discussion about how early childhood settings affect relationships between adults and children, we begin by examining an excerpt from Rachel's fieldnotes:

> Michelle – an educator – sat on a chair looking down at her 'story group'. These eight children sat silently on the carpet in a semi-circle in front of her as she read a storybook.
>
> On one side of the semi-circle, in the periphery of Michelle's vision, a small scuffle began as Aakif and Cecilia tried to position their bodies to better see the raised book which – because it was held up towards the centre of the circle – was slightly out of their line of vision. The jostling intensified – one push lead to another – until Aakif declared loudly, 'I'm going to shoot Cecilia. Because she's naughty.'
>
> The sound of his voice cut across the room, and Michelle took obvious notice for the first time, although she may have been aware of the issue earlier but hoped it would be resolved without intervention. She looked over at the two and before returning to the book, Michelle commented: 'I thought we were all friends here.' As she continued reading, the scuffling – rather than calming – began to escalate in earnest. Michelle turned and said firmly: 'Sit up now. You are all going to big school soon.'
>
> (Rachel Rosen, Taboo play)

On the face of it, this would seem to be a fairly 'typical' story session in an early childhood setting in England and probably familiar to many across the 'First

World/North'. We suggest that it tells us much about early childhood settings as spaces for the care and education of young children. As Prout (2005) has noted, generationing intersects with spatial locations in myriad ways. Here, the spatial positioning of the educator on the raised chair is indicative of her more powerful, adult educator position in the setting and children, as a social group, are distanced spatially from adults and more specifically from her as educator.

Space also serves to insulate and distance children from the world of adults more broadly (James et al., 1998), and Michelle's plea that 'I thought we are all friends here' represents the idea that the early childhood setting is somehow insulated from the harsh realities of the 'outside' world. The idea of an early childhood setting as a separate space away from the home charged with the care and education of young children has a long history. As this has had thorough examination elsewhere (e.g. Whitehead, 1972, discusses the evolution of the nursery school in the UK context), we do not intend to replicate this here beyond making what we believe to be a few salient points in relation to our discussion.

Historically, the inception of schooling in England and much of the 'First World/North' developed to serve a number of key purposes: to relocate children into an idealised, spatial, and temporal world of 'childhood' away from the exploitative workings of early industrialisation and the world of 'adulthood' (James et al., 1998); to 'civilise' children's bodies in order to produce a more economically productive workforce (Evans, Davies, and Rich, 2010); to enhance what Bourdieu refers to as children's 'cultural capital' (Webb, Shirato, and Danaher, 2002); and also to act as a form of social control, particularly of working-class children, by instilling discipline and order (Davin, 1996), which Hendrick (1997a: 73) further argues serves to impose on children 'their subservient role in the age relationship'. In countries such as Canada in the 'First World/North', we would also add that residential schooling served a colonialist project intent on forcibly assimilating First Nations' communities (White and Jacobs, 1992).

Owing to perceptions that education needed to be differently organised (or 'child centred') for *very* young children owing to their 'different natures', based on – among others – Rousseauian and Froebelian ideas from the kindergarten movement (Chung and Walsh, 2000), separate provision for very young children began to be developed in the late 19th century in England and much of the 'First World/ North'. The idea of the 'nursery school' in England, which developed from this movement, is one based on 'the kind of caring and educational environment characterised by the ideologies of middle-class family life' (James, 2012: 113). The learning environment in nursery schools is carefully prepared, in order to provide the 'right conditions' for growth (Darling, 1982) and this often includes small, child-sized equipment manufactured with young children in mind, reinforcing further the spatial separation of childhood and adulthood in what Zeiher (2003) refers to as 'islands of dislocation'.

Generally, there is a strong emphasis on play over more direct pedagogical strategies as a prime vehicle for learning (Alloway, 1997). Certainly the idea that children learn through play pervaded the thinking of each of our research settings *strongly* – a point we expand on later in this chapter. However, we are mindful here, that while play is a central feature of early childhood education in many countries in the 'First World/North', it is not *necessarily* viewed as a key vehicle for learning elsewhere, albeit that ideas about the primacy of play have colonised ideas about early education worldwide (Cannella and Viruru, 2004; Shallwani, 2010).

Alongside nursery education and its associated play-based pedagogy, there is a parallel tradition of providing *care* for young children, which is accorded far less status. This is reflected in the qualification levels of staff, which tend to be lower than staff providing 'education' (notably teachers) and in the low levels of public investment assigned to childcare (Penn, 2011b). In Deb's research, there was a stark contrast in the four research settings. Setting one, a funded setting, was in a purpose-built building and had a vast array of equipment, notably in relation to the outdoor area when compared to the other three settings. In addition, as it is a nursery class and part of a *school* setting, a teacher-trained educator is employed. Teachers are generally employed on a higher salary, work fewer contact hours with children, and are entitled to longer holidays than educators who are *not* trained teachers, and this relates especially to educators working in for-profit settings.

Unlike nursery education, which tends to operate on a sessional basis and/or be open for a limited number of weeks a year, mirroring the termly structure of statutory schooling, the temporal organisation of settings offering 'care' usually differs. Settings offering care are often open for most of the year and for longer periods of the day, typically in ways that are supportive of those employment patterns based between the hours of 8.00am and 6.00pm on weekdays. For example, two of the four settings with which Deb carried out her research provided full-day care. As such, they offered particularly important contexts for Deb's research on food events as children had their breakfast, lunch, tea, and snacks at these settings, unlike the two other settings which only provided snacks.

Historically, there has been a bifurcation of early childhood settings along the lines of education and care (Daniel and Ivatts, 1998); although demarcating a precise boundary between 'caring for' and 'educating' children in day-to-day practice is regarded as problematic (Whalley, 2007). The 'proper' place for the provision of 'care' is deemed, in England, to mean the home. The *free* provision of childcare places is reserved for families perceived as not fit to care for their children in some way (James, 2012); indeed, this was one of the central tenets for determining funding for the 20–30 children in full-time attendance at the setting in which Rachel conducted her research. Rather than addressing poverty and the struggles of working-class families to meet the ever rising cost of childcare in the absence of low cost or freely available provision (Penn, 2011b) – conditions which, for 'black and minority ethnic' families, are exacerbated by structural and institutional racism (Moller, 2002) – the 'solution' to their difficulties is located within state-sponsored parenting classes (James, 2012). In addition, owing to the 'hybridity' of early childhood provision, many parents in the 'First World/North' (primarily the English-speaking countries) have to negotiate a combination of provision based on whatever local arrangements are available, which for children can mean discontinuity as they are moved from one place to another (Penn, 2010: 51). It should be noted, however, that in the English context there have been moves to combine care and education, most recently in the development of Sure Start children's centres; although, the funding of these has suffered significant cutbacks since 2010 under the Coalition government.

The final point to make here is that early childhood settings might also be regarded as occupying a particularly liminal space between the 'private' and 'public', not least in the way in which many educators are expected to provide the closeness often associated with 'motherly love' within the context of 'for-profit' organisations (Colley, 2006). Further, the early childhood setting is often charged with managing the movement between the home/family and the wider world (Ben-Ari, 1997). As Golden (2005: 182) observes, early childhood settings serve to 'familiarise children with a non-familial and unfamiliar world'. In not being the child's 'home', but equally not quite like 'school', early childhood settings represent a particularly permeable space in the education system and are considered preparation sites for children in relation to their future schooling – the notion of 'school readiness' (Dahlberg and Moss, 2005).

It is this sense of preparation for 'big school' that provided the more insidious backdrop to the comments made by Michelle in the critical moment at the beginning of this section. Efforts to ensure children's 'readiness for school' can be seen in the 'spatial disciplining' (Holloway and Valentine, 2000) of the children, including enforcing behaviour such as not touching, sitting still, sitting up, as well as paying attention in a particular way – in this case, ensuring children are seen but not heard, as here it was the *voices* that were unacceptable to Michelle. The 'threat' of 'big school' looms large in this example and seems to regulate both the educator and the children, and the use of the term 'big school' identifies the significance placed on the movement to statutory schooling. Metaphors of size are enmeshed with ideas about children's status and competence (James, 1993), which impact on the relationships that might develop within these settings such as the degree of responsibility given to children or the degree to which educators are expected to ensure the children's 'readiness' for the next phase in their schooling (Dahlberg and Moss, 2005).

Given this discussion, when undertaking research, it seems remarkable that early childhood settings are regarded as a 'naturalistic' context in which to study children (Buchbinder, Longhofer, Barrett, Lawson, and Floersch, 2006; McGee-Brown, 1995). The idea of the 'early childhood setting' is a relatively recent phenomenon and in its different guises serves very different purposes ranging from preparing young children for statutory schooling; enabling parents to work; nurturing the child sensitively according to his or her 'needs' in a specially prepared, child-oriented play environment; or providing parenting education for families regarded as 'requiring' such intervention. The potentialities of relationships between children, families, educators, and researchers, we suggest, are both enabled and constrained by the chronotopes shaping early childhood provision.

Relationships with(in) neoliberal early childhood settings

Having explored the idea of the early childhood setting, a more thorough examination of the structural conditions that serve to shape early childhood provision is now needed. Our intention, then, is to elaborate on how the late capitalist, neoliberal economic context impacts on the kinds of relationship that are possible in early childhood research. While much has been written about neoliberalism and education (Ball, 2006; Moss, 2012; Penn, 2011b, for example), we will confine ourselves to exploring how this global context intersected with the specific chronotopes in which our research was carried out. Here, we will argue that the intensification of interest in early childhood needs to be viewed within the context of neoliberalism and its associated elevation of market principles (Penn, 2011b).

Essentially, neoliberalists see the role of the state as being confined to facilitating the operation of the marketplace, such as promoting 'free trade' and the production of entrepreneurial and enterprising individuals able and willing to compete in the marketplace (Olssen, 1996). As such, neoliberalism promotes privatisation, deregulation, and re-regulation for market purposes, liberalisation, and 'efficiency'. Neoliberalism holds that, alongside these processes, it is the primacy of 'consumers' exerting their right to choose from a variety of goods and services that serve as the prime drivers of 'quality' (Ball, 2008; Lauder, Brown, Dillabough, and Halsey, 2006). On the face of it, neoliberalism could be seen as divorced from the day-to-day relationships between adults and children in early childhood settings, but we suggest there is a strong association between the two. In particular, we will consider how neoliberalism's emphasis on consumer relations; efficiency and governance (Dahlberg and Moss, 2005); and social investment produce particular (im)possibilities for relationships in these settings.

'Choice' and marketised relations

We will begin by considering the notion of 'choice' and the idea of the 'consumer' in relation to ECEC, for it is essentially consumer interactions between purchasers and providers that characterise relationships in the marketplace (Apple, 1999). In each of our research settings, there was a range of activities on offer to the children and an expectation that children would be able to choose (and choose 'wisely') from this range of options. In Setting three of Deb's research, each day commenced with a formal registration time, after which each educator told the children what she would be doing that morning and where she would be based, such as 'I'm going to be doing "finger-painting" with you in the workshop area' or 'I'm going to be making models with you outdoors'. Following this, the educators would ask individual children which activity they would like to choose. The stating of activities 'on offer' was akin to a sales pitch at the start of each day, yet despite children having a 'free choice' of activities, these 'choices' were constrained by the fact that they could only choose from those options available at a particular time.

Kjorholt and Seland (2012) have likened such organisation of space in early childhood settings to a 'bazaar' in which there are clear parallels with neoliberal theorising about the primacy of the marketplace. The framing of early childhood practice in this way creates a sense that young children are 'customers' free to move around and 'purchase' what they desire amongst myriad resources and opportunities 'on offer' in the setting. Here, the early childhood educator becomes a 'salesperson' ready to respond to her 'customer's' wishes and needs (Kjorholt and Seland, 2012: 171).

In Setting three of Deb's research, the educators expressed disappointment at the end of a session if few children had joined their activity – as if, somehow, their 'sales' pitch' had not been persuasive enough in comparison to that of their colleagues. As researchers coming into early childhood settings, on occasions it felt as if we too were positioned as 'competitors' for the children's attention. If children were drawn to spending time with us then this took them away from activities with educators – the implications of which we develop in Chapter 4 especially. Similarly, there were times when we were collecting data relating to a particular play episode and this would be curtailed by a call from an educator to engage in a particular planned activity.

Finding it hard to choose or not choosing at all was viewed by educators as highly problematic in many of our research settings. In Setting one of Deb's food events' research, this was seen most starkly with Shahrusaad and Hamdi who, for the first few weeks of attending the nursery class, sat on the bench where their coats were situated and surveyed the nursery from this vantage point, only moving when it was time to set up for snack time – an activity they participated in with enthusiasm. Their 'inactivity' was seen as a key issue to address, and in their early meetings that term the educators set 'goals' for these children and discussed ways to support them in their choice making. A curriculum based on learning through play, seemingly 'free' (at least on the surface) and unencumbered by adults, posed a real challenge for these two children. The 'real' activity of preparing and sharing snacks and the more instructional style of the educators at this point of the session seemed to engage these children far more than play (cf. Brooker, 2010). By constructing their non-engagement with choosing from a range of play options as a 'problem' – after all, in the English context 'play' and 'choice time' are valorised as of prime importance – these children and their interests/experiences were marginalised.

Choice, we argue, in such a context is also framed around individual activity as opposed to relationships with others. In the exemplar just given, in asking children what they were going to do – as individuals – the activity and not the children or educators with whom the child spends time was elevated. Thus, mirroring neoliberal philosophy, the notion of the individual liberated from the 'confines' of the collective and able to exercise individual choices in relation to her own life is reified. To expand, the idea of a rational, self-sufficient, detached, self-interested, and autonomous person who is enterprising enough to choose also downplays (or even negates) myriad ways in which human beings are interdependent (Sevenhuijsen, 1998a). Neoliberalism also aggrandises individual responsibility, advancement, and self-interest over collective well-being and social justice, separating the individual from any sense of responsibility for or reliance on others (Davies, 2005). And, more broadly, an unbridled 'faith' in the market leaves social inequities – based on, for instance, class, gender, and 'race' – unaddressed (Salazar Perez and Cannella, 2010). This, we argue, is problematic: from a Bakhtinian (1990; 1993) perspective, the self is *always* in relation to and answerable to others.

So far, our discussion of early childhood settings has focused on them as localised sites of consumption, but they can be viewed as embedded within the market economy more broadly. ECEC is increasingly a site for profit making; for example, the for-profit market in the UK increased by 70% between 2002 and 2008 and is valued at £5.3 billion (Penn, 2011a: 153). This profit orientation can also be seen in the proliferation of large chains providing childcare and in the development of a market for specialist materials and products geared towards early childhood settings and families/carers. Such enterprise operates on a global level but also at a more local level. To some extent, each of the settings in which our research was undertaken 'marketed' its work through the use of glossy brochures, for instance. While this was most evident in Setting four in Deb's research (a for-profit nursery that is part of a chain), this was observed in each setting and represents the positioning of early childhood settings as in competition with one another and ECEC as a business enterprise, albeit that this positioning does not sit comfortably with many educators (Osgood, 2004). Penn (2011a: 159) argues that such for-profit approaches to ECEC are 'volatile' because they are 'dependent on local markets for the uptake of places' and are ethically questionable as provision is driven by cost–benefit analysis rather than questions of well-being. Such factors can impact on relationships in early childhood settings as they create significant turnover and stress for children, families, and educators (Penn, 2011a).

The child as 'social investment' or 'human capital'

ECEC is not only a site of consumption but can be viewed as a site of *production*, as can be seen in an excerpt from Deb's fieldnotes. Vera, one of the educators in Setting three, described the importance of play in the 'role play' area, which had been transformed into a 'bakery', in the following way:

> And play helps children develop positive attitudes. We had a baker's *(role play area)* on Monday and I was really proud of it. One boy said "doughnut shop" – they didn't all know the word "bakers"! We put the dough in the baker's shop – they didn't know bread came from dough.
> Play like this teaches children about different types of food . . .
> Play with food like the bakers is good to encourage talking and it helps meet the Early Learning Goals . . .
> Even though it's play, the children are learning things that are important for when they go to school – they learn so much in the early years.
>
> *(Deb Albon, Food events: Setting three)*

Vera's narrative tells us much about ECEC and how the earliest years are viewed as a time worthy of social investment. This raises an important question: Why such a focus on *early* childhood?

First, we intend to provide some brief background to the idea of seeing young children as 'human capital' before moving on to explore the excerpt from Deb's fieldnotes in some detail. The term 'human capital' relates to the 'knowledge, information, ideas, skills and health of individuals' (Becker, 2006: 292) and it has been suggested that we live in an 'age of human capital' in which the skills and knowledge of *everyone* as opposed to a few individuals drive the economy and impact on the wealth of nation states as well as individuals (Brown and Lauder, 2006). Because of this, education is positioned as key in this drive for economic competitiveness on the world stage (Ball, 2008), and curriculum content globally is shaped by the demands of 'post-industrial' economies (Lingard, 2009). International economists compare the educational attainment of nations in order to examine their respective 'stock of human capital' (Barro and Lee, 2001: 542) as governments seek to develop particular knowledge and skills linked to production in a period of late capitalism (Dahlberg and Moss, 2005). More critically, human capital theory examines and promotes the economic productivity of *individuals* in given spatial and temporal locations, disconnected from any sense of collective responsibility for addressing issues of social justice such as economic inequities on a local or global scale (Penn, 2010).

Human capital theorising, therefore, positions the education and care of the child as *crucial* in contributing to the development of a highly skilled, competitive, and innovative future workforce, fundamental in determining the future economic wealth of a particular nation state on the world stage (Lauder et al., 2006). Support for ECEC is advocated as a way of 'maintaining a stable, well-prepared workforce today [through providing care for workers' children] – and preparing such a workforce for the future' (Kagan et al., 1996, cited in Dahlberg et al., 2007: 44). Here ECEC produces particular subjects, such as 'specialised' (Qvortrup, 1985) and 'flexible' (Fendler, 2001) workers prized in the global economy.

Framed within a discourse of marketisation, young children's importance is as *future* human capital: important for what they will *become* as opposed to what they are now – Chapter 1 noted that Qvortrup (1994) coined the term 'human becomings' as opposed to 'human beings' to demonstrate how children are viewed in this respect. Moreover, positing children as a 'social investment', in addition to the many other subject positionings possible for children, such as 'innocent' (Mills, 2000), has implications for the kinds of provision made for children and families/carers (Dahlberg et al., 2007) as well as the relationships that are possible in such spaces.

But crucially, for our discussion, it is necessary to explore why there is an increased focus on children's *earliest* years. Vera's commentary – with which we opened this section – explicitly links the first few years of life with a surge in learning and development. On one level, of course, it serves to bolster her position as an early childhood educator – a job that is often afforded low status (Osgood,

2012) – but it also draws on dominant narratives about the significance of the earliest years of life.

In part, the backdrop to the escalation of interest in *early* childhood has been the growth in work around the significance of the earliest years of human life, notably the first three years. Such work professes that it is imperative to invest in the lives of very young children as early childhood is a 'critical period' for brain development; the ability to learn and regulate emotion (neuroscientific studies reported in Shore, 1997; see also Center on the Developing Child Harvard University, 2010); and for health and well-being more generally (see, for instance, Marmot et al., 2010). Indeed, the early childhood period is now considered to be of such pivotal significance for human lives as a whole that there appears to be international consensus that there should be investment at this key time of life (Penn, 2011b). As a consequence, the aims of early childhood settings have extended beyond caregiving and education to other areas of societal concern and are now regarded as a panacea to an ever widening range of social problems (Gulløv, 2012).

However, this position has not been without criticism. Bruer (1999), for instance, debunks what he sees as the 'myth of the first three years' (taken from the title of the book) and, in particular, questions the uncritical use of neuroscience by educators and policymakers. One argument he puts forward is that although the first three years are considered to be a 'critical period' in terms of synaptic growth, there is evidence from neuroscientific studies that points to much synaptic pruning in the first and second years of life as well as the plasticity of the brain *throughout* life.

On a more global level, poverty and inequities are excluded from computations that dispassionately assess the economic benefits of ECEC in given places (Penn, 2010). The World Bank, for instance, has sponsored the development of an 'Early Child Development calculator' in order to facilitate the computation of cost against benefits of investing in early childhood provision (Penn, 2010). Moreover, as Penn (2010: 61) has persuasively argued, children are positioned as 'creatures to be manipulated' in pursuit of their role as future entrepreneurial subjects able, as individuals, to lift themselves out of poverty. This can be contrasted with alternative forms of relationship between states and individuals marked by partnership and *collective* responsibility.

As early childhood is framed as an *especially* significant period in human life, we suggest this has particular implications for the kinds of relationship that are possible between children and educators. It is through early childhood educators, as professionals and managers, that young children are steered towards predetermined outcomes. And it is this very desire to tame uncertainty and control the future that underpins much of the human capital policy imperatives in relation to early childhood education and care at the current time.

Returning to Vera's commentary on the 'role play' baker's shop provides an interesting lens through which to explore the topic. Play, sometimes thought of as spontaneous and romanticised as 'free' and 'innocent' (Ailwood, 2003; Grieshaber and McArdle, 2010), is cast here as an 'instrument of rationality' (Phelan, 1997:

81). Specific learning is targeted through play – notably in relation to language – with a view to achieving the prescribed 'goals' of England's *Early Years Foundation Stage* (EYFS) (DCSF, 2008; DfE, 2012). This reflects a dominant narrative in ECEC in England and much of the 'First World/North': a belief in the primacy of play in children's learning and its significance in forming the bedrock of young children's future educational career (Ailwood, 2003; Rogers, 2010). And we would argue that, in the English context, this is exemplified explicitly in the EYFS document (DfES, 2007: 10 of practice guidance), which states 'a high quality early years' experience provides a *firm foundation* on which to build *future* academic, social and emotional *success*' (emphasis added).

The corollary of conceptualising the child as 'social investment' is a view of young children's play as needing to be 'well-planned' and 'purposeful' in meeting required 'goals' as opposed to being gleeful and desirable for its own sake (Kjorholt and Qvortrup, 2012). Thus, through the seemingly 'invisible' pedagogy of play, children are subject to intense scrutiny (Bernstein, 1975) – a point we develop in more detail in our critique of observation practices in Chapter 6. Moreover, 'good play' – play that meets predetermined learning outcomes such as prescribed levels of language development deemed important for future schooling (as noted in Vera's commentary) – is viewed as generally needing the regulatory presence of the educator in order to maximise the learning of the children (see Smilansky, 1990, on 'play tutoring', for instance). Although not stated explicitly, Vera emphasises her role in developing the area and extending the children's language with the use of words like 'baker' or knowledge that bread is originally a dough mixture. Furthermore, children are discussed in terms of what they do *not* know, and their relationship with the educator is conceived as one of learning *from* them, not *with* them.

However, we would want to be cautious here in our critique as we should not underestimate the personal and professional investment of educators in endeavouring to develop a stimulating learning environment for children, often outside their paid work hours, neither would we deny the pleasure many children derive from such environments. In addition, we are not suggesting that children do not learn through play or that educator involvement in play is insignificant. Our point here is that children learn in a variety of ways (including play) and with a variety of different people (including adult-educators), and that adults and children learn from each other.

A 'strongly governed' market

Our discussion thus far has concentrated on neoliberalism and the early childhood setting as a site of both consumption and production, but this neglects the way that ECEC in England is subject to high levels of regulation and central control. Moss (2012: 129) usefully employs the term 'strongly governed markets' here to describe the marketisation of ECEC in England – a process of 'decentralisation/centralisation' (Ball, 2006: 120). The centralising tendencies in relation to ECEC have at their root a fear that lack of regulation (if a market were truly 'free') might result in a drop in 'standards' and the EYFS (DCFS, 2008; DfE, 2012) is a significant example of this shift towards greater regulation. It is 'highly prescriptive' with a 'detailed network of norms and criteria' (Moss, 2012: 135), which leaves little room for input or negotiation despite the incredible diversity of educators, children, and families in England, not least in our research sites. Among an array of other critiques that might be put forward in relation to the EYFS, Anning, Cullen, and Fleer (2004) point out that *universalist* approaches to standards and curriculum reproduce deep inequalities by 'privileging' dominant groups.

In part, this heavily controlled environment has its basis in conceptions of childhood vulnerability. Although 'choice' is ostensibly an important principle in the marketplace – albeit that for affluent families/carers, there are far greater 'choices' in relation to the care and education of their children (Penn, 2011b) – significantly, the *child* as 'consumer' is considered *vulnerable*. As such, the state is viewed as needing to mediate the 'quality' of the service on her behalf. Young children as direct 'consumers' of early childhood services are often considered to be *especially* vulnerable, not least owing to their physical immaturity and greater dependence (as a social group) on adults and older children to provide for their physical care (Albon, 2011). As Shallwani (2010: 236) notes: 'The category of "the child" is differentiated from the category of "the adult", with the child conceptualised as vulnerable and primitive, and the adult conceptualised as saviour and civilised.' Appeals to intervening in children's and their families' lives are often premised on the perceived vulnerability of very young children (Shallwani, 2010), but children can also be regarded as competent as we will argue throughout this book (see also Lahman's (2008) discussion in relation to research).

Rigid and prescriptive regulations are not only justified by young children's 'vulnerability', but also have their basis in mistrust in the abilities of early childhood educators to deliver 'quality' ECEC owing to their often low levels of qualification (Penn, 2011b), despite the fact they are simultaneously perceived as crucial in delivering 'success' (Osgood, 2012). The corollary of this conundrum is intense scrutiny of the work of early childhood educators, which, in England, is particularly associated with the regulatory and inspection body known as OfSTED. The centralising tendencies aimed at improving 'quality' have also resulted in a range of 'technologies', involving copious amounts of paperwork, designed to regulate the work of educators and also to 'fix' or normalise the child (Dahlberg and Moss, 2005) – a point to which we return in Chapter 6. Rachel's fieldnotes exemplify this:

> At lunch, the educators sat in the staff room eating. Dhurata – one of the educators – came in and rather than getting food began working on 'transfer reports', documentation which accompanied individual children moving on to primary school. It was 'lunch break', but Dhurata was clearly not having a break and it was so 'normal' that no one even commented. I began asking questions about the reporting: Who was it for? What did they think about the process? Dhurata responded: 'We only get 2½ hours per week for records

and we have to do them for about 8 children each. Sometimes I just don't bother but then I start to get worried about how behind I am. You just never feel that you have caught up.'

Those simple comments opened a floodgate. For the rest of their lunch break, the educators told stories about staying late, coming early, and bringing developmental profiles home – but not getting paid for it. Dhurata continued: 'It used to be worse. I used to bring work home – cutting out and pasting photos until 2am. My husband would get so mad. He said I would wake him up when I would come to bed that late and I wasn't even getting paid. So I just stopped bringing it home and now I do it at lunch.'

(Rachel Rosen, Taboo play)

There are *many* other examples we could have drawn on here in which educators talked about their fears of OfSTED inspections and concerns over other aspects of paperwork such as that relating to health and safety regulations, notably risk assessments. Our point here is to stress the immense pressure that educators are under to conform to a multitude of paperwork exercises that takes them away, ultimately, from their direct work with young children and families/carers or from their time for relationships with their own families, friends, and colleagues away from work or when taking a break in the working day – as can be seen in Dhurata's commentary. Moreover, we question whether this weight of paperwork results in 'better' understandings of children – a point we take up again in Chapter 6.

The geography of early childhood settings

So far we have demonstrated that – situated within neoliberalism – *early* childhood is viewed as a time worthy of social investment as the child is considered to be *especially* vulnerable; *especially* dependent; and *especially* malleable (less agentive) in comparison to the older child. Because of this, early childhood settings are spaces that are charged with ensuring children's 'school readiness' – a position that cannot be overemphasised at the current time. To conclude this chapter, we intend to turn our attention to examining some of the physical characteristics of early childhood spaces and their impact on research relationships. We begin with an excerpt from Deb's fieldnotes:

Today I was observing a group of children at play in the home corner, but from outside of what is a small space in a converted cupboard area. After a while, Charlie and Hamid collected some large wooden blocks and from the inside of the home corner, made a wall which obscured my view of the play, giggling as they did so.

(Deb Albon, Food events: Setting one)

This critical moment highlights a number of spatial issues: the early childhood setting as a space in which children are under surveillance; the creative use of physical space (the cupboard) on the part of the educators; as well as, the agency of the children in transforming the space from one on view to the researcher and educators to a more private space – perhaps one of direct challenge to Deb as an adult-researcher. In that moment, Deb read the children's giggles as an invitation to play and so lifted blocks at random in order to see the children tucked away in the now private space of the 'home corner'. Children joined in with this play, peeking out at the various peepholes they made for themselves by removing the blocks. Whatever their intention – and whether Deb had understood this (assuming there was a collective 'intention' here) – the children's agentic use of space and her response to this sabotaged the collection of data, and Deb's actions may have disrupted the children's play.

Although spaces more generally have become demarcated as 'public' or 'private', spaces pertaining to the body – especially bedrooms and bathrooms – are viewed increasingly as *private* spaces (Elias, 1994). However, as young children are perceived as especially vulnerable and educators are often fearful of the potential for accidents (notably in the English context), a high degree of surveillance is often deemed necessary in early childhood settings. As a consequence of this, the geography of many early childhood settings facilitates the surveillance of children's activities and relationships even in what are considered the most private of spaces. In Rachel's research, for example, the below-ground bathroom spaces were made visible – via windowed ceilings – to anyone (i.e. adults) over three feet tall.

In this sense, space in early childhood settings can be conceptualised as an exercise of power in the way it both contains children but also enables surveillance of them (Leavitt, 1994). As noted in the excerpt with which we opened this final section, the space designated for 'role play' (a small cupboard transformed into a 'home corner') was regularly closed off if there was no educator available to sit near to the door. Yet, educators rarely, if ever, entered the 'home corner' area as to do so would drastically limit their opportunities for exercising responsibility for children in the classroom overall. Given the intense scrutiny of the work of educators in England, we found many educators were fearful of the possibilities of accidents in the spaces they were responsible for at a given time. Thus, prospects to forge relationships with children through shared participation in 'role play' activities were foreclosed and the careful placement of educators within the room was based foremost on being able to cast an all-seeing-eye on the children, wherever they might be, as opposed to being able to extend the interests of young children wherever those interests were enacted.

In another example from Deb's fieldnotes in Setting two, the lack of demarcation of space served to foster friendships between children across age ranges; sustain relationships between siblings attending the setting; and enable children to maintain physical proximity in relation to their preferred educators. Furthermore, the large, central hatch that made the kitchen space visible assisted children in forming relationships with kitchen staff to an extent not observed in the other settings in her research. Children regularly transported a chair to the hatch and would converse with the cook about what she was doing and she, in turn, would proffer occasional titbits of food. This suggests, then, that the time/space configurations of early childhood settings are implicated in the extent to which children are able to develop and sustain relationships.

The material environment also has the potential to produce particular feelings, such as of subjugation or empowerment (Lenz-Taguchi, 2010). By way of example, in Setting four in Deb's research, in one of the toddler rooms, the children were expected to find the chair with their photograph fixed to the back when sitting down for a meal or snack. This spatial organisation had been established with the express purpose of separating children deemed 'troublemakers' from one another and to secure their closer proximity to an educator. In a context of intense scrutiny, the ability to manage children's behaviour 'appropriately' is particularly salient for educators, whose skills as an educator are often judged on the basis of such 'performances' (Phelan, 1997).

Rather than finding herself in close proximity to educators indoors, as Deb's focus on food events inevitably led, Rachel's research offers a contrast. The spatial configuration of educators, children, and researchers is likely to differ according to one's research focus. The children's play, when focused around themes of death and violence, was often loud and physically active, resulting in admonishment from educators indoors where the preservation of a quiet 'soundscape' (Schafer, 1977) was prized. Children engaging in such play were often encouraged to go outdoors where such play was relatively removed from educator involvement and often took place in hidden spaces, enabling different types of interaction.

To sum up, in this chapter, we have argued that early childhood research cannot be divorced from the chronotopes within which it is located. In particular, we have argued that neoliberalism, with its elevation of market principles, impacts directly on early childhood settings. Within such contexts, the child becomes framed as a social investment – important (indeed precious) for what s/he will become. This, in turn, has implications for the kinds of relationship that are possible in the early childhood settings that researchers enter. But what is missing from our discussion so far is a sense of the *negotiations* that take place between child-participants and adult-researchers within these settings. Just what do we make of each other? How does the body and bodily relations impact on the research process? It is to questions such as these that the next chapter turns.

3

CHILDREN AND ADULTS, PARTICIPANTS AND RESEARCHERS

What do we make of each other?

In this chapter, we will explore what child-participants and adult-researchers make of one another in the research process. We will expand on Chapters 1 and 2, which emphasised that research relationships are shaped by conceptions of childhood as well as physical, social, political, and economic realities. We will argue that the *specific* conceptions of childhood operating in early childhood settings and the highly constructed nature of early childhood spaces create a *particular* contextual field for researcher–participant negotiations. We will begin considering how the institutional structure of such settings frames the negotiation of research relationships considering: What does it mean to be an adult-researcher in early childhood settings? What relational positions are available, possible or desirable in such contexts? How are research relations between adults and children affected by, and how do they affect, the generational order in early childhood settings?

We will argue that all researchers (as well as participants) bring something of themselves to research, but new understandings and subjectivities are co-constructed in the process. Reinharz (1997: 6) argues that both these 'brought' and 'situationally created' selves are fundamental to how research progresses including which participants relate to the researcher and in what ways. Reinharz (1997) is insistent that selves shift and change in the research process and that even the manner in which these 'brought selves' have import is relational: how participants interpret a researcher's 'selves' – including what they find meaningful – is dependent on the time/space configurations in which the research is undertaken.

Further, we will consider what matters or comes to matter to child-participants and adult-researchers in the process of negotiating research relationships. Here, we will consider relationships as an embodied practice considering how our corporeal presence and interactions inform what we make of each other. We will consider: What role do bodily relations play in the research process? How do these relations shape and how are they shaped by the material, social, and cultural spaces of early childhood settings? What is the relationship between embodied research relations and transformative research practices? Bodily matters – particularly in relation to pleasure and the 'carnivalesque' (Bakhtin, 1984b) – are often considered difficult and challenging topics within early childhood. As a result, they are often downplayed or left unacknowledged (Tobin, 1997a). Yet, we will argue that conducting research with a relational ethic involves acting with answerability (Bakhtin, 1990; 1993) that is not just verbal but also corporeal and embodied.

In many ways, these topics relate to issues of access, entry to the field, and impression management that are discussed throughout research method literature. We do not intend to rehearse the broader discussions here, but suffice it to say we will argue with those who critique technicist approaches (e.g. Coffey, 1999) that often emphasise face sheet characteristics and exterior presentation. Such approaches imply a more orderly relationship progression than the messy situations of day-to-day research allow and absent the body and researcher's self from the process. Importantly, we will emphasise the contextual and shifting nature of what researchers and participants make of one another and note these issues are not only of concern in relationships with adults but also children.

'Who are you?'

One of the initial questions many empirical researchers ask themselves centres on the 'role' they will assume in the field. Participants are often interested in related questions (Christensen, 2004) and both of us were repeatedly asked: 'Why are you here?' and 'Who are you?' Considerations of a researcher's role often centre on questions about the level of involvement a researcher will play in participants' lives, typically framed as a continuum from 'complete participant' to 'complete observer' (Johnson and Christensen, 2008). Considerations – particularly in ethnography – also include questions about the position the researcher will assume within the organisational structure of the research setting (Hammersley and Atkinson, 2007).

In research *with* children (as opposed to research *about* children), debates about the 'role' of the researcher have typically taken Mandell's (1991) notion of the 'least adult' as their jumping-off point – either as a basis of explanation or critique. In brief, the 'least adult' role in research is one in which the adult-researcher seeks to take a complete participant role and 'suspends all adult-like characteristics except physical size' (Mandell, 1991: 40). Such characteristics are assumed to include 'authority, verbal competency, cognitive and social mastery' (Mandell, 1991: 42). This attempt to literally 'become' a child involves engagement in activities children undertake such as playing with children in the sandbox, swinging with children, and engaging in extended imaginative play. Such an 'insider' role is considered important in attempts to gain intimate knowledge of children's understandings and activities that are otherwise, literally and metaphorically, hidden in the secret corners of early childhood settings (Warming, 2005).

While offering a methodological approach to researching children's social worlds from their perspective, the 'least adult' role has come under a series of sustained critiques including that it is difficult to maintain (Thorne, 1993) and diminishes possibilities for considering how differences in generational experiences affect children's lives (James et al., 1998). A more fundamental problem is that the 'least adult' position is based on a series of potentially patronising assumptions – for example that children can be 'duped' into a belief that an adult-researcher is a child. This belittles children's existing knowledge of the signifiers of and social status related to adulthood, and implies that children can be easily convinced to dispense this understanding of the social world as the result of one adult's actions. Children are very aware of social differentiations between people – including both adults and children – as their daily experiences are shaped by 'dislocations' and power imbalances, with generation 'looming large' in the way children make sense of and experience the constraints and possibilities of their daily lives (Mayall, 2002, 2008). As such, Mayall (2008: 110) notes that the 'least adult' position is based on an assumption it is possible to 'dilute' or 'diffuse' generational inequalities just by the way a researcher behaves. Christensen (2004: 173) concurs, arguing we cannot merely 'wish away the complexity of the differences and similarities between children and adults as they are currently constituted'.

Alldred (1998: 151) offers an even more scathing critique suggesting that adult attempts to 'enter' children's peer cultures are little more than colonial enterprises constituting children as exotic 'little aliens'. She is critical of the assumption that it is possible to 'suspend' adult interpretations by taking on 'children's perspectives' arguing that this is impossible epistemologically – due to adults' subject positions – and ontologically given that she does not accept a particular peer culture exists beyond the researcher's presence. We would agree with Alldred (1998) that a researcher's presence indisputably affects the research field; however, we do not hold her 'strong' (Sayer, 2000) social constructionist conviction that the peer culture is merely produced by the researcher. While the peer culture will be different with and without a researcher's presence, the people and spaces that form this peer culture have an ontological presence that exceeds the researcher.

Overall, what these debates suggest is that the 'least adult' role can at best be considered naïve and at worst reinforcement through silent dismissal of the generational inequities and power imbalances between adults and children. As a result, Mayall (2008) argues in support of a position that engages with – rather than downplays – generational issues. In her research interactions with children, Mayall makes explicit that although she has experienced her own childhood she is interested in children's practices and knowledge of *contemporary* childhood. In extending this argument, Christensen (2004) argues that she positions herself as an 'unusual type of adult' in her ethnographic work.

In the discussion that follows, we aim to critique and extend this earlier theoretical work. To begin, we will consider the danger of slippage into essentialist understandings of 'childhood' and 'adulthood' in both conceptualisations of the 'least adult' role and its critics. Becoming a 'least adult' involves putting aside social mastery and capabilities when entering children's worlds (Mandell, 1991). This is underpinned by a derogatory assumption linking adulthood – as opposed to childhood – with competence. One only need look to studies of children's caring work to appreciate children's diverse and changing capabilities – such as supporting friends and family members through difficult times (Mayall, 2002). Adults too have shifting competencies dependent on context and relationships: there is nothing artificial about walking into a setting as a researcher and not knowing about taken-for-granted practices. For example, in Deb's food events research (Baby room: Setting four), she found herself constantly perplexed as to when the children were permitted to go outdoors as there seemed no 'pattern' to this activity; neither was it based on responding to the vagaries of English summer weather.

Ironically, critiques of the 'least adult' role run a similar risk of naturalising socially constructed distinctions between children and adults. For example, conceptualising adults' participation with children as 'pseudo-colonialist' (Alldred, 1998: 151) or citing adult-researchers' playful participation with children in sandpits as examples of 'pretending' to be a child (Christensen, 2004) includes an implicit assumption about an entirely natural separation between childhood and adulthood. These critiques imply that activities such as imaginative play are the stuff of childhood. While we are not suggesting that these authors use this distinction to *devalue* play and childhood – a move that could be made in relation to this argument – we are suggesting that these critiques run the risk of reinforcing a false binary between adult and child activities. Implying that when adults-researchers play with children it is disingenuous or inherently invasive does not take into account the presence of playfulness and play activity in the lives of both adults and children.

The opposite can also be pointed out: children – even the very young – engage in labour as paid workers (Morrow, 2010) and/or as unpaid workers involved in their own care as well as that of their families (Mayall, 2002) and within the education system in the 'work' of developing skills, knowledge, attitudes, and subjectivities needed for the labour market (Qvortrup, 1985). Perhaps an even more fundamental difficulty with such distinctions is they assume the distinctiveness of play lies in the *type* of activity undertaken rather than the *attitude* of the person, in essence creating an unhelpful dichotomy between work and play. As Bruner, Jolly, and Sylva (1976: v) argue: 'The main characteristic of play – whether of child or adult – is not its content but its mode. Play is an approach to action, not a form of activity.'

While attempting to 'work with' generational issues, Christensen's (2004) proposal of the role of 'unusual type of adult' also essentialises adulthood. It presupposes that there is a *usual* type of adult. Yet, from a very early age, children learn to recognise, respond to, and even utilise the nuances of different adults. While adults in early childhood settings may fulfil particular roles and be imbued with greater social and institutional power than children – about which more later – these adults still bring different expectations and ways of being to relationships and children can become quickly aware of this. For example, in Rachel's research, while children initially attempted to enlist her help in soliciting apologies – the dominant expectation in the setting when a 'violation' occurred – they quickly realised that she would not make such demands on the 'offending' child and rarely sought her out a second time for such support.

Further, Christensen (2004) describes the 'unusual adult' position as involving a refusal to intervene and direct children's activities or resolve their conflicts. While these may be common responsibilities of adults, the notion here seems to be that these are not roles *children* assume, which contradicts diverse empirical studies documenting children's efforts to influence others (e.g. Löfdahl and Hägglund, 2006). Indeed, both of our studies included countless examples of children intervening and directing the activities of other children and educators. In Deb's research, for example, while observing lunchtime in the baby room of Setting four, Deb noted John getting increasingly distressed at not being served his food as Nadiya – the educator – had started to serve the food at one end of the table and was working her round to each child in turn. Another child – Emily – observing this, started directing who was getting their food with her hands and gestured to John what was happening to show him that he would be next to get his food, which seemed to assuage his anger. We do not see such instances as examples of 'unusual children' to invert Christensen's (2004) term, but view these as examples of the *many* ways in which children are agentive in the life of the settings they attend.

A second point of elaboration is that there is a need to consider early childhood settings as neoliberal spaces when considering researcher roles. Early childhood settings operate within a context of high regulation and surveillance, an emphasis on particular forms of 'human capital development' and as a redemptive force tasked with compensating for supposed 'lacks' in children's home lives (Dahlberg and Moss, 2005). Another significant feature of early childhood settings is the entirely artificial age separation. Such polarisation – rather than a continuum of age groups – is mirrored by a sharp division in roles and responsibilities. Educators in these settings are deemed responsible for the 'civilisation', 'schoolification', and development of young children. While children may have experience with a variety of adults in their wider communities, within early childhood settings in the 'First World/North' adulthood *largely* equates with being an 'educator'.

As a result, we suggest that the position of 'least-educator' is a more helpful way to distinguish the role of a researcher in 'outsider' research. The 'least-educator' role encourages researchers to consider ways to position themselves outside of the institutionalised responsibilities and authority embedded in an educator role, instead working towards what Edmiston (2005, 2008) refers to as 'sharing authority'. Rachel attempted to take up such a role in her taboo play research, which included abstaining from running any 'educator-led' activities or group times or enforcing setting rules. Moreover, it meant not entering into interactions with children motivated by pedagogical intentions. While we would suggest that all relationships are ultimately pedagogic – where both children and adults are learners and educators – the distinction we are trying to make here is one of *explicit* pedagogical objectives (see Suissa, 2006). Further, a least-educator position does not deny the 'adultness' of the researcher. So Rachel would, for example, read to children if asked or tie up a child's shoes, drawing on her own competencies, as Deb did in her research. Taking up Mayall's (2008) point about engaging with – rather than denying – generation was an important part of this role. This involved reflection about how conceptions of childhood and adulthood shaped our interactions.

Despite suggesting the role of 'least-educator', our final point is that however well (pre)prepared, such a role inevitably shifts and changes as the researcher interacts with different people. As Rachel noted in her fieldnotes:

> I had planned not to interfere in the way children resolved problems – a common educator practice in the setting. But it is hard in the middle of fights where children may be actually hurting each other. On some level, I feel that I need to take some responsibility for my presence as it seems to bring 'unlikely' children together. Do I stick with my naïve idea to let the children handle things as they 'normally' do and expect that the peer culture rules transverse the nursery? At the same time, I wonder how much of my concern about keeping things under control in some way has to do with my sense of myself as a 'competent educator' who can 'maintain order and discipline.
>
> *(Rachel Rosen, Taboo play)*

As this indicates, the role of 'least-educator' is not an easy position to inhabit, particularly for researchers who have previously been educators. Prior experiences cannot just be suspended as they have helped to shape the way we think about and move through the world, becoming in some ways part of our educator 'habitus': 'A system of lasting, transposable dispositions which, integrating past experiences, functions at every moment as a *matrix of perceptions, appreciations, and actions*' (Bourdieu, 1977: 82–83). While a particular habitus is not inevitable, we would argue that we do move through the world with a certain amount of – (un)conscious – constancy in our persons.

The role(s) a researcher inhabits also need(s) to be considered within the context of particular research foci. Deb's research brought her into closer proximity with educators owing to its focus on food events, which were generally managed by adult educators. The 'least-educator' position would have been far more difficult to maintain in such a context (a point we pick up again in the next chapter) as such events are often characterised (for adults and children) by a level of formality and 'body rules' (Leavitt and Power, 1997) unlike the play episodes Deb participated in during the course of her research and which were the primary focus of Rachel's research.

Ultimately, we would argue that attempts to adhere to a predetermined role – even that of 'least-educator' – are not only difficult but close down possibilities for dialogic relationships to form. As Bakhtin (1993) warns, the minute we move into abstract theorisation – in this case about relationships and our role within them –

we cease to be answerable. While the least-educator position offers some helpful ways of considering adult–child research relationships, planning to inhabit a particular role cannot substitute for the negotiations that take place in the fluid and demanding world of early childhood settings.

Holding on to a predetermined role in some sense represents an attempt to stabilise and categorise relationships that are ultimately 'unfinalisable'. It also implies that if researchers just take on a particular role, children will desire a relationship with them. Such a move is one of homogenisation, reinforcing a view of children as a group as engaged in some kind of tacit agreement as to the role of the ethnographer (Warming, 2011) or indeed adults more generally. This negates children's diversity and the wide variety of competent readings of *and* changeable responses to others in their lives.

This is evident in the following exemplar from Deb's research. In one of the toddler rooms in Setting four, Constantine called her 'bee lady' ('bees' denoted any small creature) as she was always willing to seek out and handle small creatures in the garden with him – indeed, his mother asked one of the educators who the 'bee lady' was as she tried to make sense of his talk about Deb when at home. However, the 'bee lady' positioning was not shared by all children in the nursery and was only assigned by Constantine after a few weeks of Deb's coming to the setting – he would not have 'known' her shared interest in 'bees' before then.

Rachel also noted children's various and changeable readings of her and her research. Some children approached her immediately and acted as 'sponsors' (Reinharz, 1997) into particular peer groups; for example, Paul would often ask Rachel on her arrival: 'Are we going to do *cool* play today?' This opened up possibilities for researching with a new and larger group of children as Paul was considered a desirable child to play with. Some children took more of a 'gatekeeper' role evading participation by absenting themselves, turning away or actively denying Rachel entrance to particular groups verbally; physically, such as through barricades built with blocks around play areas; or by recourse to their character's abilities, for example growling loudly as a dinosaur – expressions of dissent, which Rachel certainly respected. At other times, these same children sought Rachel out for conversations or play.

Researchers also desire different relationships with participants at different times. There may be children who are of particular interest to a researcher, for example due to their insights and involvement with the research topic or the feelings they provoke in a researcher. For example, we both reflected that we found ourselves drawn to children who regularly spent time with other children allowing us to research peer cultures, not just children's individual activity. For Rachel, peer groups were not only the focus of her study but she found it 'easier' to take a less dominant role in the play when there were many voices determining the narrative. For Deb, her focus on food events as a source of sociality (Shilling, 2005) also generated an interest in *groups* of children when engaged in play with a food theme as well as during the 'real' events of meal and snack times where groups of children are more 'managed' by educators.

To summarise, while we suggest that the 'least-educator' role offers a helpful starting point in terms of considering researcher positioning, ultimately relationships are based on far more complex negotiations than the 'role' taken by the researcher. Instead, we are arguing that acting with a relational ethic involves listening to the children we are in relationships with – through fallible acts of interpretation, active responses, and openness to unexpected replies.

Bodied relationships

Regardless of the ways in which a researcher positions him/herself, relationship negotiations are not just cerebral but also deeply embodied experiences (Coffey, 1999). In the following sections, we will discuss three aspects of corporeality that came to matter in our research relations with children: *size, hair, and bums*. We are not arguing that these will matter in similar ways in other settings or for other researchers as we recognise the 'emplaced' nature of bodies in their inter-relationship with the mind and the environment (Howes, 2005b). By way of example, we note that one reason 'skin' may not have come to occupy a central concern for either of us is due in large part to systemic racism. As white women, we were potentially less aware of the resonances of skin (and the 'naturalisation' and privileges of whiteness in particular) than a non-white researcher given the 'business-as-usual forms of racism that people of color confront every day' (Delgado and Stefancic, 2000: xvi). In other words, skin mattered, but our whiteness made this less apparent to us. Other bodily matters also had significance: Deb (Albon, 2010) noted the importance of taste and food allergies, and Rachel has written elsewhere about the semiotic and affective acoustics embodied in 'the scream' (Rosen, 2012). As a result, what we are arguing here is that – although we are focusing here on size, hair, and bums – bodily characteristics, interactions, and proximity in general are central to the negotiation of research relationships. In other words, bodies *matter*.

We should acknowledge that such a play on the word 'matter', highlighting that bodies have import in our lives, are multifaceted, and have a material presence, is not new or original. Indeed, Butler's (1993) well-known book is titled *Bodies that Matter*. However, as Shilling (2003) and others (e.g. Schlichter, 2011) point out, there is a tendency within Butler's writing, as well as other discursively focused work on the body, to replace the 'biological' body with the 'social' body inscribed by structures and categorisation that misplaces the material presence and active experiencing of the fleshy body. In contrast, in the discussion that follows, we aim to work with Shilling's (2003: 11) conceptualisation of the body as an 'unfinished biological and social phenomenon which is transformed, within certain limits, as a result of its entry into, and participation in, society'. Thus, we will consider what matters to child-participants and adult-researchers and how what matters, as well as the matter of bodies themselves, come to change in the embodied experience of negotiating research relationships.

Size matters

Over time, we both began to notice that size mattered a great deal to the children we sought to build relationships with. Similarly, James (2000) notes that height was important in her ethnographic work with English primary school children, often acting as a marker of status in part due to the conflation of height and adulthood. Noting height differences between children and adults may seem almost a tautology, as one way of distinguishing the two groups has to do with physical growth and size. Even Mandell (1991) noted in relation to the 'least-adult' role that size was the one factor that could not be mediated through impression management. Perhaps because of the ostensible 'obviousness' of size as a factor in the positioning of adults and children, some of the particular ways that size does matter in research have been less examined. At this point, it seems essential to point out that such 'obviousness' is, in fact, also open to question. Children can be both larger and smaller (and here we refer to both height and weight) than adults, depending on genetic makeup as well as social and environmental factors. With that caveat in place, size still matters in complex ways.

As we discussed in Chapter 2, one of the notable features of early childhood settings in much of the 'First World/North' is the presence of small 'child-sized' furniture, equipment, and spaces. Size matters in terms of access to the spaces and use of this equipment; it is one way in which the activities and movements of adults can be readily distinguished from those of children. Children often squeeze under tables, in nooks and crannies beside shelves, and in the small spaces of 'home corner' furniture. Many children fit their bodies together in close proximity in 'cave-like' structures. Access to such spaces is barred for adults who are larger, creating spaces of possible relationship building and spaces that are out of reach. While neither of us would ever go into a space unless invited by children, as a fairly small woman – by both Canadian and English standards – there were no spaces in the research setting that Rachel was unable to enter due to size.

As Rachel noted:

> My size is certainly something that I am aware of as I negotiate the small confined spaces where much of the children's play takes place. Today, I followed the children to a small space underneath a raised tunnel in a dash to escape a ferocious monster. The children piled in underneath and I went to follow. Cary, a child who I didn't know very well said from inside, 'You can't come under here.' Faiza – who I had spent a great deal more time with – replied firmly, 'She can.' It is possible that Cary and Faiza were merely commenting on my size in relation to the small space. But I wondered whether there was something more to it. Had this become a 'children's space' – an escape from prying adult eyes and dominating presence? Here size might work to children's advantage!
>
> *(Rachel Rosen, Taboo play)*

Rachel's small size meant that there were not many physical barriers to children including her in their activities in spaces other adults in the setting were physically restricted from entering. This gave her a picture of the play from *inside* the spaces rather than out. These small spaces inevitably prompted close bodily proximity and physical touch, which – as we will discuss further later – were important parts of the way in which research relationships developed.

We do not mean to suggest here that researchers must necessarily be small in size in order to cultivate relationships with child-participants or even that being smaller in size supports 'better' relationships. We are merely suggesting that an adult-researcher's size does matter in the way research relationships are negotiated, as Deb's experiences further demonstrate. During fieldwork in Setting three, Deb lost a great deal of her body weight. When she first visited the setting she could not get into the role play area as she was too big to get through the door, despite many children's invitations to play (this was also the case for most of the educators). There were also occasions when she feared to sit on small furniture – unless it looked particularly robust – for fear it would break. Standing up and looking over the role play area emphasised her large size in comparison to the children and prompted Deb to reflect in her fieldnotes:

> As adults we are unusually 'big' in the 'unnaturally' small world of early childhood settings. The relative inactivity of my work as a lecturer in comparison to the physicality of my work with young children in the past has piled on the pounds. Perhaps it is this or my years since being in a setting on a regular basis that has prompted this reflection.
>
> (Deb Albon, Food events: Setting three)

As a consequence of losing weight, Deb's body size and shape changed and she became increasingly aware that she was now able to move into spaces that were once out of bounds to her. Because of this, she needed to attend to ensuring she *negotiated* access to the role play area rather than assuming entry based on her excitement at the possibilities her new size/shape afforded her.

Hair matters

Head hair was another 'bodily matter' that seemed to fascinate children in our studies. We would suggest that one reason hair assumes such import in bodily relations is its sensual and textural qualities. As Rachel noted in her fieldnotes:

> Children will often lean their bodies against me when I am crouched down talking; stroking, twirling, rubbing, and plaiting my long hair. Often, children will not say anything, but will make their presence known – and in fact indicate a connection to me – through touching my hair. Today, I was deep in conversation with a group of children. Paul approached with two of his friends, listened for a moment, and then turned and began speaking with his

group. Although his back was to me, he began to gently stroke my hair, occasionally rubbing it between his folded fingers. After a time, he left with his group on a different adventure, smoothing my hair down against my back before leaving.

(Rachel Rosen, Taboo play)

Manning (2007) might refer to Paul's stroking of Rachel's hair – and similar experiences within Deb's research – as a 'reaching toward'. She argues that: 'At its most political, to reach toward is to create a concept for unthinking the individual as a discrete entity. . . mov[ing] toward something that is not yet' (Manning, 2007: xviii). 'Reaching toward' and touching Rachel's hair not only offered Paul an opportunity to make a *corporeal interconnection* with Rachel, but also to create, come to know, and embody a *new sense* of the relationship.

This bodily proximity in relation to hair is exemplified most obviously in the spread of head lice. On a number of occasions in Deb's research, she found the presence of 'nits' in her hair, which she had not had since leaving her work as an early childhood educator. In some sense, although an unwanted impact of proximity, the presence of 'nits' seemed to say much about the *corporeal* connection Deb had with children and served as a tangible reminder of the interconnectedness of the people in her research.

While hair matters in relationship negotiations in part due to its materiality, it also occupies an important boundary position socially and biologically. Synnott (1987: 404) argues that: 'Hair not only symbolises the self but, in a very real sense, it is the self since it grows from and is part of the physical human body.' While we have been alluding to a much 'leakier' and relational sense of the body than is contained in his work, we would argue that the 'publicness' or visibility of 'private' hair – to draw on Synnott's (1987) distinction – is actually an indication of the porousness of bodies and is pivotal in what children made of us as researchers.

In Setting one of Deb's research, Hamid called her 'the lady without this bit' (meaning her forehead, as her fringe (bangs) hangs long to her eyebrows). Sometimes, Deb would deliberately raise her fringe when he said this and they would play a 'peek-a-boo' game – 'now you see my forehead and now you don't' to peals of laughter. As her hair was far longer when researching in Setting one – and perhaps as it was far longer than that of the educators and also a different hair texture to most of the children and their families/carers owing to differences in ethnicity (Deb is white and most of the families/carers were black) – Deb found her hair was the subject of much interest. By the time she was researching in Setting four, some years later, her hair was shorter and most of the educators had very long hair. In this setting, most of the children were white and the educators were primarily of Bangladeshi origin but residing in the UK. On the occasions that their hair was uncovered, Deb noted many children stroking, smelling, and generally 'reaching toward' these educators' hair.

We argue that hair is also a central feature in relationship negotiations because of its figurative value. From the highly gendered Brothers Grimm classic

Rapunzel – where her flowing locks are a mark of her unsurpassed beauty as well as the means for mediating her contact with others – to 'the Natural', a radical and psychically powerful icon of the anti-racist movement in the USA and beyond, hair is a highly charged social and political symbol. However, as with other signs, hair does not hold a fixed meaning. Synnott (1987) notes that hair's transformability is part of what makes it an arena of contestation and, we would add, its position as a material of intense observation, speculation, and interaction for children. For example, the day Rachel walked in with her hair tied in a ponytail, Aamil stared at her for a long moment, his head tilted to the side. 'You're different,' he shouted from across the outdoor space.

However, we want to suggest that hair also affects what adult-researchers make of children. As Rachel wrote in her fieldnotes:

> I keep finding myself surprised by Emily's play. There is something that always strikes a discordant note for me when she fluffs back her long, curly blonde hair, like a model in a photo shoot, and then raises her arm in the air to kill the dragon with her flaming hand. It's embarrassing, and revealing, to realise how much I have categorised her based on the way that she looks.
> (Rachel Rosen, Taboo play)

For Rachel, the process of experiencing and considering reflexively the way hair mattered for children in her study, made her aware of the way that hair mattered in the sense she *too* was making of others and herself. These issues were brought to the surface by the embodied relationships and children's 'excess of seeing' (Bakhtin, 1990). This 'excess' is very literal: children are able to view us from perspectives we can never experience – behind, on top, and below. The 'excess' is also more intangible: it brought to light that one of the reasons we noticed hair mattered to children was that hair matters to us. Deb noted during our discussions about coming to see how hair matters: 'My hair is part of my identity. I know that I am recognised at a distance by my hair. And it is a bit of me that I actually *like* unlike some other parts of my body.' Due in part to a rise in consumer culture and increasing ability to transform it, the body is increasingly tied to self-identity and imbued with particular value (Shilling, 2003).

Bums matter

A final point about how bodies matter in negotiating adult–child research relationships relates to the 'bottom' and its excesses. As Rachel noted in her fieldnotes:

> My bum is an area of sustained interest, especially for a small group of boys. It manifests as friendly slaps on my bum, 'bumping into' my bum, pushing me by my bum when manoeuvring in play, and peals of giggles when Jesse said 'I saw your bum!' (despite it being completely covered). When it first

happened I felt desperately uncomfortable, uncertain how to respond to these 'intimate' interactions with young children.

(Rachel Rosen, Taboo play)

One of the reasons such situations can be uncomfortable for adult-researchers is that they collide with conceptions of childhood that claim it as a time of innocence. Boundaries between adulthood and childhood are often marked by a distinction between childhood 'purity' and 'healthy' adult sexual knowledge. Robinson and Davies (2010: 251) argue that: 'Sexuality is constituted as irrelevant to young children's lives, and yet, at the same time, a "danger" to them.' They note that adults are often positioned as the 'gatekeepers' of childhood innocence leading to uneasiness when confronted by children with questions or actions that are related to sexuality. In her reflections, Rachel noted that this dominant way of conceptualising childhood continued to resonate in her interactions, despite theoretical commitments otherwise.

Further, Rachel noted the conflation of childhood and innocence made it difficult to even write about such experiences. This is exacerbated by the highly charged atmosphere in early childhood settings surrounding abuse, which, in principle, we applaud given the horrors of living with and beyond sexual abuse. However, this has led to an increasingly implicit or even explicit prohibition on physical interactions between non-familial adults (men especially) and young children (e.g. Pole, 2007). In their study of American early childhood settings, Leavitt and Power (1997) note that touch has become limited to behavioural guidance, rather than comfort or intimacy. Yet, these and other authors in *Making a Place for Pleasure* (Tobin, 1997b) issue impassioned pleas for a return of pleasure and caring touch in the early childhood world, arguing that these are important aspects of relationships.

Regardless, the context of heightened concerns about child protection creates particular conditions for researchers of childhood experience, creating the need for an 'embodied reflexivity' and consideration of questions of where research interactions take place, how researchers present themselves, and, most importantly, the comfort level of participants (Pole, 2007). As Rachel's research continued, the 'bum' moments continued to occur and Rachel noted: 'I haven't exactly become more "comfortable" – and perhaps discomfort is a good thing for provoking an embodied reflexivity – but I have tried to worry away at my initial reactions, questioning in part the "adult" spin I was putting on the children's actions and fascinations.'

It is here that we would like to suggest a number of possible ways of analysing these 'bum' moments starting with the point that if the word is always 'double-voiced' (Bakhtin, 1981), perhaps actions are as well. In this sense, a variety of potentially contradictory ideological and embodied sources can be traced in both the words and actions we cite and the audiences and contexts we address. On a very basic level, perhaps part of the children's interest related simply to height differences: Rachel's bum – when standing – was right at the boys' eye level. Further, the type of play that Rachel was investigating often took place in small spaces prompting close physical proximity. In contrast, bums mattered less in Deb's research, perhaps as she was regularly in a seated position as is usual for meal and snack times. These spatial reflections on their own, however, do not account for these children's sustained interest in the 'bum'.

We would suggest that there is a gendered dimension to the attention: a particular expression of the eroticisation of the female body under the male gaze. Here then was a possible way for the boys to draw on derogatory notions of a sexualised female body, available for male viewing and 'use', to challenge Rachel's adult authority, much in the way that over 20 years ago Walkerdine (1990) described young boys' attempts to shift inequitable relations from adult–child to male–female in order to position themselves more powerfully in relation to educators. The group of boys may have been considering how Rachel would respond to such a 'challenge' to her generational status, a test of Rachel's least-educator positioning in the setting.

Yet, there was something more generally alluring about bums for this group of children. As an adult participant in the peer culture, it is possible that Rachel became privy to some of the peer culture attempts to make sense of the body and sexuality. As Robinson and Davies (2010) note, adult discomfort about discussions of sexuality with children mean that children's attempts to construct such knowledge are often met by others in their peer group. While we would never suggest that either of us has become a 'child' peer, Rachel's positioning as least-educator did involve her in children's peer cultures in ways that were different from that of many of the educators.

The bottom was an ongoing site of physical contact between children and a small group of boys, in particular. Rachel noted many instances of thumping another child's bum, reminiscent of male sports' figures who slap their teammate's bottom in encouragement or exuberance, and the bottom featured centrally in imaginative play. Reed and Brown (2000) suggest that in rough and tumble play intimate physical contact between boys is accepted whereas in non-play situations physical contact may be questioned or even refused. They argue that such play is a type of 'camouflage for expressions of intimacy and care' arguing that 'suppression . . . may be a further illustration of our culture's homophobia' (Reed and Brown, 2000: 114). Rachel's study was not specifically about rough and tumble play but perhaps imaginative play also provides a cover for intimate physical contact.

While we can question the need for such a masking, because of homophobia and misplaced conceptions of childhood innocence, we would argue that the desire for such caring touch is important in forming research relationships. Whether interest in the 'bum' was particular to the settings and research topic, more generally what children make of us as a researcher seems in part to do with such physical intimacy. Sitting in close proximity, hugs of welcome, physical touch in healing play themes, hair stroking and fluffing (as discussed previously), and hand holding were common occurrences in the way children made sense of us and worked to build relationships.

The bottom's 'waste' was also a matter of importance: fart and excrement jokes abounded. In both our research projects, children made frequent comments about excrement throughout their interactions such as: 'I see your poo!' or 'I'll fart at you!' to other children acting as 'baddies' in pursuit. In Deb's research examining food events, this was especially prevalent as might be expected given that farting and excrement are inevitable by-products of eating and drinking. The ability to fart at will was accorded a great deal of kudos in each of her research settings yet was never something she or any other adults felt able to join in with.

According to Bakhtin (1984b), refuse expulsed from the body throws into question the individual and autonomous subject – excrement and flatulence exist neither purely inside nor outside the human body. They are a physical manifestation of the body's porousness and interactivity with the wider world. Bakhtin (1984b: 322) goes on to suggest that 'classical concepts of the body' – one of a contained corporeality – lead to behavioural controls seeking to halt, limit or sequester these bodily flows as part of what Elias (1978) refers as the 'civilising process'. We are at pains to note here that we are not attempting to naturalise a derogatory distinction between the 'civilised' and 'uncivilised', but suggest that what is considered 'civilised' is based on a particular notion of the separate, autonomous, ordered, and rational subject. Such premises are often used to position children, women, working-class people, and (post-)colonial subjects as uncivilised in their purportedly 'closer' connection to the senses and body (Howes, 2005b) – arguments that have been used to justify brutality and inequity (see Connell, 1987; Shilling, 2003). One notable impact of the accumulative social taboos demanding the sequestration of bodily functions is increasing 'distance' between adults and children (Elias, 1994) with educators charged with 'civilising' children's bodies (Phelan, 1997).

Potentially then what makes bums and their excess a source of fascination for children is the sense of taboo surrounding both intimate body parts and bodily waste. As Douglas (1966) notes, 'taboos' exist to deal with 'matter out of place' or matter which breaches attempts to order and categorise the world. Intimate attention to the buttocks and their excesses in an early childhood setting can be seen as 'matter out of place' from a number of perspectives: conceptions of the inappropriateness of sexuality for 'innocent' children, homophobic ideas about caring physical contact between boys, bodily refuse as matter out of place in the clean and ordered public spaces of early childhood settings, and matter that challenges individualism and clear demarcations of the corporeal body. And this is exacerbated as children get older and have more experience *within* a setting. In Deb's research, babies and toddlers often had their nappies (diapers) changed in public view, whereas toileting for *older* children became a progressively more private matter, in part mirroring how settings are charged with managing children's movement to the expected, more 'civilised' behaviours of the wider (adult) world (Ben-Ari, 1997).

In our respective research projects, we both noted a sense of bonding through a humorous use of the taboo. For example, in Deb's research, on one occasion an educator farted loudly during snack time, which was accompanied by a strong smell. At first, she pretended this had not happened but gradually, the hilarity the children clearly felt about the situation encouraged everyone to simultaneously break into peals of laughter – a temporary liberation from the 'order' prized during the setting's snack times. Similarly, in Rachel's research, children occasionally used 'toilet' humour to break up tension in moments that felt as if on the edge of slipping into angry, physical fights.

These exemplars are reminiscent of Bakhtin's (1984b) notion of the 'carnivalesque'. According to Bakhtin (1984b: 317), the medieval carnival was an event filled with 'grotesque realism' where bodies – including their forms, functions and 'sensuousness' – were 'subject to positive exaggeration, to hyperbolization' as a way to transgress the 'confines between bodies and the body and the world'. Jokes and laughter, which centred on the grotesque real, were times when people parodied the ideological authority and domination of royalty and those in officialdom. However, more than just parody, Bakhtin suggests that the carnival is an act of renewal, offering new possible ways of being and new social relations.

This suggests in some ways that responses in moments of bodily jokes and engagement are crucial. Part of what children make of us and how our relationships with child-participants shift and change is impacted by the ways in which we navigate these taboo topics and bodily expressions. Rachel noted:

> I have tended to avoid children's references to bodily waste because I don't want to 'condone' or negate it. But silences do speak. And if such talk and joking is a part of some of these children's peer culture: Am I communicating that I don't care what they have to say? Am I ignoring an important aspect of the group humour? Am I losing out on both the research potential and the chance to form stronger connections? Is poo really such a 'terrible' thing to joke about?
>
> So, I had a play with 'toileting humour' today just to see where it would go. I was with a small group of children who were making a plan to trap a terrifying monster. Rafiq approached us and said to me, 'Yuck! The monster smells: poo-poo.' Deciding to have a go, I responded: 'Oh that smelly monster. I guess he doesn't have a toilet.' Many of the children laughed and Rafiq joined the group's play for the first time that day.
>
> (Rachel Rosen, Taboo play)

Perhaps then, we can see moments of pleasure and laughter as being central to the negotiation and formation of research relationships, rather than moments to be avoided. Humour, and parody in particular, rely on a sense that all is not as it appears, creating a space for the possibilities of Bernstein's (2000: 30) '*yet to be thought*'. Without intending to valorise humour or deny its potential for bigotry and ostracism, we do suggest that it offers an important opportunity for challenging reified dichotomies (such as between adulthood and childhood) with their attendant inequitable practices and effects.

To sum up, in this chapter, we have argued for an embodied and situational approach to 'impression management' where the body and senses are an important part of negotiating relationships and where selves, relations, and positionings are ultimately unfinalisable. We caution, however, that such *proximal* and *emplaced* interactions require continued reflexivity as well as verbal and embodied answerability to children – particularly given our place as adult-researchers in an inequitable generational order. However, what is missing from our discussion of what matters in research relationships with children is a sense of how these 'matters' are impacted by the *wider web* of relationships in which negotiations take place. We will take this up in the next chapter, considering specifically what matters in relationships with educators and the ways relationships with educators impact on relationships with child-participants. This new avenue of inquiry introduces a further layer of complexity to the negotiation of research relationships in early childhood research.

4
A WEB OF RELATIONSHIPS

Encounters between researchers, educators, and children

So far we have begun to explore researcher–child relationships in early childhood research, but, of course, research relationships extend *beyond* the researcher–child–participant dyad. Most obviously in the context of early childhood settings, these 'others' include adults who are paid to work with the children as educators, families/carers, and other children within the setting. Crucially, relationships between children, families/carers, and educators will usually exist prior to, during, and after research has taken place, and these adults are significant both as 'gatekeepers' to researching with children and as key contributors to research. Therefore, rather than viewing relationships as a series of separate dyads, we prefer to conceptualise them in terms of a complex network – or web – of encounters (Degotardi and Pearson, 2009) that rub up against one another in different ways and at different times.

In this chapter, we will be exploring these ideas through a focus on researcher relationships with *educators*. We note, however, that this in-depth interrogation of the impact of relationships with educators on relationships with children is not an indication that we prioritise educators above families/carers or value what happens within early childhood settings above interactions beyond such spaces. Our choice of focus for this chapter is largely pragmatic: the result of our respective research questions and the limited involvement of families/carers in the day-to-day workings of the settings in which we carried out our research.

Our focus in this chapter, then, is on 'outside' researchers coming into a setting and negotiating research relationships, but in the course of our discussion we will complicate the notion of 'outsideness' and 'insideness' in relation to research. In brief, an 'outsider' status in research is often afforded to those who do not share some characteristics of the research community such as professional status or ethnicity; however, it should not be assumed that there is uniformity of understandings and actions of those who share 'insider' status (Gregory and Ruby, 2011).

We wish to further complicate the idea that the self is ever completely finalised in the way that a static positioning of 'insider' or 'outsider' suggests, as our own experience was that at times we were 'insiders' and other times 'outsiders' during the course of our respective research projects.

While there was commonality between us and the educators in the settings in which our research projects were undertaken, particularly because we have also both been early childhood *educators*, given the diversity of participants in our studies – in terms of, for example, class, 'race', gender, age, body size, and health status – there were *inevitable* differences between us that impacted on the research in different ways and at different times (cf. Skeggs, 1994; Osgood, 2010). By way of example, in Deb's research, she was markedly 'other' to the educators in Setting four, who were primarily Bangladeshi women (Deb is white and British); considerably younger than Deb (Deb was in her mid-40s at the time of the study); were parents (Deb is not a parent); and mostly lived in social housing in inner London (Deb owns a flat in a relatively affluent London suburb). Although Deb shared an ethnic background with the majority of children and their families/carers in this setting, differentials in income were *marked* as they were far more affluent in comparison.

There were also many experiences (and *in*experiences) that we shared with particular children as opposed to educators, such as 'being new' or not understanding the 'rules', and (in)experience was a state of being that fluctuated throughout our respective research projects. When new members of staff joined or when new students started their placements, we were often positioned as more 'experienced' in a setting. At other times, we were both viewed as 'students' as educators tried to make sense of what we were doing in the settings. And this fluctuation between 'insider' and 'outsider' positions was affected by a number of 'matters'.

In the previous chapter, we examined how size, hair, and bums mattered in our relationships with children, and linked the notion of 'matter' to wider discussions about relationships as corporeal as well as cerebral and embedded within a material context (Howes, 2005b). Extending this further, here, we will be arguing that, as with children, navigating relationships with adults – for our purposes, educators – is an *embodied* practice, constantly negotiated during the course of fieldwork interactions and has direct bearing on researcher relationships with children. In this chapter, then, we will be exploring the following questions: What mattered in our negotiations with educators in the research settings? Why did these areas come to matter and others not? How do relationships with educators impact on relationships with child-participants? In exploring these questions, we will make further reference to the neoliberal context of ECEC in the 'First World/North' including the intense surveillance and regulation of the work of early childhood educators. We suggest that this is a vital consideration as it is within this 'chronotope' (Bakhtin, 1981) that researchers negotiate relationships in early childhood research.

'Roles' matter

The first 'matter' for discussion is one of 'roles'. As we are both early childhood educators, we have found it useful to explore our 'educator' identities or 'brought selves' (Reinharz, 1997) and the fluidity of such positionings in relation to our research projects. We noted differences between being researchers from 'outside' a setting and our former experiences of being educators with day-to-day responsibility for groups of young children: as former educators, we recognised much of the day-to-day work that educators did in our research settings. The organisation of the environment to include a role play area, an area for books and reading material, an area for art/craft activities, sand and water, and constructional play (as examples) was very familiar to us, as was the temporal organisation of the session or day into blocks of time for play and more 'structured' times such as group story times or mealtimes. We also recognised the style of discourse adults used with the children and the kinds of assessment tool used, albeit that there was not a *direct* parallel to our own prior practice. Further to this, we also observed a mirroring of the neoliberal practices within the early childhood settings with developments in higher education where we now work.

Yet we acknowledge, following Watson (2009: 105), that empathy is a 'notoriously slippery' practice as it can mask the difference between the self of the researcher and the participants. Being answerable – in the Bakhtinian sense – involves an accompanying 'outsideness' or return to oneself after empathising with another's position. Indeed, pure empathy is regarded as passive as it is the polyvocality and *dialoguing* between the self of the researcher and the participant(s) that enables new and creative understandings to be generated (Bakhtin, 1993). Furthermore, the presumption that we might feel *exactly* as the educators in our research by virtue of being 'educators' is, Van Loon has described, an 'impossible vanity' (Watson, 2009: 107) and one not conducive to *rigorous* research.

With this in mind, it is important to differentiate what our 'researcher' status enabled in comparison to our prior experiences as early childhood educators. The key difference we both noted was the luxury of not being responsible for the overall education and welfare of each child, as well as the large amount of other work that takes place in any early childhood setting such as preparation for impending inspections and external scrutiny. Although, like all researchers, we are governed by ethical requirements laid down by universities and governing bodies, such frameworks do not carry with them the weight of *accountability* to parents, children, and the state for children's welfare and progress accordant with being an early childhood educator.

As we have detailed in Chapter 2, framed within a neoliberal context, educators are positioned as both a 'problem' and the 'solution' to a perceived crisis in ECEC, which, in turn, has resulted in a range of policies and instruments designed to objectively measure the 'quality' of education and care provided (Osgood, 2012). Underpinning this is a notion of the early childhood professional as a 'technician' (Dahlberg and Moss, 2005), able to 'deliver' a prescribed curriculum with its associated assessment instruments in order to meet centrally determined performance standards (particularly in the English context, where both of our studies were carried out). Moreover, 'technologies' have been developed to measure the 'outcomes' of early childhood provision. In England, the Office for Standards in Education (OfSTED) oversees the quality of early childhood provision, and assessment of a setting's work is expressed as if a scientifically 'objective', and thus a 'true', measure of performance (Dahlberg and Moss, 2005; Fenech, Sumsion, and Shepherd, 2010). We both found that educators in our studies were often fearful of the possibility of inspection or of being reported to OfSTED.

Further to this, hegemonic ideas about what it is to be an 'educator' are taken up by individuals and educators as a group to the extent that they embody or 'perform' those bodily practices, often uncritically (Holligan, 2000). As Ball (2003: 216) argues:

> The performances (of individual subjects or organizations) serve as measures of productivity or output, or displays of 'quality', or 'moments' of promotion or inspection. As such they stand for, encapsulate or represent the worth, quality or value of an individual or organization within a field of judgement.

For Colley (2006), this sense of 'performance' – and indeed actually changing oneself in ways that are often disempowering and subordinating – needs also to be viewed as the 'ability to labour with feeling', in which educators use particular 'emotional capital' in their (low) paid work. And this is further intensified in the division between those educators who work in 'daycare' (in England they are often known as 'nursery nurses' and have different training from that of teachers) as opposed to teachers, who usually work in 'education': the former is accorded lower status and lower pay, despite longer working hours in the less secure parts of the sector.

To expand this point further, the work of early childhood educators is deemed 'hyper-feminine in public discourse' owing to perceptions that it is a mere extension of the skills and attributes of mothering (Osgood, 2012: 15), and this is notable particularly in relation to nursery nursing. From its inception, the work of 'nursery nurse' educators has been perceived as akin to a devotional, romanticised form of motherhood, which was enmeshed with concern that children were being left to the care of 'ignorant women during their most impressionable years' (Lawrence, 1952: 75). Yet the devotional discourse associated with nursery nursing conceals the fact that working with young children can be demanding and tiring, and implies that educators have to be 'nice' all the time (Whalley, 1992). As a result, educators are charged with a double bind of 'civilising' children's bodies, with their own bodies similarly 'civilised' towards a set of bodily performances deemed 'appropriate' for the early childhood educator (Colley, 2006; Phelan, 1997).

A key 'performance' expected of educators at the current time is that of 'risk manager' (Tobin, 2004). Constant vigilance in relation to health and safety regulations, an obsession in the 'First World/North' (Penn, 2011b; Tobin, 2004), was not our concern as researchers but weighed *heavily* on the work of educators. While researchers are required to abide by health and safety legislation, this, we argue, is very different from the statutory and institutional responsibilities educators have for the welfare of *every* child in the setting (and if holding a leadership position, for adults on the site, too). Thus, there is a distinction to be made here between the responsibility of educators acting *in loco parentis* and the work of researchers who come in to a setting, despite arguments we will be making throughout this book for 'answerability' (Bakhtin, 1993) as a form of political and ethical responsibility.

In addition, in order to see how 'normal' and 'school ready' children are becoming, early childhood educators are expected to undertake *copious* observations of *all* young children in their care designed to order, classify, and assess their progress. Jones, Holmes, MacRae, and MacLure (2010a) argue that the high levels of recordkeeping early childhood educators produce in relation to young children has led to a construction of the 'paper child': a child who exists in this paperwork. While we return to this area in depth in Chapter 6, the point we wish to emphasise here is the implications this has on the amount of *time* available for relationships: the time taken for observation, planning, and recordkeeping impinges directly on the time educators have for participating directly with young children in their activities (Kjorholt and Qvortrup, 2012). And this was crucial in both our respective research projects.

As researchers, we were able to spend long periods engaged in play with a single child, without needing to cast an eye on what was happening in the rest of the play space in or outdoors. This opened up different possibilities for being with children than we had generally experienced as educators. Deb's fieldnotes demonstrate a specific example of this:

> Bhupinder asked me to play 'rockets' with him this afternoon. This involved making a rocket from Lego or any such available material. But his prime focus appeared to be on the *movement* of the rocket through space not constructing the rocket itself. Once hastily built, and following Bhupinder's lead, our rockets soared into the air accompanied by a zooming noise and we travelled round and around the large hall space (the nursery occupies a very large church hall space).
>
> I followed behind Bhupinder: sometimes our rockets were low in the 'sky', sometimes high. We did not talk at any point but continued making zooming noises – the amplification of which was related to our rockets' position in the 'sky'. We did this for more than half an hour, travelling round and around the large space. It felt almost hypnotic, divorced from the reality of all around us. When all other children went outside to play in the garden area (there is a 'set' play time outside as the space doubles up as the vicar's garden and car park space for members of his congregation) we were able to stay inside in our 'bubble' of rocket play and did not stop until tea time.

> It felt incredibly luxurious to be so immersed in one child's play – not needing to look at what others were 'getting up to' or the need to help get coats on to go outside and not needing to verbalise what we were doing.
>
> *(Deb Albon, Food events: Setting two)*

Reflecting on these fieldnotes further – as following Bakhtin (1993) to merely co-experience is not enough – we want to highlight the seeming *luxury* of being able to respond to a child in this way. Often, observation of children by early childhood educators is conducted at a *distance* when the educator is simultaneously observing, undertaking some activity with children, and maintaining a watchful eye over a group of children engaged elsewhere. As researchers, we had no such responsibility and this afforded greater opportunities for being 'in the moment' with children (Elliot, 2007).

This provoked a range of feelings in the educators in our studies, including envy and frustration. In Setting three in Deb's research, educators all commented on her relationship with a child new to the nursery: Beth (aged 2 years). Beth's key person, Katy, commented: 'It's nice you have time to play with her – I am always so busy with other things.' (On a Thursday, Katy was 'on toilets' as it was known, denoting an entire session spent in the bathroom area, ready and available to respond to children's needs.) Deb spent long periods engaged in food-related role play with Beth each time she visited the setting, whereas educators told her that, regretfully, they spent very little or no time in the area. Indeed, the manner of their expression of regret was akin to *jealousy* of Deb's relative freedom in being able to respond to this child's spontaneous play.

Perhaps as a consequence of their relationship, during the setting's morning 'coming together' session, Beth would invariably seek out Deb to sit on her knee for this period, which often triggered a jokey response from the educators such as 'her favourite person's back again!' Over time, Deb realised that this appeared to trouble Katy:

> It is noteworthy that today, just prior to the morning's 'coming together' period, I deliberately busied myself with something to prolong physically sitting down with the children – a point when Beth usually seeks me out and sits on my knee. I hoped she would seek out Katy and then I could sit down quietly out of the way.
>
> *(Deb Albon, Food events: Setting three)*

In this critical moment, Deb was concerned that her relationship with Beth was being seen as a usurping of Katy's role as Beth's 'key person'. The key person role is now statutory in England following the introduction of the *Early Years Foundation Stage* (EYFS) (DCSF, 2008; DfE, 2012) and actively promotes a close, trusting attachment relationship between a designated educator (as key person) and child (and his/her family). Moreover, the key person relationship is conceptualised as pivotal for the young child's emotional well-being in the 'life' of the early childhood setting she attends (Elfer, Goldschmeid, and Selleck, 2003).

But this role, we suggest, is sometimes understood by educators to mean an *exclusive* relationship between a child and a key person, with the key person having sole responsibility for a key group of children, which, in turn, emphasises a dyadic form of adult–child relationship and negates the idea that children form many different kinds of relationship (not least with their peers) when attending an early childhood setting (Degotardi and Pearson, 2009). There is also an expectation inherent in the EYFS that the key person will 'know' their key child more intimately than other educators (and indeed researchers). However, in our research projects we found that the key person role was often regarded simultaneously as an administrative burden by educators in terms of keeping on top of the paperwork they associated with the role (despite the role being conceived as far more than this and essentially about promoting close relationships – see, e.g., Elfer et al., 2003). Perhaps as a result of such a framing of the key person role, Katy seemed happier when Deb asked if educators wanted her to share observations of their key children. Katy 'read' this positively as saving herself paperwork – indeed, she came to expect observations to put in Beth's file, often saying 'what was Beth doing today?' at the end of sessions. Yet, as we will discuss in Chapter 6, the sharing of observations is not unproblematic.

Educators were put in an impossible situation in our research settings: key workers were expected to 'know' a child well and have formed a close relationship, yet were impeded by institutional practices that effectively tied them to particular spaces or activities through a rota system intended to provide 'cover' for the setting. This allocation of roles was underpinned by views of educators as 'risk managers', seeking to control the perils associated with conceptualisations of young children's bodies as 'unruly' and 'disruptive' (Grosz, 1994: 3) through a close and permanent adult presence. This had significant impacts on educators' ability to form relationships with children who moved from space to space in a way that educators, by virtue of these institutional policies, could not. In Rachel's research, the children's play involved rapid chase scenes and adventures to different parts of the setting that became new 'worlds' afforded by the varied characteristics of the physical environment. As a researcher – unimpeded by institutional requirements about 'cover' – Rachel was able to move fluidly around the space, in ways foreclosed for the educators. This then allowed for relationships to be negotiated *across* spaces, pivotal given the children's nomadic play.

Our 'outsideness' illuminated these differences in the 'role' of educator and researcher in these settings. However, this inevitably raised complex issues with regards to relationships and ethics. Should a researcher challenge the spatial disciplining of educators, which limited possibilities for forming relationships with the very children with whom this was expected? Should a researcher share written observations with overworked educators, 'colluding' with a conceptualisation of the key person role as administrative? While we will discuss the issues of researcher 'intervention' in more detail in Chapter 7, suffice it here to say that we would wish to acknowledge the value of *doubt* in our interactions with research participants. Summarising Bakhtin's writing in this area, Bender (1998: 191) states:

> Doubt is not an activity that arises in reflection in spheres of meaning, but rather is a constitutive part of acting. It is a creative moment that helps craft the outcome and tone of concrete acts.

But, this implies a degree of intentionality and reflection in given moments that is not always present in fieldwork. We suggest that doubt enables us to dialogue further after we act, when reflexively writing up or sharing one's experiences with another person.

Our actions as researchers in these 'ethically important moments' (Guillemin and Gillam, 2004) are inevitably intertwined with the people and situations we encounter, which Seigworth and Gregg (2010: 2) helpfully describe as the 'shuttling intensities' of encounters and their affects. In the case of Deb and Beth, for example, educators worked for little pay in a shared community space, which had to be set up in entirety every day. The educators had few qualifications and were mostly bewildered by the vast array of 'guidance' documentation that they were expected to enact. Yet despite this, children and parents generally seemed very happy with the setting and the educators were passionate about their work. Unsettling educators' confidence further when they were working in a difficult institutional and structural context seemed insensitive, and on a practical level may well have jeopardised Deb's access to the setting. However, we both continue to experience lingering unease about some of our in-the-moment responses, feeling that in such situations we may be acting with arrogance in assuming our points will not be 'understood' or that we 'side' with one group (such as adult educators) over another (such as children). In short, our responses to issues in situ were not always ones that sit comfortably on reflection (Barbour, 2010).

Finally here, it is important to note that there is not one universal 'educator' (or 'insider') position with commonalities of understandings and interpretations of practice (Gregory and Ruby, 2011). We both observed instances of educators and other members of staff positioning themselves outside the 'technicist' discourse relating to 'performing' as an early childhood educator. In Deb's research, in Setting two, Sharon worked in part as a cook and as a 'spare adult' (with no formal training) in the nursery. In her role as a cook, she refused to monitor food temperatures or wear the 'required' clothing in the kitchen stipulated by health and safety requirements. Unless hot food was being cooked, Sharon opened the doors of the kitchen to children and welcomed them in warmly, encouraging them to join her in sneaking to the refrigerator to 'steal' bits of food, hide in the cupboards or raid the fruit bowl. Deb sat at different tables for lunch over the period of her research in this setting, but looked forward especially to the days when she had lunch at Sharon's table.

When Deb observed other educators at mealtimes, they often seemed concerned with 'performing' as 'educators', but Sharon showed no such concerns in being under Deb's watchful 'gaze' (cf. Foucault, 1977). However, 'gaze' worked both ways. When sitting down to lunch on a small table with a few children and an educator, Deb – the researcher – was *also* under close scrutiny, so she generally adopted the 'body rules' (Leavitt and Power, 1997) of each table and in so doing, noticed shifts in her relationships with children. On Sharon's table, there was an overwhelming feeling of being liberated from the need to overly manage the children's bodies whereas on other tables, where children were expected to talk quietly, keep clean, keep their bodies apart from others, and eat 'nicely', it was difficult not to support the (gentle) reinforcement of these 'rules' in order to maintain relationships with educators. Ultimately, the idea that as 'researchers' and 'least-educators' we were not compelled to 'control' or 'manage' the children – a pervasive practice in early childhood settings (Millei, 2005) – was more difficult to achieve in the field, especially when in close proximity to educators.

Experience matters

One of the similarities we have noted between our research practices is that when approaching potential research sites we both stressed our qualifications and experience as early childhood educators rather than our lecturer/researcher status. Perhaps here we were concerned with presenting ourselves as 'insiders' – a term we continue to problematise – despite our 'outsider' status as researchers who work in a university and who are not paid to work as educators in the setting. Such experience, we would argue, *was* an important aspect of our acceptance in early childhood settings. In Setting three in Deb's research, the manager approached her after an hour in the nursery on her first day, stating loudly: 'I can see *you're* a practitioner!' Deb's style of interaction with the children (and we suspect her 'teacherly' discourse in that moment) provoked a positive response from the manager and ensured her presence in the setting was not only permitted but welcomed. Inevitably our educator 'habitus' (following Bourdieu, 1977) was impossible to shake off in entirety (see also Jones et al., 2010a).

Our prior experiences as educators also meant that on occasions we were both left alone with children and were even considered part of the 'cover' for the spaces of the setting in which we spent time. This indicates a high degree of trust in us, based in part – we would argue – on our credentials as early childhood educators, but it was also highly gendered. In Setting two, while Deb would be left alone with children – such as in the case of playing 'rockets' alongside Bhupinder noted earlier in this chapter – the same was not the case for a male educator, despite the fact that he was a full-time member of staff and a key person to a small group of children. This made some activities possible for Deb (as a female researcher) that were not open to a male educator and potentially, as Pole (2007) suggests, a male researcher.

This 'insider' status meant also that, on occasion, we were asked to help in ways that we may not have been had we not had professional experience and qualifications. On one such occasion Deb was asked to run three consecutive group story and drink sessions to free up educators who had a difficult deadline to meet in relation to completing baseline assessments for each child. Because Deb was seen to manage the sessions 'successfully', both children and staff in the nursery seemed to view her differently – as someone who could *really* do the job of being an 'educator'. This enabled her to ask the educators in the setting for their time on matters connected with her research more easily, and she found children, with whom she had not previously had a lot of interaction, spontaneously sought her out. We also suggest that some children may well prefer to engage with an adult who is 'more like an educator' than the 'least-educator' positioning we have put forward thus far. However, we can never know whether other children *avoided* Deb following her facilitation of the sessions and cannot state with any certainty the extent to which such actions closed down other ways of relating to the children.

In retrospect, our extra efforts to help out were likely an attempt to present our common credentials – at least *to educators* in the setting – as early childhood educators who were still able to 'get our hands dirty' despite now working in a university environment. Crucially, however, there are a number of tensions involved in these attempts at emphasising 'sameness' with participants in the research site. As we noted earlier, Bakhtin (1990) stresses the importance of 'outsideness' for answerability to take place. Attempts at 'doing sameness' can also cause a researcher to miss or even minimise the differences between 'insiders', essentially homogenising their experiences. And – as Abell, Locke, Condoer, Gibson, and Stevenson (2006) note in relation to researcher attempts to gain access, 'quality' data and rapport with participants in the interview context – 'doing similarity' can ultimately end up 'doing difference' because such efforts are fundamentally contingent on participants' interpretations, as became apparent in Rachel's research.

Although her educator experience did mean that educators often left her alone with children, Rachel's attempts to take a 'least-educator' role with children disrupted her attempt to 'do similarity' with educators. Rachel's research focused on play that was, although mildly tolerated in the setting, generally considered by many with trepidation: as one educator commented, she was concerned about the possibility of injury because the play was often 'frenzied' and 'uncontained'. As a result, Rachel's time with the children was often subjected to the 'gaze' of educators. While she thought she had made it clear in discussions with educators that she would not assert rules with children unless she was worried about physical safety (a difficult position to negotiate and which we discuss in further detail in Chapter 7) and that they should continue to run the setting as they preferred, Rachel's attempt to do 'similarity' with educator experience created a tension when she did not 'manage' children's disordered and physically active play as educators in the setting expected. In an interview with Rachel, one of the educators commented: 'I have concerns about physical play. There is a thin line between pretend and real. I usually observe from a distance when you're here just to make sure the children are OK. You don't really set rules or boundaries with them do you?' The trust Rachel's 'common' experience engendered was fragile, particularly when she acted in unexpected ways, such as not seeking to 'manage' children's bodies or maintain the prized calm of the nursery setting (Phelan, 1997).

Tensions in negotiating relationships with educators inevitably affected relationships with children. In Rachel's research, this was particularly apparent in the inside space where educators had more explicit 'body rules' based on the value placed on hushed and sedentary activity in this area. As a result, Rachel often felt that if she stayed indoors she would be specifically flaunting the 'body rules' of the setting. She would often go immediately outside when entering the setting, foreclosing opportunities to form relationships with children who stayed inside. As time went on, children also often suggested going outside when they saw Rachel in the setting. We do not know if this is because they connected Rachel with the outdoor space or they too felt that the play would soon be censored or stopped indoors.

(Non-)motherhood matters

Perhaps unsurprisingly in an 'early childhood' context, motherhood surfaced as an issue in relationships with educators. Neither of us is a mother, which 'mattered' substantially in Deb's research, but seemed to have far less import in Rachel's research. We have reflected that this may be due to Rachel looking decidedly younger than Deb or perhaps also has its roots in Deb wearing a wedding ring and being in a heterosexual relationship or even in her more 'motherly' rounded body shape. However, not only did these aspects of our 'brought selves' (Reinharz, 1997) affect what mattered in our negotiations, but the focus of our different research was also crucial. While Rachel's research focused on 3- to 4-year-old children and their 'independent' play, Deb's research focused on food events, which were often managed by adults and also involved infants and toddlers. And it is here, we would argue, that the slippage between motherhood and ECEC becomes central. Very young children are more intensely conceptualised as in need of 'motherly' care, something keenly demonstrated through practices centring on food and feeding – the focus of Deb's research.

Many educators in Deb's study were mothers (the two men in her research project were young and childless) and ascertaining information about whether she was a mother or not was a source of interest to many of the educators in the early stages of her research. The following fieldnotes demonstrate an example of this:

> Nadia and Ambia (educators) have both asked me whether I am a mother this morning. When I reply that I am not, this provokes questions as to why. On the one hand, this feels quite rude and personal (given they hardly know me) but I strongly think that they are trying to make a friendly connection with me. When I don't immediately answer, they both assume that there is something 'wrong' with my reproductive system and take great pity on me. They assume that this is something I would 'naturally' want, perhaps because I am an early childhood educator (and so *must* want my *own* children). And although it was a conscious and positive decision not to have (our) my own children, I cannot face telling them this. Perhaps this is exacerbated by Ambia

> being heavily pregnant and about to go on maternity leave coupled with the babies and young toddlers who envelop the space with their presence. How could I *not* want my own child?
>
> Rather than appear 'abnormal' in my conscious/positive choice of non-motherhood, I settle for being pitied (wrongly) for a biological 'abnormality' that is out of my control. This is not the first occasion this has happened to me – and not just in a research context – I feel guilty as this feels like I am not being totally honest.
>
> (Deb Albon, *Food events: Setting four baby room – first morning*)

At that moment Deb felt the need to be accepted and be seen as sharing some aspects of the educators' beliefs – to 'pass' (Paechter, 2003: 52) – even though it masked some of her views, such as the idea that motherhood must 'naturally' follow from marriage or from the status of being an 'early childhood educator'. Would such concealment – although not *intentional* but occurring in the intensity of that moment – have occurred in research carried out in a bank or office or spaces in which she was not surrounded by babies and toddlers, a heavily pregnant educator, and 'early childhood' paraphernalia? We suspect not. However, we recognise that in daily life people share and conceal aspects of their beliefs and practices, and research is no different. There are some details about oneself that may only emerge gradually – after all, few people 'tell all' to a new acquaintance.

In addition to the gradual emergence of information that occurs in relationships, notwithstanding that the rate at which one discloses information is likely to vary according to each relationship, there are cultural differences in what we might ask of each other or share about ourselves when a relationship is newly formed. Further, researchers were traditionally not expected to share *anything* of their own lives with participants owing to a view that it would 'spoil' the field and consequently, pollute the resulting data: all 'sharing' was on the part of the participant (Okley, 1996). Although this position has been challenged, we would argue that 'sharing' is far more nuanced and complex than is often presented in research manuals (Coffey, 1999). What to share and how and when to share it is difficult to decide a priori in research as we cannot know what might be asked or the context in which it might be asked. Thus, in a particular moment, decisions are made and crucially have to be made regarding what to share (or not) – whether we are a researcher or a participant. For Bakhtin (1993), this relates to the unavoidable and pressing nature of relationships in the real 'once-occurrent' world as opposed to the world of objectivity, neutrality, and distance.

The backdrop to 'not sharing' in the particular moment in question can also be related to the long association of ECEC with maternalism (see Ailwood, 2008). As we noted earlier, the maternalistic discourse is pervasive owing to a perception that the kinds of skills needed to be an educator are a mere extension of those attributed to mothering (Osgood, 2012). While maternalism is viewed as out of place in the world of a 'professional', educator narratives indicate a perception that *lack* of mothering experience is an impediment to trainee educators, who are deemed as wanting for the experiential knowledge of caring for babies and very young children formed through caring for their own children (Osgood, 2012: 115). In the fieldnote just quoted, Deb's lack of motherhood experience was akin to a 'guilty secret' sitting uneasily with the professional work of being an early childhood educator. While we would not wish to denigrate in any way the experiential knowledge and skills acquired through motherhood, we suggest that *non-motherhood* is a status that is considered 'odd' in the sphere of ECEC.

On the face of it, this may seem to have little bearing on negotiating research relationships with children. However, as Deb's research meant she spent many weeks in the 'baby room', it was highly significant. When Deb fed one of the younger babies, as she often did, it was under their watchful eye as they assumed she would not know what to do even though Deb has fed numerous babies in the course of her professional and personal life. This meant that the educators made their practice explicit, taking the trouble to explain to Deb the reasons why they held babies in the way they did or fed them in the way that they did, drawing on narratives of their experiences as *mothers* as support. Had Deb shared an 'insider' status as a mother, it is doubtful whether she would have learnt as much about their perspectives on feeding practices.

But this also had a deleterious effect on Deb's relationship with John, a young baby new to bottle feeding. On one particular occasion, in trying to support Deb with bottle feeding, Nadia punctuated John's bottle feed (as Deb fed him) with constant alterations to his body positioning. John seemed niggled by these many adjustments and made this clear with agitated vocalisations and wriggles. This prompted Nadia to gather him up warmly and feed him herself, saying: 'I've got you now' – interrupting the relationship Deb was negotiating with John. Feeding children was inextricably entwined with the relationships Nadia had with the children in her care, and while this has been noted in research into feeding relationships between mothers and infants (Keenan and Stapleton, 2009), we suggest this is less explored in research focused on early childhood settings.

Food and weight matters

Food is a key theme in our final section in this chapter. ECEC is an embodied practice for educators as much as for children (Tobin, 1997b), and food and body weight were *constant* topics of discussion among the educators in our research settings. Food was a major source of sociality (Shilling, 2005): meetings and lunchtimes were an opportunity to bring in cakes and biscuits to share with other educators. We both found that food served as a means through which each team bonded together (see also Valentine, 2002) and sweet foods, especially, were pivotal in cementing relationships. For example, in Deb's research in Setting three, one of the educators had been a school cook and made 'school puddings' of jam roly poly and spotted dick for lunchtime eating, and in Setting two the manager took great pains to find out details relating to everyone's favourite 'treat' foods and stocked the staff cupboard accordingly.

Given that Deb's research focused on food events, it is not surprising that food and weight featured highly in her negotiations with educators. In Setting three, Deb was working hard to lose weight (losing three stones), resisting the temptation to snack on high-calorie foods. As a result, she increasingly became an 'outsider' to this group of educators in a way that she had not been in Settings one and two of her research as in the previous settings, she had eaten the same foods as the educators (and children if a mealtime). Deb's fieldnotes state:

> I seem to have got a lot of kudos in the group as being able to stick to a diet and lose weight. It seems to reinforce a view of me as someone different, with a will of steel and the team seem banded together in both jealousy and camaraderie of 'naughty eating'.
>
> Today, Sadie brought round some mince pies mid-morning and I didn't eat one. By the end of the morning, there was one left so clearly everyone else in the team had had theirs and I was the only one to refuse. When Fay asked (accusingly) who had not eaten their mince pies, I had to own up and it felt like I had rejected a very kind offer – after all, mince pies are linked with the Christmas festivities and conviviality. It feels like I am always rejecting their kind offers of food.
>
> *(Deb Albon, Food events: Setting three)*

Food was far less important in Rachel's research negotiations with educators: she does not eat sweets and her fast metabolism gives the impression of being 'outside' struggles with weight that are particularly predominant among women in the 'First World/North'. We suggest, therefore, that our two different experiences in this area indicate the need for embodied reflexivity in relation to research participants.

While sweet foods served as a source of bonding for educators, great trouble was taken to bring delicious treats to planning sessions away from the children, particularly in Setting one of Deb's research. When 'frontstage' (Goffman, 1969), performing as an 'educator', the educators took great pains to act as role models of 'healthy' eating and any allergies and food preferences (of adults) were kept secret for fear that the children may take up these ideas and replicate them in their own eating behaviours. This can be seen in the following comments by educators in Deb's research:

> Merryl: 'Take tomatoes . . . I don't eat tomatoes but I will eat it. It doesn't matter but I will eat it even though I don't like it. I will eat it with a *straight face* with an *enjoying it face*, you know, just to encourage them to try it. It's like Hamdi (child). She don't like oranges. You'll be going "Oh it's *juicy*, oh it's *sweet*." That is some of the tricks.'
>
> *(Deb Albon, Food events: Setting one)*

> John: 'We try – we usually try to eat – even if we have to grin and bear it. We have a bit – and then we can say "Just try a little bit." If you're saying

"Try a little bit" and you've got something on your plate and you haven't tried it then it's like – you're sort of being a *hypocrite*.'

(Deb Albon, Food events: Setting two)

Yet children seemed *intensely* interested in who was able to eat what as well as the likes and dislikes people had in relation to different foods. Unlike adults, children's allergies were in the public domain. In Setting two, they were written on placemats, and in Setting four, the educators talked of a baby who had his allergies written onto his T-shirt as a highly visible reminder for educators in case they fed him foods that would cause an allergic reaction.

By way of contrast, Deb has a minor allergy that makes her skin swell if it comes into contact with a lot of citric fruit juice. On one occasion, in Setting one, Deb was asked to peel oranges for a snack time but had to refuse and stated why. She was admonished by one of the educators in the setting for speaking about her allergies in front of the children: Emma told her to '*shhh* – the children will hear you and won't eat their fruit'. The children did hear and showed a lot of concern, so much so that at every snack time from that day on, Charlie – in particular – *always* remembered her allergy and Deb noticed how this seemed to change their relationship. Formerly at snack times, Charlie would jump up against her or on to her quite forcefully in a way not observed with other adults; but, after this, when food was around, Charlie would initiate conversation in order to tell her to 'take care', often accompanied by a gentle stroke of her hand or arm. We suggest that in sharing something of herself that expressed vulnerability, Charlie found a way to interact with Deb in a more attentive, less confrontational way. Furthermore, on no occasion did Deb observe the children refusing to eat the fruit themselves following Deb's allergy revelation.

Earlier in this chapter we noted that researchers make decisions – sometimes unwittingly – about the information they share or choose not to share in relationships, particularly when they are newly formed. Information about the bodies of adults (in this instance: allergies) is often hidden from children in contrast to the vast array of sharing of information that takes place in relation to *children's* bodies. We would argue that in doing this, the vulnerability of children's bodies is emphasised and adult bodies are falsely positioned as 'finished' and invincible. Furthermore, as Hammersley and Atkinson (1997) note, scrutiny of the private lives of children (we would also add working-class families) by middle-class professional adults is considered legitimate when compared to adults, and we suggest is further exemplification of generational and class inequity.

In addition, the fun, sociality, forging, and maintaining of relationships that is derived from food was regarded as something to be *hidden* from the children and a 'front' maintained of 'healthy' eating. The 'role model' discourse, we argue, pervades food and eating practices in ECEC but is premised on a view of young children as 'dupes', who passively, unproblematically, and uncritically take up the 'healthy' behaviours in front of them – particularly if modelled by adults such as educators or family members. Moreover, role model theorising ignores the way that children take up as well as reject the range of discursive positionings that are open to them (Grieshaber, 2004). Yet, this idea pervades much of the health literature in relation to early childhood and, as Albon (2011) has argued, the corollary of such a viewpoint is a high degree of regulation of educator's bodies.

Before leaving this issue, it is important to note that not all educators in each setting hid their food preferences and/or allergies from the children's view. In Setting two, Deb noticed Sharon on a number of occasions leap up from the lunch table and state loudly: 'I can't eat that – I'm going to make myself a sandwich. Anyone else want one?' (a general comment made to adults and children present). This was noteworthy as it was refreshingly different to the practice observed of many of the other educators in the research and seemed to give adults and children permission to state their food preferences and share information about themselves – moreover it did not result in a mass rejection of the meal in front of them.

In conclusion, this chapter has argued that relationships with children are negotiated among a web of other relationships both within and beyond early childhood settings, albeit that for the purposes of this chapter we have focused on relationships with educators. Navigating relationships with educators – as with children – is an important part of research in early childhood settings, but is never easy or 'finalised'. We have examined instances of how our 'brought' and 'situationally created' selves (Reinharz, 1997) impacted on and were impacted by educators, who, in the English context, work within a highly regulated and scrutinised environment, and we have suggested that 'sharing' is more nuanced than is often acknowledged in research texts notably in relation to 'generationing' (Mayall, 2002). In particular, we have troubled the notion of 'insider/outsider', focusing on the blurred boundaries between an 'outsider' researcher and 'insider' participants. We will continue to trouble this distinction in the next chapter, interrogating the notion of the 'insider' in relationship negotiations undertaken during educator-research.

5

THE EDUCATOR AS RESEARCHER

Implications for research relationships

Thus far, this book has examined research relationships between adult-researchers and child-participants in projects where the researcher is someone 'outside' or 'external' to the early childhood setting. In this chapter, we will turn to studies in which the researcher is an 'insider' and, more specifically, an educator. Though the issues discussed elsewhere in this book are certainly relevant for educator-research, we argue that this type of research raises a number of *particular* concerns. This is not the least because relationships between educators and children usually exist prior to and continue beyond the boundaries of the research project. Further, the positioned practices associated with being an educator provide an additional, powerful layer to the already unequal power relations between child-participants and adult-researchers (Alldred, 1998).

While other chapters in this book focus primarily on data generated during our doctoral studies about food events and taboo play, this chapter introduces and elaborates on two additional research projects in order to explore research relationships in *educator*-research. In brief, the Froebel Blockplay Research Project (FBRP) was carried out in southwest London in the late 1980s under the directorship of Tina Bruce and research assistant Pat Gura. It involved educators and children from six early childhood settings (including Deb's) who had a common interest in collaboratively exploring children's learning through use of a resource (wooden blocks) commonly found in early childhood settings, but at that time one that was often neglected. Crucially, researchers were interested in the kinds of pedagogical approach that might enhance the children's learning (see Gura, 1992).

The second educator-research project we will discuss was carried out in a preschool setting in British Columbia (Canada) between 2008 and 2009 and was entitled 'Transforming assessment practices' (henceforth referred to as TAP). In this action research project, Rachel's team of four educators sought to transform their year-end assessment process from a summative, developmental approach – inherited from previous educators at the setting – to one that involved children, parents, and educators in collaboratively reflecting on learning and meaning making within the setting.

A very brief comment on the Canadian early childhood context is in order here, given that our primary focus thus far has been on settings in England. Without a national early childhood education and care (ECEC) programme, and with the lowest rankings among 25 OECD countries in terms of 'suggested standards' for provision of ECEC (UNICEF, 2008), ECEC in Canada has been referred to as a 'patchwork of uneconomic, fragmented services . . . often without a focused child development and education role' (OECD Educational Directorate, 2004: 6). Care of children is generally considered a private family responsibility and ECEC is primarily provided by the private sector – in both not-for-profit and for-profit settings (Beach, Friendly, Ferns, Prabhu, and Forer, 2009) – which operates largely within the neoliberal framework discussed in Chapter 2.

By way of example, the setting in which the TAP project was carried out was a private, not-for-profit preschool run by a volunteer parent executive board. Costs for the sessional preschool were primarily shouldered by individual families and through collective fundraising efforts; a negligible proportion of families qualified for government subsidies that were available for only those families living in extreme poverty. At the time of the TAP project, government regulations focused primarily on qualifications of staff, staff–child ratios, health and safety, and recordkeeping. There was no statutory early years' curriculum in British Columbia, Canada; therefore, each setting implemented its own localised approach to curriculum. Rachel's preschool, for example, drew heavily on sociocultural (e.g. Fleer, 2002) and inquiry-based approaches to teaching, learning, and assessment.

Returning to the focus of this chapter, our intention is not to rehearse arguments developed elsewhere in relation to the efficacy of educator-research in early childhood settings (see for instance, MacNaughton and Hughes, 2009; Mukherji and Albon, 2010) or the 'techniques' that might be employed (see, for instance, Schmuck, 2006). Similarly, our purpose is not to present a critique of approaches to educator-research that reify a modernist project of continuous 'improvement' and 'action' over critical reflection and deconstruction of practice (see, for example, Brown and Jones, 2001). For although we would generally concur with this critique – with the caveat that *both* 'thought deeds' and 'real deeds' (Bakhtin, 1993) are necessary, notably in the case of educator-research dedicated to social transformation – expanding on it is not the aim of this chapter.

Instead, however, we will explore a range of questions relating directly to research relationships between educator-researchers and the children in their care, namely: How do the positioned practices of being simultaneously an 'educator' and a 'researcher' enable or constrain relationships with children? What does 'consent' to research mean in the context of prior and/or continuing educator–child relationships? These, we suggest, are the kinds of pertinent questions that are rarely articulated in relation to educator-research. Exploring the issue of consent through the lens of *educator*-research raises some particularly challenging issues and for this reason is taken up in this chapter, keeping in mind that consent is significant more generally in research with children.

Educator-research: A different context – a different relationship?

Bakhtin's (1981) notion of the 'chronotope', outlined in Chapter 2, provokes consideration of the impact of space–time configurations on our beings and ongoing acts. It is here that educator-research differs significantly from the research projects outlined thus far in this book. By way of explanation, the first point we wish to raise relates to the temporal differences between educator-research and research carried out by an 'outside' researcher. We contend that these temporal variances between 'educating' and 'researching' are key factors impacting on research relationships between children and educator-researchers.

In both of the educator-research projects outlined at the outset of this chapter, we had worked in our respective settings for a number of years and so had a relationship with children and their families/carers that spanned years prior to, during, and after the research. Thus, undertaking 'research' was sandwiched between and was part of generally longstanding relationships with children, families/carers, and the setting. This differed from our doctoral research projects as the period of data generation was, for both of us, inevitably far more *bounded* and it was reasonably clear from the outset when we would be 'leaving the field' (in the sense of not visiting the setting regularly).

There was also an expectation that our respective educator-research projects would impact on our practice *after* the research. For example, in the FBRP, there was a hope that the kinds of interaction Deb and her team had been having with children in the blockplay area would continue to be enhanced and extended to their practice as a whole. Likewise, the educator-researchers Rachel was working with had the specific intention of changing their observation, documentation, and assessment practices based on the findings of the TAP project.

A second difference between educator-research and 'outsider' research relates to the responsibility and power inherent in the educator-researcher subject positioning, which has particular implications for relationships in early childhood settings. Notably, the educator-researcher has *ongoing responsibility* for the education and care of the children; towards the children's families/carers and colleagues working with/in the setting; to the setting's governing/managing body; and to local and/or national government. One of the central responsibilities of an educator is the need to form and facilitate relationships with and between others, notably with children – see, for instance, Kernan and Singer (2011) in relation to peer relationships, and Elfer et al. (2003) in relation to attachments between children and a 'key person' (an adult) in the nursery. Certainly, there is general agreement in the field of ECEC that fostering close and supportive relationships with and between educators, children and families/carers is the bedrock on which learning and development take place (e.g. Gandini and Edwards, 2001; Manning-Morton and Thorp, 2003), albeit that there are differences in their theoretical underpinnings, for example attachment as opposed to sociocultural theorising (Degotardi and Pearson, 2009).

Undertaking educator-research, where there are shifts in practice, inevitably results in changes to these relationships. Rachel recalls one child – Sam – who had joined the nursery 10 months before the research began with whom she had not formed much of a relationship prior to the TAP project. Sam had spent a lot of time spinning and twisting objects on his own, and when he interacted with others he did so primarily through animal noises such as barks and growls. He was 4 years of age and rarely used recognisable verbal language in the setting. Prior to the research, the preschool had contacted his family to discuss having him assessed as he had been highlighted as 'of concern'.

Yet, Sam was one of the first volunteers to engage in TAP research activities designed to encourage reflection on learning at the nursery. He was especially keen to take photographs (a non-verbal language) and loved looking at his portfolio book, which documented his and other children's learning. Part of the TAP research involved meeting with children and their families (as will be expanded on later) and the educators were unsure how successful this would be in Sam's instance. Challenging all prior conceptions of him, Sam stood out as one of the children who did the *most* talking, explaining and reflecting on his learning.

Overall, being a part of the educator-research project shifted Sam's participation in the setting, with Sam seemingly having access to a *variety* of ways of interacting with others not previously available. In reflecting on this experience, Rachel now believes that the bounded nature of the research, as well as the clear way 'in' to participating unlike some of the more 'free-floating' activities usually found in the setting, facilitated these shifts. Deb similarly recalls changes in her relationships with children as a result of the intense observation and dialoguing with children about their blockplay, including the development of relationships with children with whom she had rarely spent much concentrated time prior to the research. These 'blockplay relationships' also enabled further interactions with these children in other areas of the curriculum.

But in carrying out any research, some children are inevitably more interested in the project than others. Did we form closer relationships with the children who engaged in our research activities in comparison to those who were less interested in the research topics? If so, does this matter? As an 'outside' researcher, it is generally of little importance whether research activities engage with *every* child to an equal extent or enable relationships to form with *all* children in a setting, and this was certainly the case in the 'outsider' research discussed in this book. In Deb's food events research, all children were observed at some point as participants in food events at the four settings, but in the play activities during the sessions, there were some children who gravitated more towards her than others. And this was especially the case in Rachel's taboo play research, in which she engaged with those children who were exploring themes of death and violence in their play – not *all* the children in the setting.

This focus on particular children in a setting did require an interrogation of the data to evaluate whether there were significant omissions in the research findings. However, as educators engaged in research in the place of work, such omissions have different implications as there is a fundamental responsibility to engage with *all* the children in the setting in some way. There was concern expressed early on in the FBRP, for example, from some educators in Deb's setting that those children interested in blockplay were receiving greater attention from educators. Certainly – as noted in the examples already given – the educator-research projects we were involved with enabled interactions and relationships with particular children. However, the FBRP educators' concern about inequalities in 'attention' is worthy of further comment because it suggests an understanding of relationships in terms of equivalent time spent together as opposed to the *quality* of those relationships and how responsive educators are to the individual and group needs of children. Clearly, it is important that educators form relationships with children in their care, as we have noted, but measuring this out in terms of equal time for individual children is problematic and represents a technicist approach to a complex issue.

Part of the problem lies in the view of personhood contained here, for the educators' comments suggest that 'attention' is something that can be apportioned, measured, and balanced in relation to autonomous individuals. Yet, we have been arguing throughout this book for a view of human beings as connected and interdependent (Sevenhuijsen, 1998a). In early childhood practice, children and adults move through myriad different groupings and even when – on the surface – an educator spends time with one child, this is never separate from relationships with others in the nursery. By way of example, a simple activity such as the nappy (diaper) changing of one child will often involve some discussion with another passing child in the bathroom and perhaps a written note to a parent/carer (at that moment, a distal relationship between educator and parent/carer). Further, another educator in the same room may shift what s/he does with a group of children if the nappy changing leaves a space 'short' of a staff member, thus changing his or her activity with children. Crucially, however, even if we were able to spend equal time with each child, this may not result in 'better quality' relationships.

In addition to differential responsibilities in relation to forming relationships with *all* children, there are divergent *purposes* embedded in the relationships an educator has with the children in her care when compared to an 'outside' researcher. While relationships – we have argued throughout this book – are central to *research*, when the researcher is an 'outsider', the relationship does not have its basis in facilitating a particular group of children's development and learning – a group for which one has ongoing and statutory responsibilities. There is, after all, a degree of *intentionality* in the work of being an educator (Suissa, 2006); in other words, there is an expectation that educators will bring their pedagogic desire and knowledge to bear in offering different ways of thinking and knowing to young children, drawing in part on their professional training and ongoing professional development. Children *may* learn from and with an external researcher, but there are few expectations, legal or otherwise, for researcher *responsibility* beyond fairly basic duties of care. Although we urge researchers to look beyond notions of responsibility to *answerability* in terms of a relational ethics, following the work of Bakhtin (1990; 1993), this does not negate the significance of the different degrees of responsibility towards children inherent in being 'researchers' and 'educators'. 'Outside' researchers, of course, have other professional responsibilities: to their universities/places of work and to funding bodies – a detailed examination of which is beyond the purview of this book.

Additionally, when undertaking research in one's own setting, the research is one of countless other activities *beyond* the research – but, crucially, bounded within the space of the setting – that constitute the educator's work with children and families/carers. Thus, while Deb was engaged in research into blockplay and Rachel was researching ways of transforming assessment practices, they were also facilitating children's learning in other areas, both indoors and outdoors: reading stories; maintaining equipment; attending meetings – a list impossible to document in full. And many of these activities relate to the *statutory* responsibilities that govern the work of the educators. At the time of the FBRP, for instance, the introduction of the National Curriculum had instituted unprecedented regulation and control over the school curriculum (Bash and Coulby, 1989). Deb, and the team with whom she worked in the nursery, felt a 'top-down' pressure to assess children as 'working towards' prescriptive statements that had been introduced in primary and secondary education as part of the National Curriculum. These imperatives were part of the radical shift in the UK towards a 'strongly governed' (Moss, 2012) central education policy.

Of course, being an 'outside' researcher is highly complex too and often requires balancing myriad other responsibilities. For instance, both our doctoral studies were carried out in tandem with our work in the higher education context, with its own accordant responsibilities and associated activity. Moreover, we are not suggesting that as external researchers, our work was unaffected by context – for instance, the neoliberal climate – far from it (cf. Davies, 2005)! The point we wish to emphasise here is that when engaged in research as an 'outsider' in an early childhood setting, negotiating relationships with children and adults *in the setting* is relatively free from the weight of responsibility for the countless range of activities that constitute the education and care of a particular group of children on an ongoing and daily basis.

To return to the question of differences between 'insider' and 'outsider' researchers, we now wish to explore the power that is associated with the educator position, as the additional responsibilities inherent with being simultaneously an educator *and* a researcher bring with it particular implications for adult–child relationships. Unlike some forms of 'insider' research undertaken by adults with *adults* (albeit that these too are riddled with ethical and political dilemmas associated with power (Gregory and Ruby, 2011)), research undertaken by adult-researchers with child-participants embarks from a position of *unequal* power relations (Alldred, 1998). We contend that this asymmetry of power is manifest more strongly in the context of educator-research owing to positioned practices as well as a legal mandate associated with being an 'educator' in relation to a group of children. This is exemplified in the practice, in some (notably school) settings, of calling educators by their last rather than first names (Taylor, Ntsoumanis, and Smith, 2009), which sediments the 'distance' expected in relationships between educators and children and their families/carers.

But perhaps the most obvious manifestation of adult power over children in the education context is the statutory requirement that *all* children of a certain age range spend a great deal of their time in school (Robinson and Kellett, 2004). In constructing children as 'pupils', with their schooling a matter of national concern, schools act as a powerful reminder of the 'child' as distinct from 'adult' (Hendrick, 1997b). Johanssen (2012: 102) further testifies that 'children are structurally as well as situationally at the mercy of adults' arbitrariness, more or less the property of their parents or other guardians and later of the school system.' While ECEC is not statutory (in the sense of compulsory daily attendance below the age of 5 years), children's involvement in decision-making about whether to attend a setting or not is likely to be rare; yet, children are generally expected to take responsibility for their learning and participation in these settings (Mayall, 2002).

In addition to this, educators generally carry with them the power of the state to 'measure' individual children. In England, there are statutory assessment instruments in early childhood, the power of which should not be underestimated (Dahlberg and Moss, 2005). However, even the use of profile books and other more 'friendly' documentation carries with it the power to classify the child (see Grieshaber and McArdle, 2010) as well as families/carers. 'Outside' researchers have no similar institutional authority in relation to an individual child. This, we suggest, represents a significant difference in relationships between children and adult-researchers: for instance, the educator (as researcher) holds powerful sway over reporting progress to families/carers over the academic year. An educator reports on *this* child in *this* context and, in the English context, the measurement of an identifiable setting – based in part on the assessment of children in the setting (including that made by OfSTED inspectors during their inspection) – is reported nationally as a supposedly 'objective' measure of its 'performance' (Dahlberg et al., 2007).

Of course, issues of power also permeate the role of being a 'researcher' and the process of undertaking research (Christensen, 2004), including the power to categorise, normalise, and silence through representations of children and families/carers in published work – a *particular* concern when privileged researchers represent marginalised communities (Alcoff, 2009). However, research classifies in a generalised manner as there is an expectation of anonymity and confidentiality in a research context, which differs markedly to the responsibilities of an educator. We would argue, then, that when the researcher is simultaneously the educator *and* the researcher, s/he holds an especially powerful position in relation to children both individually and more broadly as members of marginalised collectivities.

Negotiating consent in educator-research

It is made clear to anyone undertaking research that participants should give 'informed consent' to any research activity involving them. Research committees and associations, as well as texts on the subject, will emphasise this as a *crucial* component of any piece of research. 'Insider' knowledge of a particular community developed over time, it has been argued, is especially useful in navigating consent to research with key gatekeepers and participants (Coghlan and Casey, 2001). Generally, we both noted how our 'educator' positions – spanning beyond the spatial and temporal boundaries of the research – both enabled and were problematic in negotiating consent to the FBRP and TAP research. Two critical moments from our research highlight these issues and, in the process, unsettle the notion of 'consent' in the context of educator-research.

Alderson (2004) states that it is preferable for children to 'opt in' to research rather than 'opt out' as it is more respectful of their individual choice making. But in the context of educator-research this can be especially problematic as there is often an inextricable tie between some aspect of the curricula and pedagogy of the setting and the research itself (Waller and Bitou, 2011). This was certainly the case with the educator-research projects we undertook examining and transforming blockplay (FBRP) and assessment practices (TAP). Given the blurring of boundaries between 'educating' and 'researching', in *educator*-research children may see little difference between the 'research' and their usual experiences in the setting: a key difference between these activities often lies in the *type* of scrutiny and *publicness* of the representation of these activities, processes that often occur when children are not physically present. In contrast, children may well regard 'outside' researchers and their research activities as 'different' to the usual goings-on of the setting. Perhaps, in being 'different', the 'outside' researcher's intentions have greater *visibility* for children and, as 'outside' researchers do not hold institutional power over children as an educator does, it is therefore *easier* for children to withdraw their consent to the research, and it is to this issue that this chapter now turns.

Our purpose now is to examine a critical moment from the TAP project in order to explore the issue of 'informed consent' and a child's withdrawal of consent in more detail:

> When we first began working on our action research project to transform assessment practices, we thought carefully about the issue of consent. We felt that it was important to gain consent from families as we hoped to use data collected about their (1) previous experiences of assessment practices (this was for returning families only), (2) participation in the new assessment process

that we were seeking to develop in the project, and (3) their interpretation and evaluation of this new process. We also felt that it was important legally to get consent for their child's participation in the project. All families quickly indicated agreement signing the consent forms we distributed.

We also felt that it was important to gain consent from children for their participation: we sought to treat children as competent participants rather than objects and extensions of their families. We recognised that while a parent may consent, a child may not (and vice versa). To gain consent, early on, we explained the project to the children and described what their participation might involve. Whenever we began a new research 'activity' as part of the project we asked for 'volunteers', viewing the process of seeking consent as an ongoing negotiation rather than a hoop to jump through at the beginning of the project.

(Rachel Rosen, TAP)

This extract raises a number of ethical issues: as is usual and generally required in research involving young children, consent was sought from families/carers acting on behalf of the child. However, in accordance with more recent developments in research, Rachel and her team elicited the consent of the children themselves, which has its basis in re-conceptualisations of children as participants in, rather than objects of, research (Woodhead and Faulkner, 2008). The children's consent was seen as something in permanent flux, requiring a sense of ongoing accomplishment (Cocks, 2006) or 'ethical radar' (Skånfors, 2009), and no child – on the surface – was coerced to participate. The children and their families/carers were told about the proposed research project, which aimed to explore learning that was happening in the setting and how it could be 'assessed'.

As Skånfors (2009) has argued, whilst the idea of gaining children's consent to research is rightly considered imperative, in recent research trends framed within the social studies of childhood a dilemma is often expressed around young children's understanding of what they are actually consenting *to*. For Cocks (2006: 253) the notion of 'informed consent' is problematic as underpinning the idea of presenting a proposed project to children in an understandable way is a presupposition of a 'mainstream child, who is presumed to have some age-appropriate channel of communication that adults know and understand'. Dockett and Perry (2007: 55) further problematise this issue by arguing that 'too much information can be as confusing as too little', and it is difficult to alert child-participants (we would broaden this to *all* research participants) to 'possible positive and negative outcomes of research participation.' One child – Cynthia – and her story from the TAP project add a further dimension to this complex and 'messy' process of negotiating consent, specifically in the context of educator-research.

Cynthia was one of the first children to volunteer for the TAP research by raising her hand during a group time when the project was introduced. She volunteered to join a focus group with Glecy – an educator with whom she had a particular connection. Glecy had supported Cynthia in her transition to nursery and Cynthia often chose activities that would bring her into close proximity with Glecy. Looking back on this project, Rachel noted:

> While Cynthia had ostensibly consented to participate, what exactly had she consented to? In this moment: Was Cynthia consenting to being involved in this research project? Was she consenting to participation in an activity that would provide her with an opportunity that promised to allow her to 'excel' as she had in previous small group discussions which were part of our curriculum activities? Was her assent an indication of her desire to spend time with Glecy, a trusted and important person to her in the nursery? Or was her raised and waving hand a response to a combination of these and potentially other factors?
>
> *(Rachel Rosen, TAP)*

One of the issues that emerges from this fieldnote relates to the question of visibility – or in this case *lack of visibility* – in educator-research. The proposed research was introduced during a group discussion time, which was a typical occurrence in the nursery and closely tied in with the pedagogy of the setting. However, generally these in-depth dialogues were stimulated by the children's interests and the educator's reflections on these, whereas the TAP research project was primarily an *educator*-driven initiative. Further, this was a piece of research that Rachel and her team explicitly intended to take *beyond* the walls of the nursery – subjecting their joint conversations and practices to a level of public scrutiny and critique that was not an integral aspect of their everyday projects with the children. Was Cynthia aware of these differences? Had the educator-researchers provided sufficient information to the children to make the differences between their everyday and research practices clear? This was a blurry line for the educators to maintain sight of, let alone for the children who were substantially less involved in planning and reflecting on the research process.

During the small group discussion with Glecy and two other children, Cynthia participated vocally in the conversation. She noted that learning happens when 'someone teaches you stuff and then you know it' as well as through observing and then practising: 'Learning is trying to do it by yourself. That is how you know you are learning: trying something by yourself.' Cynthia continued to show a strong interest in the research project on subsequent days, engaging in follow-up activities such as taking pictures of 'what learning looks like in the nursery' designed as a participative strategy for eliciting children's perspectives on a topic (cf. Clark and Moss, 2001). She eagerly spent an afternoon walking around the setting with camera in hand taking photographs and rushing back to tell Glecy about them. On subsequent days, Cynthia engaged with Glecy to look at and discuss the printed photographs.

Away from the activities with the children, the educator team met to discuss emerging themes and lessons of the research, seeking to use their reflections to develop a new process for 'assessing learning' in the setting. This activity was less visible to the children, but we would argue, again, mirrors much of early childhood practice (rightly or wrongly) where much discussion about and for children occurs *away* from them. At this point, the educator-research team felt it was important to share more widely the rich and complex discussions they had been having as a team and with children. The research 'data' were compiled in children's portfolio books and children were asked whether their families/carers might be invited into the nursery to talk about learning that had taken place in the nursery. As we noted earlier, in such practices the child is never anonymous as is usual in research, and any discussions needs to be seen in a context in which communicating with families/carers about their children's development and learning is 'recommended practice'. Again, however, the response from the children to this proposal was one of excitement and anticipation. Children began adding items independently to their portfolio books in preparation for the meeting. One child suggested creating invitations for their families and, thereafter, discussions with the children were overrun with suggestions for the meetings with their families.

Rachel's fieldnotes that follow reflect how easy it is to lose sight of the issue of consent as well as how complex an issue it is in relation to educator-research:

> It may have been the momentum of the project spurred on by a few vocal children in the group. It may have been our desire as educator-researchers to undertake such meetings with families. Perhaps both of these sources of excitement were contagious and fuelled each other. It may have been the more general difficulty of navigating between research responsibilities regarding consent and the right to withdraw versus the more universal expectations of the general nursery programme: as educators we were always concerned that no family would feel left out by the involvement of and communication with another family. Regardless, in the process of planning these year-end meetings, our focus on on-going negotiation of consent with research participants slipped from view.
>
> When the first day for the meetings arrived we – educators, children, and families including siblings and extended members in many cases – met to discuss what we had all learned from each other. In general, the children showed their families the portfolio books and spoke about the question 'what learning happens at Nursery'. As educators we shared what we had learned from the child. Family members spoke about what they learned from the Nursery and their views on their child's growing knowledge and competencies.
>
> By mid-afternoon, we were feeling on a high, buoyed by both the 'success' of the project and excited by the prospects of our new assessment process for the future. When the knock came on the front door at 3.15, it wouldn't be an overstatement to say that we were stunned into silence when Kai – Cynthia's father – said that she was lingering outside, highly reluctant to

come in to the nursery. He explained angrily, 'She keeps talking about not knowing how to answer the question: "What does learning look like?" Why would you ask her something like that?'

In the end, we met with Kai, Cynthia, and her mother and sister: Cynthia decided that she wanted to come in after we reassured her that she didn't have to talk about anything she didn't want to – including 'what learning looks like'. However, the experience was a humbling reminder about the complexities of navigating educator and researcher identities and negotiating consent in 'insider' research. We were not able to discuss the issue further with Cynthia as it was year-end and Cynthia began attending a primary school soon after.

(Rachel Rosen, TAP)

This incident exemplifies the way that in the 'life' of any research project, participants may fluctuate between eager participation to withdrawal of consent, further exemplifying Cock's (2006) notion of 'consent' as being in permanent flux. Despite endeavouring from the outset to research ethically, an unintended consequence of the research was *anxiety* on the part of this child and her family. Could this have been avoided?

The question that seemed to have prompted Cynthia's anxiety had been chosen carefully by the educator-researchers as it allowed for a wide range of responses, but it seemed – perhaps *because of* its open-endedness – to unsettle Cynthia's yearning to 'get things right'. Without wanting to 'fix' Cynthia, she was a child who seemed to enjoy engaging in activities that would demonstrate her 'school-based' competencies. Such skills were well rewarded by her 'high achieving' older sister, teacher father, and a mother engaged in many 'intensive' mothering practices shaped by a desire to do the best for her child, which as Tronto (2002: 42) asserts is characteristic of a capitalist society in which parents are urged to 'keep competitive advantage over other people's children'. Perhaps, then, the shift in consent took place when Cynthia's 'private' world at the nursery – where such questions were 'permissible' – was opened up to the scrutiny of others who she read as being less sympathetic to such ambiguities.

However, we might also read this incident as one of 'informed dissent' (Morrow, 2005: 158), which enabled Cynthia to absent herself from part but not all of the research. Certainly her family – as well as the educators – supported her right to withdraw her consent and indeed challenged the nursery in relation to the anxiety caused by this aspect of the research. But would all families have felt able to do so? Cynthia's family was middle class and her parents had social and cultural capital that made them more adept at negotiating with educators – particularly as her father was a teacher – and certainly confident that they would be listened to (e.g., see Reay, 2005). Further, some families (and adults more generally) may have viewed Cynthia's refusal to participate as 'naughty' (cf. Alderson, 2005), especially as she was refusing to participate in a project linked inextricably to the work of the setting she attended.

Regardless of her reasons, Cynthia's story serves as a vivid reminder of how laudable pedagogical goals for an entire group of children can distort research goals of individual consent and the right to withdraw. It raises questions about the distinction between research and educational practices and purposes and the challenging consequences of blurring boundaries between the two. We suggest that the educator-researcher has to work especially hard at raising the *visibility* of his/her research. Further to this, educator-researchers (like all researchers) need to engage in a constant process of sensitising themselves to the cues of individual research participants (Alderson, 2005).

One of the other issues raised by Cynthia's story centres on the question of what precisely Cynthia was consenting *to*. We suggested that there were myriad motivations that could have compelled her 'consent' and will now pursue this issue of 'compulsion' further by examining a critical moment from the FBRP and, in so doing, raise some further challenging questions in relation to the notion of 'consent' in educator-research. In the FBRP, the increased educator involvement in the blockplay area did not at any time involve an *overt* level of compulsion: for example, researchers never said to children, 'You must come and play with the blocks right now.' But did their increased spatial positioning within this area of the classroom result in a more subtle form of pressure? Did children feel *compelled* to come to the blockplay area if they wanted to be with the particular educator based in that area at a particular time (similar to Cynthia's possible desire to be with Glecy)? And, as two of the educators (including Deb) had far greater involvement in the research project and as a result spent increased time observing children in the blockplay area, did these actions *further* compel children to show an interest in blockplay or at the very least seek Deb out in this space should they wish to spend time with her?

Such questions are prompted in part by Mercedes' story in the FBRP. One afternoon, Deb recalls Mercedes coming over to the blockplay area where she was seated, sitting herself firmly on Deb's knee, and pulling her face close to Deb's own so all Deb could see was Mercedes and not the blockplay activity she had been observing and documenting in detail. Mercedes accompanied these actions with a hearty chuckle. Mercedes, it should be noted, rarely – if ever – engaged in blockplay. In this instance, Mercedes seemed to be attempting to subvert Deb's activity, copious documentation of blockplay activity on children *other* than Mercedes.

More significantly, however, this incident offers a salutary reminder that children may desire a relationship on occasions that notices them aside from what they are *doing*. Cederman (2008), for instance, in her discussion of *Te Whāriki*, has argued persuasively that *noticing* and more importantly *capturing* children's play experiences in the copious documentation of children's activities may be given prominence over children's present, relational, and embodied selves. As educator-research (and in all likelihood *most* research) tends to involve increased documentation, does it aggravate 'capturing' the activities of children over being with children?

Mercedes' action, by way of contrast, prompted Deb to act in a different way as it offered a 'refractive' angle (Bakhtin, 1981: 300) on her activity, highlighting the problematic of *capturing* children through her observations of blockplay rather than *being with them* – a point we develop in Chapter 8. In order to 'answer' Mercedes, Deb had to look (it was impossible to do otherwise given Mercedes' position!) and stop recording. She spent time chatting to Mercedes about her family, as she had observed on other occasions that Mercedes liked to do this. As we have noted throughout this book, for Bakhtin (1990; 1993), we are answerable when we try to contemplate another's experience but bring to this our own uniqueness – our own 'outsideness' – and respond. But we do not answer one another outside the cultural context: the metaphor Bakhtin uses is '*music in midst of music*' (1990: 201; emphasis in original). Thus, Deb's actions towards Mercedes were authored in the context of an educator–child relationship, so perhaps less exuberant than had it been her nephew, but prior to the current climate where close bodily contact between children and adults is framed as 'risky' (Tobin, 2004).

After this incident, Mercedes often came over to the blockplay area to see what was happening, sometimes offering a comment to children engaged in building, but she rarely participated 'actively'. We would argue, therefore, that Mercedes' actions were indicative of a desire for *being with* other children as well as Deb, as opposed to *engaging in tasks with them*. Indeed, the FBRP (Gura, 1992) noted the important presence of 'onlookers' at the time of the research, but this was framed more in terms of children generating ideas for building with blocks and *learning* from each other – an important contribution at the time as 'onlookers' are often viewed as lacking purpose or being 'off task'. Reflecting now on such moments, we suggest that perhaps there are other more pro-social motivations for such actions, with children desiring to be with others.

Consent through the lens of answerability

Both critical moments we have outlined in this chapter highlight the 'refractive angles' children have bought to our research projects. This, in turn, has provoked re-appraisal of our own practices as researchers *and* educators in relation to 'consent'. And, in drawing this chapter to a close, we wish to pull out a number of overarching points about 'consent' in the context of educator-research. First, a thesaurus search of the word 'consent' in its various guises indicates that it can mean 'permission' or 'agreement' and even 'harmony'. But the polyvocality associated with Bakhtinian thinking implies the possibility of greater disjuncture than this presentation of 'consent' suggests, as the notion of dialoguing starts from the premise that at least two people coming together will rub up against one another and produce something *new* in this creative – but not necessarily easy – process.

As Edwards and Mauthner (2002: 25) point out: 'Ethics is about how to deal with conflict, disagreement and ambivalence rather than attempting to eliminate it.' However, intense emotions – and indeed disjuncture and conflict that often provoke such responses – are often considered out of place in early childhood settings intent on ensuring 'a secure, safe and happy childhood' (DfE, 2012: 2) through 'kind', 'warm', and 'gentle' interactions (Colley, 2006). Teaching children to 'manage' or learn how to 'regulate' emotions, particularly those which are 'negative', is emphasised in parenting literature (see Hoffman, 2009) as well as texts for early childhood educators (see Holland, 2009). While we applaud a focus on children's well-being beyond prescriptive assessment profiles and in no way seek to diminish the importance of a pleasurable and meaningful life, we argue that such a focus risks becoming a form of simplified and 'compulsory happiness' that denies the fruitfulness of dissent (cf. Suissa, 2008).

Here we would argue that while we should *not* deliberately cause anxiety for any child or participant, dissonance – while uncomfortable – can be viewed as productive, and not just for adult-researchers. In the case of the TAP project, although Cynthia was anxious about talking about learning with educators and her family at *one point* in the research, she asserted her right to withdraw from the research: as Prout and James (1997: 8) argue, children are not 'passive subjects of social structures and processes'. In this case, Cynthia's withdrawal of consent was accepted unequivocally by all concerned, an important experience providing as it did a sense of Cynthia's agency and influence contra dominant ways of framing children as 'objects' with 'lives lived through childhoods constructed for them by adult's understanding of children and what children are and should be' (Mayall, 1994: 1). In dissenting, she destabilised her inequitable position as 'child' in the face of adult educator-researchers, which – although disquieting for all concerned – opened up different ways of conceptualising adult–child relations more broadly in the setting. In expressing how she felt, Cynthia affected profound change in the way the project's educator-researchers viewed *all* children's 'consent' to activities in and outside the research.

It is critical to reiterate that we are *not* suggesting that adult-researchers should strive to cause anxiety for *any* research participant – far from it. Our point here is that 'doing nothing' in relation to others is not a possibility whether it is in research, education or indeed any other activity involving more than one human being. As Shotter and Billig (1998: 22) observe, drawing on the ideas of Bakhtin:

> Two living embodied human beings cannot exist juxtaposed for long without affecting each other in a living way. We cannot, like dead and inanimate things, remain utterly inert when in one another's presence; neither can we not be responsive to aspects of our surroundings.

To expand further, for Bakhtin, our actions *anticipate* the reactions of the others with whom we act. Applied to research, this encourages researchers to anticipate possible responses to their research activities. We may anticipate 'correctly' in many instances – and here we concur with Morrow's (2005: 161) recommendation that researchers 'read as widely as possible', including methodological accounts as well as ethical guidelines, as this can sensitise the researcher to potential thorny issues — but there will be other occasions in which, despite our best endeavours, we misjudge and misread as in the case of the creative, open-ended ended questions put to Cynthia in the TAP project. *Some* predictability of response is possible but *complete* predictability of responses to research undertakings is impossible as events are 'once-occurrent'.

Of course, this is open to the criticism that acting as if we 'know' the position of the other is possible and that there are some voices on the margins that may not be heard by us (Bernard-Donals, 1998) — a point we take up in more detail in the next chapter. Here, suffice to say that for Bakhtin (1993), awareness of and attention to difference and one's unique 'outside' position are crucial to an answerable act. As educator-researchers, our 'outsideness' can prompt us to ask questions provoked by critical moments in our research relationships with children, such as those involving Cynthia and Mercedes, not least: Are children made aware how information about them is shared and with whom? How visible can we make 'researching' as distinct from 'educating'? Whose perspectives are missed?

Traversing these issues is complex and cannot be set down as a series of tightly framed statements about what one *ought* to do in every given moment. To rely purely on ethical guidelines from a Bakhtinian (1993) perspective is tantamount to relying on an 'alibi' with no personal responsibility for one's actions — acting in such a way cannot be described as being 'answerable'. Indeed the cyclical/processual nature of educator-research complicates this further as it is difficult to be entirely transparent a priori. In this sense, we would argue that educator-research projects and longer term research projects more generally need to attend constantly, both to making developments in research visible as well as to participants' feelings about these changes. This involves continuous renegotiations around consent. Here, we suggest a shift from viewing consent as a technical practice — as a 'thing' to be achieved before entry into the field — to a *relational process*.

Again, we find the work of Bakhtin (1993: 32) instructive here as he argues that an 'interested-effective attitude' is a key component of answerability. Applied to research, we interpret this as the desire to care enough to enter into a relationship with others and ideas in *actual ongoing situations* with a view to being open to difference and change well beyond these research moments. In the TAP project, for instance, although Rachel's team was not able to predict and avoid the anxiety produced for Cynthia, they strove to 'answer' her and her family by acknowledging and accepting her dissent and shifting the focus of the family meeting. While not being able to change what happened in that 'once-occurrent' moment, in dialoguing with Cynthia's story in the years that have followed, Rachel can effect change in her own thinking and practice as well as the thinking and practice of others. In the FBRP, Deb was able to 'answer' Mercedes by 'being with' her as opposed to 'capturing' her in that moment, and she is similarly able to continue to dialogue with this event.

To conclude, the context of educator-research is an interesting lens through which to examine research relationships between adults and children. We can see that 'consent' is an area that is worthy of greater examination in this context as it leads to probing questions relating to the visibility of 'researching' in relation to 'educating', and how this enables and constrains relationships between children and adult-educators. The next chapter returns to exploring data from our doctoral research projects and examines how data are generated in greater depth in order to explore how we come to 'know' the child and what children make of the methods we use in research.

6
GENERATING DATA, GENERATING RELATIONSHIPS

From observation to *sensing practices*

We return our focus in this chapter to data from our doctoral research projects and begin with an excerpt from Rachel's fieldnotes, which highlight some of the complex and complicating practices involved in generating, interpreting, and representing data in research with young children:

> Jesse approached me right away today. Seeing my video camera, he began swinging his head side to side for the camera and declared, 'We're the funny men.' He raised his hands, gently hitting himself in the head with alternating hands: 'Donk! Donk! Donk!' Ismael jostled for position in front of the camera repeating, 'I'm the funny man.' He stuck his tongue out and waved his head back and forth, 'Ahhh!'
>
> I am really struck by differences in our interactions. Without the camera, Jesse and I have long extended conversations about the play characters he inhabits or the way a narrative is developing. Often when my video camera is out, he becomes 'silly'. He 'consents' officially to the camera – approaching me when I have it on or agreeing to being recorded when I approach him (most of the time at least). But, I wonder if it is the gaze of the camera that provokes such a performance.
>
> *(Rachel Rosen, Taboo play)*

Who is observing whom in this example? What possibilities do these observational practices open up and what do they foreclose? And perhaps more generally: How do we 'know' what we 'know' in relation to early childhood research? How do our ways of knowing impact on research relationships? And how do research practices interact with *sensing practices* more broadly? It is to these questions that we seek to speak in this chapter, as we explore the ways that child-participants and adult-researchers make sense of one another in the research process. We will return to the first example given, as well as others, throughout the chapter to help us do so.

This chapter will consider observation in particular, given its prominence in research and education; although, such a practice invariably involves and interacts with others. Warming (2011), for example, in discussing her research into Danish school children's perspectives about 'the ideal child life', argues that participant observation is both a way of generating data about children's perspectives and 'giving voice' to children. While this latter assertion deserves sustained interrogation in its own right, suffice it here to say that this assumes a particular authenticity to children's voice – an idea that has come under sustained critique (e.g. see Jackson and Mazzei, 2009) – and that children always *want* to voice their experiences, risking them to scrutiny in heavily managed and '*overcivilised*' early childhood settings. Further, claims that adults are the ones to 'give voice' merely reinforce what they claim to critique: inequality between adults and children. This aside is indicative of the nature of this chapter, which, by necessity, will not remain bound within debates explicitly tied to observational methods, but will slip into the cracks of writing about 'voice' and 'listening to children' using this as a source of and subject for critique.

Unravelling observation in early childhood settings

Angrosino's (2005: 732) proposal that observation be considered as a 'context for interactions' rather than a 'method' is the starting point of our discussion. In addition to helpfully unbinding observation from its technical practice, his point implies that it is necessary to consider the way that such interactions are experienced within the observation-rife milieux of early childhood settings. In the 'First World/North', child observation has become virtually synonymous with early childhood practice going back to pioneers such as Jean Piaget and Susan Isaacs. Entrenched as child observation is in curriculum documents as well as in educator training programmes, both observational practices and their products are highly visible in early childhood settings. In all our research settings, observational artefacts were visible in the form of books, reports, and public displays. Observational data were drawn on in informal conversations, planning meetings, and family–educator meetings. Beyond educators, there is a constant stream of other adults – including speech and language therapists, behavioural therapists, and social workers – moving through settings observing children according to their professional foci.

The following example from Head Start, an American government programme promoting 'school readiness' for low-income children, is illustrative of the way observation is promoted among educators. While we could have used similar examples from British or Canadian sources, Head Start is of particular global relevance given the hegemony of American cultural practices in the field of early childhood, not least through the 'transfer' of the Head Start curriculum to the 'Third World/South' (Penn, 2011c):

> If you make a habit of asking questions, you will get to know who a child is and can keep track of who that child is becoming . . . Not only can you observe what children know, but also how they think and solve problems.

> By collecting observations, you can find answers to your questions and build a picture of children's performance and progress without interfering with their daily activities or usual behavior.
>
> *(Jablon and Dombro, 2001: no page)*

What is at stake with these observational practices is nothing less than the child herself. By this we mean that it is not just an activity or practice that is the object of observation, but through observation educators are deemed to 'know' the child *in entirety*. Such an assumption is premised on an originatory subject with innate dispositions, abilities, and desires that are exteriorised through the child's actions (or *in*actions for that matter). This assumption misplaces the way that subjectivity is fundamentally socially as well as historically constituted and constituting: Elias (1994: 207) notes the way that self-regulation and individualisation of thinking, actions, affect, and even corporeality itself – the sense of a 'self in a case' – is produced through historically amalgamated 'civilising' processes. Suggesting that through observation we can 'know' the child also disarticulates children's practices from their relational and contextual situatedness: put simply, we do different things at different times with different people. In contrast, as the Head Start directive exemplifies, observational practices are often used to '*fix*' children, in essence assigning inherent and stable dispositions and intelligence. Such 'fixing' of children through observation has significant consequences. In the highly charged and regulatory environment of early childhood settings, observation tends to serve the function of increasing normalisation and surveillance in the move to develop 'human capital'. By way of an example, the *Early Years Foundation Stage* (EYFS) (DCSF, 2008; DfE, 2012) curriculum in England can be regarded as a document that aims to establish uniformity over educators' understandings of the 'normal' and 'abnormal' child through its explicit use of developmental stages. As a national document, the curriculum and its practice guidance sediment the idea of such stages being a 'true' measure of children's development and learning (Holligan, 2000). Educators themselves accept, often uncritically, the idea or set of ideas such as stage theories of development as objective and neutral (Burman, 2001; Holligan, 2000). This might be framed within the Bakhtinian circle's (1986) conception of 'double-voicedness' – or what we would call 'multiple-voicedness' – as the 'utterances' of early childhood educators are 'populated' with a range of other voices, not least what Jones et al. (2010a) have called the 'spectre' of developmental psychology.

As we have noted, this approach to observation serves to shift the focus from flesh and blood children to a 'paper child' (Jones et al., 2010a). However, Bradbury's (2011) work charts the even more insidious and inequitable outcomes of the associated EYFS (DCSF, 2008; DfE, 2012) assessment tool: the 'profile'. Her research demonstrates the way this observational assessment does not just record inequities but actually produces them. In the London schools she studied, educators were under pressure to deflate children's assessment scores, including through direct intervention from local government: schools were *deemed* to be adding 'value' to children through the education process if a child's scores rose during the course of his/her time at school. However, rather than a generalised deflation, educators dropped the assessment scores of those children perceived to be 'lower ability' – based on the educators 'knowledge' of children obtained through observation practices. Bradbury (2011) argues that in a racist society such observations are already shaped by discriminatory discourses of marginalised children's expendability and home deprivation, and can in part explain the low attainment levels of children of colour and those on free school meals (the proxy measurement for deprivation, in the UK).

With the importance attributed to young children's 'normal' development – where the first 1000 days are viewed as particularly critical (Allen, 2011) – the corollary is that early childhood educators are charged with maximising this development, requiring intensive observation and practices intent on ensuring prescriptive learning. As Bernstein (1975: 24) contends in relation to the predominant pedagogy of play in many early childhood settings, 'The theory gives rise to a total – but invisible – *surveillance* of the child, because it relates his [sic] inner dispositions to all his external acts' [emphasis added]. Such surveillance focuses on spaces, actions, as well as the child herself and risks subjecting increasingly diverse and (potentially) secret aspects of children's lives to scrutiny and normalising efforts (Dahlberg and Moss, 2005). This surveillance and '*over*civilising' practice is especially visible and explicit in official activities, such as the more *formal* organisation of food events when compared to the 'free play' aspects of a session in Deb's research. As Ben-Ari (1997: 104) argues: 'Mealtimes predicate a gradual harnessing of the children's bodies – their limbs, capacities for coordination, and cravings, for instance – towards actions and demeanour deemed socially "proper".' Deb's research highlights the way that children's bodies were subject to a high degree of monitoring: every nappy (diaper) change and morsel that a child ate was documented in Settings three and four and this was championed as part of these settings' risk management. If a child became ill, then there would be an audit trail as to what s/he had eaten.

We have only scratched the surface of critiques of observation in early childhood settings. However, our aim here is to set the stage for considering the significance of such an omnipresent practice on researcher–child relations, as it is in this highly scrutinised arena – with its remarkably visible practice of observation – that the researcher studies.

The problematic of research observations

Not only is observation ubiquitous in early childhood practice, but it is a primary methodological tool in nearly any empirical research project to the extent that it is characterised by Adler and Adler (1994: 389) as 'the fundamental base of all research methods' in the social sciences. Observation takes both explicit and implicit forms in research: for example, while observation is not always formally identified as a part of a research interview, it is essential for interpretation of body language and vocal tone (Angrosino, 2005). Indeed, observation of children and adults was crucial in our research, in part because observation is one of the primary ways to generate data about *very* young children, given their lack of verbal language.

Warming (2011) broadens the point here, arguing that children – even those who can – do not always prefer to engage in verbal communication, but rely instead on bodily productions to express perspectives. Here, observation is essential for considering embodied action such as movement, voice quality, and touch. Attention to these various modes is also important as they may contradict the visual and verbal and therefore potentially denaturalise categorisations (cf. Schlichter, 2011). Observation brings to light taken-for-granted practices, changes in people's practices such as the earlier example of Jesse and the video camera, and contradictions in the way people interpret and represent these practices.

However, it is here that we wish to begin interrupting this discourse of observation, considering the tensions within such research practice. For example: How do we think about these moments of contradiction? What authority generates analysis and representations of these contradictions? What are the implications for research relationships? These questions are prompted by a long tradition of critique levelled against assertions of unbiased and 'naturalistic' observation in the social sciences, critiques that hold particular salience in early childhood research: 'naturalistic' observation in the 'unnatural' spaces of early childhood settings is somewhat of an oxymoron, as we pointed out in Chapter 2.

Further, these critiques suggest in no uncertain terms that observation is 'generated' by the researcher's paradigmatic orientations, habitus, and interests (Mason, 2002). Critiques of naturalistic observation stress that practices under observation are necessarily affected by the researcher's presence, even in non-participant observation (Robson, 2002). The context of activity also affects the practices under observation as Tizard and Hughes' (2002) influential study of children's talk at home and school demonstrated. Working-class children in particular exhibited greater confidence, engagement, and ability at home, given the very different communication styles practised in their homes in comparison to formal educational environments. This research challenged taken-for-granted ideas within the educational system about linguistic 'deprivation' within working-class homes. Such work also supports the earlier discussion about the dangers of 'fixing' participants through observation.

In addition, the *way* we record observational data is not a mirror of reality but a selection, shaped by our categories of thought. Jones, Holmes, MacRae, and MacLure (2010b: 483) argue that observational notes should be seen as 'scribbles' with all the incompleteness and lack of detail such a term implies; such gaps, they argue, are then 'cleansed' in translating scribbles to data. Acknowledgement of the always partial and perspectival nature of observation has in part led to the 'crisis of representation' and debates about the authorial authority of the researcher coming out of post-colonial and feminist literature in particular (Alcoff, 2009; Skeggs, 2007;

Spivak, 1988). Such debates are particularly pronounced in the field of ethnography, given its racist and sexist traditions of inequitable relations of knowledge production, representation, and dissemination under the colonial gaze of the researcher (Ahmed, 2000).

We would like to use this necessarily quick gloss of contemporary critiques of research observation to begin to analyse the fieldnote about Jesse with which we began the chapter. Here, we note that Rachel seemed to assume that moments of self-presentation in front of the video camera are performed in a way that they are not in un-tooled observational situations. Rachel seems to be searching for the possibility of 'finding' the authentic subject if only the methods are 'right'. Such yearnings may in part have been shaped by her educator 'habitus', including the underpinning assumption that observation provides a reasonably straightforward way to 'know' the child. However, productive consideration of the 'opacity and inconsistencies' (Jones et al., 2010b: 489) of the observation prompts a different line of inquiry. Here, Jesse's 'extended conversations' with Rachel could have just as easily been a performance as the 'silliness' in the video situation, shaped by the recognisable 'serious' and educational form of adult–child interactions in the setting and serving to achieve a connection with Rachel – an interested adult. How was Rachel different in her relationship with Jesse in these moments? What were the effects of Jesse's 'silliness' on him and his relationships? In this fieldnote, Rachel's unintentional commitment to finding Jesse's 'originary self' stalled such lines of inquiry. But her commitments also shaped relationship negotiations: in reflecting on this fieldnote, Rachel realised that she would often turn to Jesse to verbally explain the play narrative, to the neglect of other participants in the play and non-verbal modes of communication. This, we suggest, is indicative of the problematic nature of observation in research practice.

The blurred boundaries of observational practices

In the discussion thus far, we have noted the ubiquity of observation as a practice of both educators and researchers in early childhood settings. In this section, we will argue that there is a blurring between these positioned practices that has implications for adult-researcher and child-participant relationships. Researcher observations cannot be readily distinguished from other observational practices in early childhood settings and, as a result, the presence of observational tools plays a role in how children perceive the researcher, regardless of how the researcher attempts to position herself.

Rachel's research into taboo play provides a useful entry into this discussion. On Rachel's first two visits, she entered the setting with a large notebook and pen. She stood and sat in various locations of the setting observing and writing notes about the children's activity. Although children occasionally glanced obviously at her – and this was often when doing something 'forbidden' such as throwing a piece of Lego at another child – during neither visit did children approach her or speak directly to her. Rachel returned nearly four months later to begin her research proper. Again, she placed herself on the edge of the setting close enough to observe children's play at the water table but without any obvious tools of observation. Within 10 minutes, a small group of children had formed engaging her in conversation and play. As it was months after the initial visits, and the children did not make reference to having seen her before, increasing familiarity with Rachel cannot account for this change. Instead, we suggest that the presence of visible observational tools created a particular 'context of interaction' accounting in part for the children's different responses. As a recognisable material symbol in a setting pervaded by adult observation, we suggest that the children read Rachel's notebook as indicative of an adult inhabiting a particular subject position: adult as a detached observer, assessor or regulator of children's activities.

Notably here, observational tools are not just symbolical barriers, but also real physical barriers to participative interaction as they can impede movement, limit proximity, cause distraction, and erect a material boundary between people – concerns also voiced by educators in our studies. The video camera, in the critical moment that began this chapter, certainly assumed this role. For despite Rachel's efforts to use 'ethical radar' (Skanfors, 2009) and feminist approaches to visual ethnographic production – such as turning the camera gaze onto herself as well as the child-participants (Pink, 2007) – the video camera introduced a prominent, *visible* separation between her and the participants.

The objectifying gaze of an observer where the child becomes a 'describable, analyzable object' (Phelan, 1997: 85) has been widely commented on, particularly when aided by apparatus such as cameras and video cameras (e.g., see Twigg, 1992). It is perhaps the violence of such gaze that Jesse was alluding to when he commented to Rachel a month after the observation above: 'Your camera's weird. It looks like a gun,' demonstrating how the camera with its open view-finder perched on top of a tripod could be used as a machine gun: 'Ptchew! Ptchew! Ptchew!' Jesse's responses were also suggestive a displacement of the 'established' social relations between Rachel and the children, where she became more of a documenter and interviewer than co-player. The video camera became a symbol of this changed role, additionally highlighting generational and classed distinctions between Rachel and the children: most of the families in the setting could not afford video equipment and children certainly did not bring such tools into the setting.

We are *not*, however, suggesting these points indicate observational methods – including those involving video – should be abandoned entirely. Grasseni (2004: 14) argues that while visual methods of data collection do not present an 'unproblematic record of reality' given the way the framing and gaze of a camera orders the viewer's attention, they do help researchers consider how a communities' visual attention organises and shapes their particular world view. Further, we suggest that observational tools can engender different forms of conversations and even serve as a catalyst for relationships, as the following exchange between Deb and Avleen, a child in Setting three, exemplifies:

Avleen: 'Are you writing again?' (*She had often observed me writing.*)
Deb: 'Yes – I'm writing about what I see in the home corner again.' (*I had been coming to the setting for two terms.*)
Avleen: 'Did you write about me yesterday?'
Deb: 'Well . . . not really – not like *this*. To write observations of what you are *actually doing* I have to be able to see you.'
Avleen: 'What does that say?' (*Said while pointing to my writing.*)
Deb: 'It says: "Kyle says, 'I'll go and have my drink now.'"'
Avleen: 'Kyle just said that.'
Deb: 'I know. I found it interesting, so I wrote it down . . . here.' (*Avleen looked intently at the observational notes.*)

Avleen then asked about lots of other notes in my fieldwork book and borrowed my pen to write her own notes on my pages. The pages are now littered with many children's writing.

(Deb Albon, Food events: Setting three)

In this instance, Avleen's interest in Deb's fieldnotes prompted some deep joint reflection on the nature of observations as written in 'real time', in situ, and then elaborated on later. We noted in Chapter 5 how much of the reflection and writing in research occurs *away* from children, but in this example we can see that Avleen expressed an interest in what was being written and who Deb was writing about. Moreover, Deb's use of the phrase 'I found it interesting' is also striking: Why are some things more noteworthy than others? And *whose* actions are more noteworthy than others? As a result of this exchange, Deb began to reflect more intently on what her observational practices communicated to children about who and what she found of 'value', and how that impacted on the potential for relationships. This exemplar unsettles notions of children's (in)competence in relation to adults and their supposed inability to comprehend the methods researchers adopt (cf. Robinson and Kellett, 2004). Deb recalls feeling that her relationship with Avleen had shifted to be more equitable. Following this moment, Avleen would often sit and write next to Deb, asking her questions about her fieldnotes; this prompted Deb to share far more information about what she was writing and how she was using fieldnotes than she had originally envisaged doing.

As with any observational practice, the effects of the researcher and her observational tools on the setting cannot be evaded. However, Hammersley and Atkinson (2007) suggest they can prompt new lines of inquiry – in this case, consideration of how observational tools shift relationships says something about participants' perspectives about both the technologies and their uses in highly surveilled settings. In the example with which we opened this chapter, Jesse's use of humour displaced the potentially invasive or objectifying gaze of Rachel and her camera, but also shifted relationship negotiations with Rachel and the others to one based on humour and mockery. Deb similarly noted:

Today I was in the home corner with my notebook. The children found their own writing materials and sat with me writing. When I asked what they were

>writing, they replied: 'We're doing observations.' When I replied: 'What are we observing then?' they laughed and I joined in. In parodying the observational practices used in the setting and adopted by me as a researcher, we had reached an impasse: effectively there was nothing to observe aside from observing each other observing.
>
>*(Deb Albon, Food events: Setting one)*

Tobin and Grace (1997: 184) suggest that opportunities to laugh about, parody or engage with the Bakhtinian 'carnivalesque' – an amplification and even overturning of the 'prevailing truth' and 'the established order' (Bakhtin, 1984b: 10) – can open up spaces to 'renegotiate' the 'highly stratified societ[y]' of the educational institution of which the researcher is inevitably a part. In this way, we would suggest that observation practices can never be seen as unidirectional or participants as passive victims of an inherently colonial research enterprise. Observational practices as well as their tools and artefacts are taken up and transformed – 'domesticated' (Howes, 2003) – in often unexpected ways, as Jesse's humorous attempts to unsettle Rachel's removed observational stance and Deb's fieldnotes of children parodying observation practices demonstrate. We recognise these as moments of contestation and 'agency we all experience, however multi-layered, fictional, and constrained it in fact is' (Alcoff, 2009: 121).

It is, in fact, this *appropriation* of observations that forms our second line of argument in relation to the blurred boundaries between educator and researcher observation practices. The point here is twofold: there is rarely a clear division between who has access to the observational artefacts generated in research, and this leads to a further blurring of pedagogical and research practices. We have discussed this in relation to children's appropriation of observational *moments*, such as in the example with Jesse, but this happens with observational *data* as well. Deb, for instance, shared many of her observations with educators and children's families in her food events' research as she found their comments often added an additional layer to her understanding, but this 'sharing' is not unproblematic. As an experienced educator herself and now a lecturer, Deb found that in two settings her observations were appropriated by the educators for purposes she had not expected. In Setting two, for example, they were used in a training session for the team in 'how to write observations', unbeknown to Deb prior to the session. Following this, it was difficult not to appear as 'expert' as some educators asked for her advice in this area of practice.

This discussion is in part connected to our third point which is that, to an extent because of the competing claims to observation data, there is a blurring between observation used for research or pedagogical *purposes* (Gallacher and Gallagher, 2008). While there is nothing fundamentally wrong with teasing out the pedagogical implications of research findings and, in fact, this can often be a laudable goal of research, in the immediate setting in which the data have been generated it becomes more difficult to separate analysis from the recognisable individual child about whom the observation is written. The technical solution of using pseudonyms, a strategy that we both attempted, does not easily anonymise the child, as children were often still identifiable or at least considered to be so. But even more consequentially, in the world of early childhood – where observation is deemed as the way to 'know' – there is something very unfamiliar about attempts to move away from discussions based in children's individual psychology, particularly as educators are under immense pressure to produce normative developmental assessments.

A dialogue with educators from Rachel's research will serve to exemplify these points. While sharing observations with educators that demonstrated the way a group of children used their knowledge of cultural media as a powerful resource in their play negotiations, the discussion became diagnostically focused. Some of the educators began identifying those children who could play 'well' and those children who were 'lacking' in play skills – viewed as 'repetitive' appropriation of media scripts (a reasonably common view, which Edmiston (2008) has subjected to sustained critique). In particular, two educators commented that the children 'lacking' play skills needed an *adult* presence to help them 'move on'. Without seeking to negate any differences between educators or imply that there were unvoiced criticisms of this particular reading of the research data, the discussion in that moment essentially *shifted* to one of potential interventions to support the development of play 'skills' – an instrumental perspective dominant in the contemporary rhetoric of 'play as progress' (Sutton-Smith, 1997). This put research observations to work for a specific, not to mention potentially problematic, pedagogical purpose with specific children identified as not meeting a normative developmental profile.

As a result, Rachel began to wonder: In the neoliberal climate of early childhood, was sharing observations of individual children subjecting them to further categorisation, developmental assessment, surveillance, and '*over*civilisation'? These concerns were exacerbated by the controversial play she was observing (which included extreme physicality as well as the taboo topic of death) as there were few data being generated that would have been perceived as benign in the setting. In such situations, questions of consent become central, for it is unlikely that many people would agree to research observations that subject them to diagnosis or increased surveillance and regulation (except possibly for medical purposes). In some cases, the children made a desire for confidentiality very explicit; for example, Monica turned to Rachel and said, 'Don't tell my Daddy' in reference to one of her actions. However, there were also implicit indications that children did not want their actions to be exposed to an educator gaze. In one such instance, Abdul 'died' – lying sprawled in a supine position with arms out and eyes closed. A passing educator asked: 'What are you doing Abdul?' He jumped up, keeping his eyes carefully on her – reassuming 'death position' as soon as she disappeared from view.

As time went on and Rachel became privy to more and more aspects of the peer culture, she grew increasing uncomfortable sharing observations with children or adults who had not been involved in the moments that led to their generation. As a result, by the end of her research, Rachel made efforts to focus her dialogues with educators on general points of analysis rather than observations of *individual children* (albeit that a tension remains here with the publication of data generated in the setting). Although researching a very different topic, Deb found that she too often observed children engaged in practices that her experience in the setting suggested would not be sanctioned: notably smearing bits of banana on their bodies and comparing masticated food in each other's mouths. She chose to *tactically ignore* such behaviours rather than admonish the children or inform the educators what she had seen.

While confidentiality and attempts to avoid 'fixing' children in normative categories are important principles to uphold, there may be occasions on which these principles come into direct conflict with issues of injustice. For instance, in Deb's research, her fieldnotes noted on more than one occasion how a particular child, who was regarded as having 'additional needs', was regularly excluded from the children's play by being overtly pushed or told to move away. She felt that to keep this information to herself would have been tantamount to colluding with such acts of injustice (see also Hatch's (1995) similar account). By sharing her observations with educators who had not seen such behaviour, the team was able to work on some ideas to foster a more inclusive approach in their provision.

In carrying out research, researchers may, on occasions, see something that has been missed by educators and, similarly, educators may share information that may be helpful in a researcher's endeavours. Here, the 'outsideness' (Bakhtin, 1990; 1993) that we and educators brought to each other during our respective research projects – in effect, an *additional* level of dialogue further to those we had with children – generated, on occasion, new understandings of the phenomenon under investigation and the practice of the setting. In essence then, we are arguing that decisions about what data to share, with whom, as well as when and how are highly complex; and, while ethical and political principles can provide some direction, ultimately, such decisions can only be made in situ.

Our final point in this section is about the blurred boundary in *critiquing* observation practices. It is more than likely that any practice that comes under extended examination can be critiqued (Chaput Waksler, 1991) and critique is certainly an important part of questioning taken-for-granted assumptions and challenging inequitable practices. However, while educators and children do scrutinise researchers, it is primarily the *researcher's* representation and critique of observational practices that becomes public given the authorial authority of the researcher. There is an uncomfortable irony in doing a study that involves critiquing the way educators' observational practices may objectify, 'fix', and discipline when the researcher's own observational practices may inadvertently do the same to educators. For example, we wonder to what extent sharing observations that include educators has the unintended consequence of causing the educators to look suspiciously at each other's practices. As researchers working within the same context of neoliberalism as educators, albeit generally within higher education institutions rather than early childhood settings, it is difficult to avoid similar impetuses and implications of our observational practices. And, arguably, 'fixing' educators is something that we have done to a certain extent throughout the discussions here.

The challenge, then, for researchers, is balancing the need for critique without slipping into easy formulations of power and institutional authority – such as adult–educator versus child – which negate broader systemic issues. For example, the positioned practices of educators need to be understood within the context of the intense pressures they labour under (Bradbury, 2011) as an 'alienated' workforce (Leavitt and Power, 1997) in the high-stakes, low-status field of early childhood. Here, platitudes – such as claims to 'not blame' educators – are a beginning but are ultimately insufficient. Instead, we suggest that this process is one of teasing out the lessons that can be learned for research as well as education, focusing on positioned practices and the authoritative 'double-voices' – including of neo-liberalism – with which we speak and act rather than pathologising individual educators. We will return to these ideas later in our discussion of answerability and the non-disinterested gaze.

Negotiating relationships through *sensing practices*

To this point, we have discussed observation primarily as a practice of educators and researchers; however, we have already alluded to the fact that observation is not a unidirectional process. While young children are not typically involved in the production of observational representations of adults, they do engage in extensive observations. We have come to think of these observations as '*sensing practices*' or multi-sensorial awareness of and engagements with others in the world. In our research projects, children's *sensing practices* included attention to embodied presence, practices and interactions, and observational tools. *Sensing practices* often involved detailed observations, noting both changes and continuities. 'Jesse's not here today,' Keyan informed Rachel about a child Rachel regularly spent a great deal of time with, 'Can we play?'

Sensing practices are, we argue, an important way that children 'emplace' the researcher and others: they provide children with an opportunity to see what type of initiation or interaction strategies might work with particular people and are fodder for conversations – as highlighted earlier. Sometimes *sensing practices* are a mechanism that allows children to move from distant observation to more proximal interactions, providing a spatial–temporal pacing to relationships as the following example illuminates:

> Emily and Ali noticed me sitting on a bench observing the outdoor space. They began circling around the large area, keeping their eyes on me as if to see what I was up to. Their loops slowly brought them closer until they were about three feet away. I smiled at them. In retrospect, I felt happy to be 'noticed' in direct opposition to my intention to observe 'unobtrusively'.

They began to laugh, covering up their eyes as if playing peek-a-boo. After a moment, Emily joined me on the bench – sitting close, placing her hand on my leg, and looking out in the direct of my gaze.

(Rachel Rosen, Taboo play)

We note here the way that visual observation allowed Emily and Ali to make a connection with Rachel moving from the distal to the proximal. This became a shared visual gaze as Rachel and Emily looked out from the bench together. Similarly, the sound of the girls' laughter announced their distant presence, creating a soundscape that compelled a response (Finnegan, 2002). In some ways, the properties of sound and sight allowed for a very intimate call to relationship that contradicted the physical distance between Rachel and the girls, despite contra arguments put forward by Serres that vision, in particular, is a sense linked with detachment and separateness (Connor, 2005).

Further, reverberations of laughter resonate through the entire body making prominent the corporeal sense of 'physical and emotional presence' (Feld, 2005: 184). However, rather than a self-contained existence, the touch of Emily's hand on Rachel's leg suggests co-presence and interconnection. Emily's 'reaching toward' (Manning, 2007) created a sense of common endeavour and joint action in this moment. Such 'sensory affinities' (Davies, 2011) may appear controversial in the world of early childhood as they violate and expose strongly held notions of independence and autonomy (Phelan, 1997). Yet, we would argue that the embodied interdependence of *sensing practices* offers both a more accurate picture of subjectivity and a way to begin considering 'observation' as a meeting of subject to subject.

It could be argued here that we are reifying children's practices and suggesting that children are essentially innocent of the classification and disciplining aspects of observation. This is certainly not the case: it was apparent in our studies that children did use observations to regulate each other and themselves in line with hegemonic ideas and institutional expectations. In Deb's research into food events, this was especially marked as mealtimes are occasions imbued with 'rules' relating to bodily expectations such as washing hands prior to eating, not speaking with mouth full, or sitting with a particular group – rules that children soon learnt and applied to each other.

What we do want to suggest, however, is that our growing cognisance of the children's attentiveness to us through *sensing practices* was productive in a number of ways. First, it helped us to unsettle the notion of observation as a purely visual practice. The dominance of the visual in our thinking is not surprising given the way that sight and hearing, at least of the verbal (Finnegan, 2002), are generally the most esteemed senses in the 'First World/North' with other senses often associated with 'nature' and 'savagery' as opposed to culture (Howes, 2005b). Yet the notion of *sensing practices* posits that it is not just sight or attention to the verbal which help us come to know each other and the world, but all of the senses (e.g., see Howes, 2005a). Our earlier discussion of body matters in Chapter 3 began to open up this aspect of relationship negotiations, noting the way touch and the other sensorial experiences are produced by close proximity. The children's *sensing practices* also encouraged us to consider the way that senses other than vision and verbal hearing often slip away in the writing-up process, dematerialising what is a very sensorial and embodied world (Pink, 2009).

Second, we became more attuned to the way that we, along with the children, were engaging in *sensing practices* as part of the process of negotiating relationships with others. Importantly, we are arguing here that *sensing practices* are not just precursors to relationship negotiations, they are a fundamental part of the entire research relationship. As Howes (2003: 40) notes: 'Perceptual relations are also social relations, making culture a lived, multisensory experience.' In Deb's food events research, smell and taste were inevitably part of this process. For example, Deb noted that one of the children, Shelly, was often upset when her dinner came. Sitting near Shelly at one dinner, Deb realised that by the time dinner arrived it was cold and vile. Deb could not have understood this other than through tasting it as part of the meal experience along with Shelly. On this occasion, she went to the kitchen and found a hot bit of potato for them: a bond developed between her and Shelly from that point. Finally, an awareness of *sensing practices* helped us to challenge the way observation is often essentialised as an inherently invasive and disciplining practice, and this is the jumping-off point for our final section.

Observation through the lens of relational ethics

To this point, we have suggested that observation has particular nuanced meanings in the '*overcivilised*' and neoliberal arena of early childhood settings. We argue, however, that observation and its tools and artefacts cannot be reified as either inherently neutral or innately regulatory. As a result, critiques of observation do not mean that researchers should (or in fact could) stop engaging in *sensing practices*. Here, we concur with Gallacher and Gallagher (2008) that it is not a question of finding the 'right' method to resolve epistemological, ethical, and political quandaries – of which we have only touched the surface in this discussion – but one of 'attitude' and approach to research. In the section that follows, we attempt to sketch out some principles for data generation practices through the lens of relationship negotiations.

Viewing observation as a nuanced practice that is both historically and contextually situated is essential to this endeavour. This suggests a need for continuous efforts to understand how observation practices are produced, perceived, and experienced, for example within the observation-rife milieux of early childhood settings. The Bakhtinian circle's work prompts a number of questions useful to such an exploration: What are the citations or double-/multiple-voices at play in our observations? And here, we reiterate our point that such multiple-voicedness cannot be restricted to the level of the verbal but can be productively understood as 'multiple-bodied'. How do these multiple-voices and bodies respond to and anticipate the context? What does the context then make (im)possible? Returning to the critical moment with Jesse that began this chapter, what we want to stress is that the presence of the camera is not the barrier to unmediated 'naturalistic' situations. However, the particular tools of research methods – the video camera for example – will necessarily impact on observational interactions, not the least because people are so used to the narrative format of edited video (in movies and TV), they may often perform in such ways in front of a camera (Haw and Hadfield, 2011).

However, just identifying the tensions in our practices, such as what observational practices foreclose and make possible, is insufficient because we live in a 'world of inescapable actuality and not in that of contingent possibility' (Bakhtin, 1993: 44). Such a statement flies in the face of much of the post-structural thinking that perhaps otherwise shares some of the concerns we raise in this chapter. At the risk of simplifying, this work does not just acknowledge – but actually valorises – the contingency, fallibility, and uncertainty of knowledge. This leaves little room for consideration of the actualities in everyday research and the necessity of moving 'beyond deconstruction towards reconstruction' (Dunne, 2006: 13).

We will explore this broader trend of valorising uncertainty in the social sciences (e.g. see Britzman, 2007; Lather, 2007) by examining one relevant example: the production of a research video about how 'naughtiness' is identified and fixed to particular children (MacLure, Holmes, MacRae, and Jones, 2010). Rather than presenting a video of the 'everyday banal', the research team in this project opted to 'jar' and 'animate' the viewer by counterpoising observational videos taken during their ethnographic study with a wide variety of other cultural images and sounds – a montage of 'fragments'. The authors claim hopefully, albeit tentatively, that the film did not 'champion one point of view over another, or lead the viewer to resolution through narrative or argument' instead shifting this licence on to the viewer (MacLure et al., 2010: 553).

We do not contest the notion of fallibility of knowledge in these texts; neither do we debate the need for humility and reflexivity long argued for in feminist and post-colonial critiques of the 'expert' researcher. What we do note and take issue with, however, are the implications of such inversions – from the Enlightenment quest for certainty and 'truth' to the postmodern insistence on uncertainty and the impossibility of truth – for research, praxis, and relationships. We would suggest that such valorisation of the unknowable ends up masking, rather than displacing, authorial privilege in subtle ways. As MacLure et al. (2010: 554) acknowledge, the film may be critiqued for 'smuggl[ing] in argument and critique under cover of an illusory openness'. Certainly, their choice of particular fragments as well as the decisions about the video format were influenced by, and therefore could not escape presenting, particular epistemological and ethical commitments. While we would argue that the film does necessarily contain argument and that it is dangerous to deny this, we are not fundamentally opposed to including researcher's interpretations and arguments in research – quite the opposite, in fact. Thinking with Bakhtin, we argue that interpretation and argument are a fundamental and necessary responsibility of the researcher. Without making arguments explicit, we attempt to evade subjecting them to the critique of others and inevitably shift responsibility for interpretation and its fallout to participants and viewers/readers.

To expand, we are not arguing for a return to a dominating and all-knowing colonial stance of the 'expert' researcher, but one embedded in the notion of answerability. Seeking to be answerable to others, for example, the children with whom we research, involves awareness, attentiveness and – in fact – *sensing practices* with and of others. However, the gaze of answerability is one of subject to subject, rather than the objectifying gaze associated with the abstract 'paper child' (Jones et al., 2010a). As Gardiner (2009: 214) notes:

> For Bakhtin, a genuinely ethical relationship of answerability to the other requires a 'loving and value-posting consciousness,' and not a disinterested, reifying gaze projected from the vantage point of an isolated ego.

This suggests that it is not observation itself that is at issue, but observation undertaken from a removed and uninvolved standpoint. Alternatively, a relational ethics of answerability requires a researcher to be *engaged* with and *caring* about participants aiming towards what Bakhtin (1993: 32) calls an 'interested-effective attitude'.

This has two key implications that we wish to highlight. First, answerability in this sense involves continuous and committed attempts to bring meaning to child-participants about their desires, explanations, and experiences. It involves bringing our 'excess of seeing' to each other in the research relationship. For example, this might mean caring to observe those who are silenced or whose ways of being are otherwise marginalised in a setting we are researching. It may also mean bringing our own knowledges to bear on situations affecting participants, offering potentially more transformative explanations and possibilities for the situations they/we find themselves/ourselves in (Mus, 2012). As Skeggs (2004: 131) notes, a researcher's interpretation might draw on academic knowledge that has 'epistemological authority'; however, the particular form of 'inequality of knowledge' between researcher and participants does not negate the 'moral equality' between researcher and participants. Likewise, participants may have knowledge based on their unique experiences and observations of the researcher – as we have tried to demonstrate through the notion of *sensing practices* and, for example, the way children's responses to our observational practices and tools made us think about how and why we were engaging in particular practices.

Bakhtin (1990; 1993) emphasises that answerability fundamentally involves *acting* while still remaining *open*. In this sense, knowledge and the act of knowing are always tentative and fallible but *importantly* involves an 'effort of understanding' (Holquist, 1990: xlii). This includes taking the risk of expressing interpretations – even with the knowledge they might be wrong. As Bakhtin (1979; as cited in Todorov, 1984: 111) suggests, 'For discourse (and, therefore, for man [sic]) nothing is more frightening than the absence of answer' and in order to answer we necessarily must engage in an act of interpretation.

In relation to observation, we can think about this as a *continuing dialogue* as we return to our observational data and interpretations, and dialogue with one another's observations, in writing this book. This is not a relativist wandering, or about ascertaining the ultimate veracity of an observation. Instead, truth becomes about 'practical adequacy' rather than infallibility: 'the extent to which it generates expectations about the world and about results of our actions which are realised' (Sayer, 2000: 43). Sayer (2000) argues that while to a certain extent these knowledge claims can 'produce' the world, not just any old idea will do in this regard because the referent – the materials, people or institutions, and places – has particular characteristics that are not infinitely contingent. However, the practical adequacy of interpretation is not something that is predetermined, by the position of the researcher for example or 'authenticity' of the participant voice, but something that can only be judged through reflexivity and in relation to methodology and the phenomenon under study.

To conclude, we have offered a critique of approaches that reify observational practices, arguing that 'sensing practices' helpfully extend understandings of observation, for example in recognising multi-sensorial ways of knowing. While we have problematised 'knowing' – in the sense that this privileges the power of the researcher as 'knower' and 'all knowing' – we have argued that being answerable in research relationships inevitably *and necessarily* involves 'interested-effective' interpretation, however tentative and fallible one's conclusions. As we have begun to explore, being answerable demands consideration of the broader social, political, and economic contexts of interpersonal negotiations, which, we contend, suggests that answerability has the potential to transform not just individuals but the spaces, institutions, and relationships being researched. This will be the focus of our remaining chapters and we turn next to exploring two particularly contentious ethical moments in some detail, considering questions of intervention, social justice, and the relationship between politics and ethics in research.

7

'CIVILISING' CHILDREN, CONFRONTING INEQUALITIES

Navigating narratives of the 'good researcher'

In previous chapters, we have indicated that research negotiations are typically more complex, messy, and uncertain than generally presented in methodology texts and professional ethical guidelines. In continuing to develop these points, this chapter will focus on those situations in which relationship negotiations are particularly 'contentious', throwing ethical dilemmas into more extreme relief. We have chosen to focus on two types of *contentious ethical moments*, 'dangerous' transgressions and injustices, which have brought us in direct conflict with narratives of the 'good researcher'.

Our use of the term 'good researcher' refers to dominant ideas about what a researcher should be like and should do which, as we have noted throughout the book, often becomes entangled with narratives of the 'good educator' – as 'civilising' force and risk manager – given the relatively small number of adults in early childhood settings. The 'good researcher' narrative often stresses 'neutrality' and efforts to 'eliminate cues' as to the researcher's own perspective and subjectivity (Robson, 2002: 274). Indeed, traditional – and arguably still dominant – ideas in social science research distinguish 'naturalistic' from experimental research based on its non-intrusiveness. Literature on research with children makes the point about influence most strongly when discussing the powerful impact adult-researchers can have over children, arguing that adult-researchers need to attend to conditions that compel children to respond in ways they believe will please the researcher (Clark, 2005). Despite suggesting that the *effect* of researcher presence can actually serve as an important data source, Hammersley and Atkinson (2007: 72) imply that a primary consideration for researchers must be to contain and minimise such effects arguing: 'It may be necessary to tolerate situations, actions, and people of which one disapproves, or that one finds distasteful or shocking.' In many ways, these arguments imply that the 'good' researcher 'goes with the flow' in order to avoid 'spoiling' the field and to generate 'accurate' data.

Yet, the very presence of a researcher – particularly in longer term research projects – necessarily affects the research field, regardless of whether researchers 'go with the flow'. As a result, Dennis (2009: 131) claims that a researcher's presence involves not only the 'potential for change', but in research motivated by social justice perspectives it involves an 'expectation' of changing the research setting 'for the better'. Motivated by goals of social justice, we share this *desire* for our research (and educational) practices and publications to have positive – even transformative – impacts on the contexts and lives of marginalised participants (following Skeggs, 2007). However, the expectation that this *will be so* is certainly overstated, bordering on arrogance, and serves to mask the complexities of research interactions.

That said, in research underpinned by goals of social justice, researcher 'interventions' become a matter for political and ethical consideration rather than something to be avoided as an a priori imperative (Dennis, 2009). To expand, Griffiths (1998) suggests that social justice research involves attention to: topics related to the distribution of resources, power, as well as individual/collective rights and responsibilities; critical paradigms; and methodological approaches that pay close attention to issues of power and inequity. Thus, research is made meaningful, and indeed *improved*, by an explicit commitment to emancipation. However, Griffiths (1998) notes that while such explicit commitments helpfully unmask the values that stand behind any project, researchers must still guard against unacknowledged perspectives including those influenced by funding and access issues.

In addition to these political concerns, consideration of non-maleficence, beneficence, and justice are widely recognised ethical principles for research (Murphy and Dingwall, 2007). Read through a social justice lens, these ethical ideas imply that research *ought* to improve the lot of individuals and collectivities who have been historically marginalised or 'harmed' – in other words, contributing to social change (Sayer, 2011). Taking this into account, 'intervention' is no longer outside the purview of research but can be understood as dedication to the ethical principles of beneficence and non-maleficence to both marginalised individuals and collectivities and committed to social transformation (Dennis, 2009).

What happens, then, when researchers *intervene* in the face of troubling situations? What do researchers convey to participants, and to themselves, when instead they 'go with the flow'? How do these researcher practices affect research relations and the practice of research? It is to these questions that we now move, beginning with a *contentious ethical moment* involving questions of safety and physical risk.

Negotiating across 'dangerous' transgressions

Early childhood settings are places full of, often implicit, rules about 'proper' conduct, with everything from the layout of the setting to the emphasis on repeated routines and transitions conveying the 'rules of the game' (Connolly, 2008). Alongside rules come transgressions, and transgressions are ubiquitous in early childhood settings. Arguably, among the more contentious contraventions of early childhood social orders are currently those which involve (perceived) safety risks. Wyver et al. (2010) suggest that many early childhood settings in the UK, USA, and Australia operate within a context of 'surplus safety' as educators in these settings attempt to prevent any type of danger for fear of even the most minor injury, even if limiting such activity could lead to long-term risks or allowing it could lead to longer-term benefits.

According to Beck's (1992) influential thesis, people have become increasingly alerted to dangers in our everyday lives because our understandings of 'risk' have multiplied with growth in scientific knowledge: even the imperceptible can now be constructed as a threat. This has led to a reification of 'expert' knowledge, which has resulted in greater *uncertainty* and *confusion* about the many different knowledge claims over what constitutes a 'risk' and what our responses to these should be (Beck, 1992). Individuals are expected to be 'risk managers' predicting, controlling, and planning for risk in relation to their bodies and selves (Shilling, 2003).

In early childhood, there is often an expectation that educators and families/carers will support or inculcate children in such endeavours (Bialostok and Kamberelis, 2010). This is underpinned by a notion of children as pre-rational as opposed to 'fully developed' deliberative adults (Burman, 1994). At the same time, Bialostok and Kamberelis (2010: 300) argue that in this 'insecure' period of 'new' capitalism, risk taking is valorised as people are encouraged to develop an 'enterprising spirit', 'embrace risk', and be open to change in order to 'bring adaptability and flexibility to jobs that are constantly changing'. The 'good educator' then is one who insulates children from potential harm, through an ambiguous combination of 'surplus safety' (Wyver et al., 2010) and 'good', managed risk taking (Bialostok and Kamberelis, 2010).

Negotiating research relationships needs to be seen within this backdrop of anxiety about safety and is our starting point for accounting for the following excerpt from Rachel's fieldnotes:

> Cecilia was standing on a raised wooden platform about two feet off the ground. She had wrapped a long rope around her waist, finishing it off with a knot. She hung from the taut rope dangling from the platform, calling 'Help! Help!' to a group of children in front of her. Sean responded immediately: 'I can help you!'
>
> At that moment, Cecilia saw me walking by with obvious interest (and some concern) and said to the children around her: 'Let's do it again.' She repeated the performance, this time dropping her head to the side and closing her eyes (recognisable symbols of death in the setting) as she hung suspended over the drop. The gathered children began clambering for her attention: 'I can save you!' and 'I can help!'
>
> When the rescue was complete, Kakali asserted: 'Ok, it's my turn.' The other children jumped up on to the platform behind her – presumably all wanting a turn. Kakali died quickly on the rope, saved herself, and jumped

down from the platform. The action continued as other children stepped into the role; although, no one else demanded the same rescue response from others as Cecilia.

Charlene was excited to take her turn, having waited impatiently for the other children to finish. 'I need to wrap myself up,' she explained, working with Kakali to tie the rope at about chest height around her body with a firm knot. From across the space, an educator called out: 'Charlene, Charlene! Off your neck!' Charlene hastily removed the rope from her body. But she watched until the educator looked away, quickly tying the rope back around her chest and laughing loudly.

Charlene hung down, swaying slowly over the small drop with her arms and upper body hanging out of the rope. Seeming unsatisfied with the position, she moved her arms out of the rope bending them to get a firm grasp in order to keep the rope away from her neck. She tipped her head to the side and issuing a strangled sound: 'Ehhhhhhh!'

Although Cecilia's original use of the rope had put me in mind of a 'damsel in distress' narrative, by the time the rope had come to Charlene it seemed to me the narrative had moved to a public hanging at a gallows pole. I was disturbed by the image – reminiscent of a mixture of bloodthirsty crowds and the heroic efforts of a few comrades at the public display of death sentence. When watching such dramatised scenes in movies I often have to close my eyes or turn away.

I was aware in this moment that at least one educator had a concern about safety. While I was disturbed by the *image* of such a horrific death, given what I had seen so far I didn't share the educator's safety concern. The drop down was small. The landing was a soft surface. The rope was arranged into a circle akin to a noose but the knot held firmly in place rather than slipped. And, because of the narrative, the children's use of the rope was purposeful. As a result, I said nothing but continued filming from a spot on the ground about 10 feet away, watching and speaking with children who approached me.

All of a sudden, Charlene jumped down from the platform. With her arms positioned outside of the loop, the rope slipped up her body catching momentarily just before her feet touched the ground. As she landed, she bumped her back on the platform.

I jumped up in alarm and ran over with the nearby children. (After the initial intervention, no educator had stepped in or come close.) Charlene was not hurt, but she seemed shocked. After being comforted and checked by myself and the group of children, she got back up and set out to the nearby drawing table. It took me longer to calm myself down, and I still can't watch the video without gasping when Charlene jumps. Kakali was also disturbed. She approached me when Charlene had left asking repeatedly: 'Was it my fault?'

(Rachel Rosen, Taboo play)

While this play was transgressive in a number of ways, not least because of the presence of themes of death which contradict dominant ideas about childhood innocence and instrumental attachments of play to rationalised learning, we will focus here on risk and harm. In this *ethically contentious moment*, Rachel had remained in the vicinity of the activity and had neither verbally supported nor censured the children. Such 'non-intervention' (aside from when children are in immediate danger) is explicitly justified in research as an attempt to assume non-authoritative positions with children (Galbraith, 2007; Keddie, 2001), but is also implicit in accounts that advocate – to varying degrees – avoidance of 'spoiling' the field. However, the example of Charlene suggests that such prescriptions are inadequate in the messy arena of 'real-life' research where such considerations are punctuated by the researcher's ethical obligations, habitus, and conceptions of dangers and childhood. The critical moment raises questions such as: Who is responsible for assuring safety and averting harm? Is there an expectation that any adult would assume such a role, regardless of their position as researcher or educator, or is such responsibility more complex and nuanced?

Given that Rachel had initially decided she would only impose setting rules in the case of physical danger, this situation required her to evaluate the potential for harm. Although she felt concern for the children when she had first approached the 'gallows pole', she had quickly ascertained that the rope was tied into a large loop with a secure (rather than slip) knot and that the children were carefully manipulating their bodies in keeping with their narrative. Further, she was generally concerned to avoid letting dominant conceptions of children's need for protection, in contrast to adult invulnerability, frame her responses to children. Christensen (2000: 40) argues that vulnerability has virtually become a 'master identity' for children, with their capabilities for dealing with risk minimised.

Although Charlene was generally unharmed in this situation – at worst enduring a sore back and a bit of a scare – we suggest that a sole focus on children's competence and capability may have the opposite effect intended, where researchers may neglect responsibility for their presence in risky situations. In effect, this may *invert* rather than challenge dichotomous views of childhood and adulthood. As adults are typically the ones who verbally pronounce the existence of risk in early childhood settings, the presence of an adult who does not set such limits is significant. In this context, such actions could imply that a situation is *safe*, in effect, condoning or even encouraging participation. As Kjorholt (2005: 168) points out, discourses of children's competence, many of which are rooted in notions of Western individualism, 'imply leaving the responsibility to children for their own social life'. Overemphasising children's 'autonomous' ability to 'manage risk' serves to distance people rather than developing the interconnections and desire for answerability that we have been arguing for throughout this book. It is these individualistic assumptions that lead Kjorholt (2005: 168) to question whether an emphasis on children's competence 'represents adults' abdication from a caring relationship with children'. In the context of research relationships, we are left wondering how a distancing from notions of vulnerability squares with a researcher's ethical responsibility to child-participants in terms of 'benefice' and 'non-maleficence'.

While we would support critiques of the conflation of vulnerability and childhood, it would be both irresponsible and inaccurate not to acknowledge young children's *particular* vulnerability, not least because they have generally had fewer experiences than adults (Lahman, 2008). Here we would add that vulnerability is not only physical, but also *emotional*. This can be said for Charlene most obviously, in regard to the fear that came with the fall, but we would argue that such emotional risk is also present for others involved when someone is hurt. For example, Kakali blamed herself for the incident and Rachel continues to agonise over the situation, including how her actions will be construed within the context of academic study and work in higher education and, more importantly, whether – ethically – she should have done something different given that more extreme consequences would have had severe impacts on the children, setting, and broader field of research with children.

Given these points, we argue that adult–child relationships can be viewed as constituted by mutual vulnerability and competence. This implies that adult-researchers, in seeking to be answerable, have responsibility to others – adults and children – which, we suggest, includes bringing their potentially 'outside' knowledge of risk to negotiations. However, it is equally imperative that research relationships are not only shaped by constructions of powerless and vulnerable child-participants. As Wyver et al. (2010) note more generally, an emphasis on 'surplus safety' can 'stifle' relationships as the focus of adult–child interactions becomes solely about curtailing children's risky play.

In this last example, an intervention from Rachel to decrease the 'danger' may have had the effect not of ending such play but of pushing it into the hidden corners of the setting, a notable occurrence with transgressive activities in early childhood settings (Corsaro, 1985; Holland, 2003). In effect, this distances children's efforts to experience and understand phenomena from more general community spaces where adults and children have the *potential* to co-construct meanings about powerful ideas and images together. Edmiston (2008) makes this argument powerfully in his work on adult–child play about liminal and disturbing topics; he suggests that by engaging in 'radical dialogue' as co-players, adults can support children to form compassionate and ethical identities. While we are generally persuaded by his argument, we would add that children have the potential to do this for and with each other. Further, such dialogue does not have unidirectional impacts but also has the potential to develop adults' ethical identities.

What we are suggesting, therefore, is that prescriptions for researchers to intervene only when child-participants are in immediate physical danger, for example, are *deceptively* clear cut. Instead, in the 'once-occurrent' moment of being there is always a responsibility to others that cannot be abdicated or determined in advance, but this involves a complex negotiation of ethical principles and the 'emotional-volitional' tone of the moment (Bakhtin, 1990).

An added layer of complexity in such *ethically contentious moments* is the web of relationships in which the researcher finds her/himself a part of. A researcher is not only responsible to the child-participant, but to multiple others in the setting and potentially even beyond. In this case, Rachel was not just ethically answerable to Charlene, but to the educators and other children involved, both as individuals and to the marginalised collectives to which they claim membership and/or are positioned within. It is here that the pressures on educators to keep children safe are particularly salient. In the intense regulatory context of early childhood settings, embedded within policy and enforced through inspection bodies such as OfSTED in England, many educators become anxious that allowing 'risky play' will lead to legal action including compensatory claims (Wyver et al., 2010) or at very least unsatisfactory reviews by inspectors. Educators may worry that low inspection ratings will lead to decreasing numbers of children being registered in the setting, given the emphasis on parental choice in the marketised field of early childhood (e.g. Kershaw, 2004; Vincent and Ball, 2005). Further, educators may be overly worried that if a child is injured during 'risky' play that they have allowed, they may be subject to disciplinary measures or worse (for example, job loss). Such concerns are further exacerbated by sensationalised media coverage of accidents in early years and other institutional settings.

We are suggesting then that regardless of whether the educator's fears of danger were accurate in this moment, the context of surplus safety created a situation where 'order and control' have become 'pervasive concerns' (Phelan, 1997: 76). In this context, we suggest that Rachel's continued presence served as an implicit challenge to the educator's attempts to stop Charlene from putting the rope around her body. For the children, Rachel's presence was likely interpreted as condoning their 'hangings': they continued with the enactments in Rachel's presence once the educator had left. Because the educator did not return to the play, despite the continuing activity that gave rise to her initial concern, Rachel's actions, we argue, were interpreted by the educator as a dismissal.

On the one hand, Rachel's actions can be seen as a challenge to the '*over-civilising*' of children and 'obsession' (Penn, 2011b: 99) with health and safety in UK early childhood settings. We question, however, the 'effectiveness' of Rachel's challenge. First, by not articulating her critiques, it effectively became Rachel's positional power and status, as a white, middle-class lecturer and researcher in relation to a working-class, woman of colour, which 'spoke'. While educators in the setting would often stop children from engaging in activities they found unsafe, they never attempted to stop Rachel and, in fact, rarely intervened with the children when Rachel was present. This may have resulted from a high degree of trust in Rachel due to her experience as an educator and lecturer, but it also may have reflected a sense of deference to her higher status positions in the early years' field.

While Rachel's implicit intervention may have challenged or 'modelled' (Dennis, 2009) ways of interacting with children that were not based on assumptions of superior adult knowledge and invulnerability, ostensibly an attempt to challenge generational inequities, we would argue it ultimately drew its 'effectiveness' from class and 'race' inequities. Second, and contradictorily, embedded within Rachel's implicit challenge was a message to the children: '*Although we have been building a relationship, don't count on me to speak up when an educator intervenes.*' As such, the mode of intervention lacked in strength of persuasion or transformative dialogue and did not actually shift inequitable relations between adults and children in the longer term. Without an explicit interaction with the educator, Rachel maintained a tacit bond with another adult; Griffin (1991: 114) refers to such collusion as 'the researcher as nodding dog'.

Reflecting on the event, Rachel felt that ultimately the 'gallows pole' events were not overly risky and that the educator's concerns were born within a context of surplus safety and '*over*civilising'. However, Rachel realised that she prioritised her 'safe' position as a researcher with virtually unlimited access to the setting over and above her concerns with social justice and transforming inequitable relationships. Researchers have a very practical need to preserve relationships with educators, as gatekeepers, in situations in which access to settings does not come easily. Rachel could have made an 'interpersonal intervention' (Dennis, 2009) by describing, for example, how the rope had become a resource whose affordances sparked an important exploration of death, and how the children had managed to competently coordinate their hanging prior to this moment. However, this type of intervention may have caused negative repercussions for the researcher–educator relationship and affected her privileges as a 'good researcher'. While both the children and educators opened themselves up to a number of potential risks, disciplining for disobeying an educator's safety demands or 'neglecting' responsibility for ensuring (surplus) safety, Rachel risked little in this moment.

Confronting inequalities in early childhood research

Researchers encounter acts of injustice throughout the course of a research project; in fact, having to deal with particularly contentious acts of injustice may be a *result* of the relationships formed between the researcher and participants, as Connolly (2008) argues based on his study about young children's racism. He argues that his presence in children's peer culture groups, as a white man *not* in a position of institutional authority, in part created a context for extremely violent, sexist, and racist comments: the children may have been attempting to build alliances with him based on raced and gendered assumptions about his perspectives. Regardless of the reasons children made the comments, Connolly (2008) felt that, politically and ethically, it was important to indicate that he did not agree, which he did by questioning the provenance of the beliefs. While this was a thoughtful response in a difficult situation, it runs the risk of suggesting that there is a reasonably straightforward, consistent, and readily available response possible in challenging moments.

A *contentious ethical moment* from Deb's research demonstrates these complexities. This observation, of two boys and a student educator, took place at lunchtime where adults and children sat together in the common space of a church hall:

'Civilising' children, confronting inequalities 109

Jeremy kissed Zach and poked him, calling him 'cheeky monkey' – more because he liked the phrase it seemed (at least at first). Zach pretended not to like it. Then, both of them pushed their fingers through their garlic bread pretending it was a wedding ring and that they were getting married – giggling loudly and kissing each other.

The student educator, Jan, who was supervising the table seemed very uncomfortable with the way this was developing. It seemed as if she was worried by the playful sexuality; the noise; and the lack of getting on and eating.

It is interesting because this was the only table where children were not allowed to have their garlic bread until they had eaten some pasta – no other table seemed to have this 'rule'.

After a while, the garlic bread wedding ring broke and for Zach, it became a mouth that opened and shut and could be used to torment Jeremy (in a playful way). Jan was clearly bothered by the use of food in this way, repeatedly telling them to stop and eat.

Zach and Jeremy returned to the 'getting married' theme, hugging each other at the table, while laughing – facing Jan directly (is it a challenge?). She told them that boys cannot get married and that they should be eating their lunch. I gently asked, 'Can't they?', and there seemed a momentary pause – I tried to say it quietly so other educators did not hear my challenge (especially as she was a student). Interestingly, this also seemed to halt the children's playfulness.

(Deb Albon, Food events: Setting two)

This brief glimpse of an 'ordinary' day at a lunch table involves a complex mixture of intersecting inequities, including heterosexism, generational stratification, and class divisions. Also present are a variety of responses, including silences and both verbal and 'playful' acts of resistance. In seeking to understand this moment and its implications for research relationships, we will begin by considering what may have accounted for the educator and children's responses and interactions.

In keeping with our previous discussion, we suggest that, in part, Jan's obvious discomfort with the situation was rooted in expectations that, as an educator, she would maintain order and calm. Because mealtimes are generally planned, initiated, and managed by educators, they are particularly susceptible to the charge of 'civilising' children, and there are few opportunities or spaces in which children can evade the 'gaze' of educators. In this case, such efforts were apparent in Jan's insistence on the seriousness of eating. Jan's status as a *student* educator exacerbated such expectations, as part of her placement within the setting involved subjecting her capabilities to the observation and evaluation of other educators. We suggest then that Jan's uneasiness in this moment circulated, in part, around concerns about being watched and found 'lacking'.

As such, Jan's disquiet may have existed regardless of the particularity of the boys' activity; however, her final comment – 'boys cannot get married' – indicates a deeper problematic. Queer sexuality, made public in the boys' physical touch in conjunction with conversations about marriage, is a particularly taboo topic in many early childhood settings owing to an 'assumed absence of gay and lesbian families' and the 'pervasiveness' of discourses and practices rooted in compulsory heterosexuality (Robinson, 2002: 416). While children's play about heterosexual weddings and family life is celebrated (at least when it does not involve sexual contact), similar activity is often deemed problematic when it involves same-sex relationships given the prevalence of homophobic views (Robinson, 2002).

There was a further complication in this moment: Jan's attempt to curtail the boys' playful engagements contradicts narratives of the 'good educator' as someone who best supports children's learning by following their interests (e.g., see discussion in Chung and Walsh (2000) about proponents of such an interpretation of 'child-centred' practice). We would argue, however, that in this case, the boys' engagement with themes of same-sex sexuality was rendered 'unnatural' in the context of the compulsory heterosexuality of early childhood settings – indicating, among other things, the way hegemonic discourses and practices belie the claims of 'child centeredness'. Jan's initial responses to the boys, which focused on *behaviour*, may have been, in part, an attempt to avoid explicitly addressing the more controversial interest in *queer sexuality* altogether. It was only when such 'sanitised' reactions did not achieve Jan's goals that she made her homophobic responses to the situation explicit.

On initial gloss, Jeremy and Zach's engagements, by the same token, can be understood as a playful exploration of sexuality. As Davies and Robinson (2010) point out, although sexuality may be a forbidden topic in early childhood settings, children do not stop trying to make sense of their own and other's sexuality. Such exploration is often pushed underground with other children's 'fragments of information' (Robinson and Davies, 2010: 250) serving to develop knowledge. In the rule-bound, non-sexualised, and *public* context of this example, however, Zach and Jeremy's play took on a joyful and exaggerated 'carnivalesque' (Bakhtin, 1984b) quality, challenging both the boundaries of the setting's (implicit) approach to sexuality and (more explicit) expectations of behaviours at mealtimes. As Grace and Tobin (1997: 160) note, such carnivalesque moments develop in relation to 'authority figures, and [are] fuelled by the knowledge that classroom norms are being transgressed'. The boys' attempts to subvert the order of the setting may have been in response to the arbitrary rule set by Jan about when the children were allowed to eat garlic bread as well as the controlled order she was trying to maintain at the table. Here the children's merriment, which accompanied their irreverent use of bread for a valued social symbol (wedding ring), can be viewed as building 'solidarity' in the face of 'disciplinary power' (MacLure, 2009: 107).

The boys may also have been playing with, even mocking, the compulsory heterosexuality reigning in the setting. Here though, we would suggest that the boys' very public performance of the wedding complicates this interpretation. The orientation of their bodies in the educator's direction suggests that this was as much a performance for Jan as it was of their own exploration. The accompanying hilarity, apparent in their increasing giggles and noise, suggest Jeremy and Zach knew their actions were perceived as threatening or challenging. It is here that Schepher-Hughes' (1992: 482) point, made in relation to the carnival in Brazil, becomes salient:

> *Carnaval* 'play' can also do the dirty work of class, gender, and sexual divisions, which by means of grotesque exaggeration are etched even more deeply into the individual and collective bodies.

We might ask then: Did Jeremy and Zach's actions challenge homophobia or just make use of homophobic ideas to challenge Jan's authority? We would like to reply affirmatively to both of these questions. The very presence of a 'gay marriage' in an early childhood context does shift ideas about childhood and (queer) sexuality by making the 'invisible visible' (Robinson, 2002), and potentially even making such acts possible by bringing them into contact with onlookers' social imaginaries. However, heading Rikowski's (1997) warning of the dangers of romanticising carnivalesque acts, we are certainly not suggesting that just because an act is transgressive it is an effective strategy for social transformation. It may offer a momentary glimpse of something different, but the temporality of the carnivalesque means that there is always a return to the hegemonic 'order'. Further, the hilarity with which this marriage was performed suggests that it was the 'abnormalness' of gay sexuality and love in early childhood that the boys were capitalising on in their challenge to the educator's institutional and generational authority. In effect, this served to reinforce the homophobic belief that queer sexuality is 'deviant' in early childhood settings.

MacLure (2009) suggests it is possible to hold on to a view of the positive aspects of humour at the same time as remaining critical of derogatory jokes. She does not, however, explore how such ambiguous moments can be navigated in the moment, focusing instead on analysing data after the fact. Yet, a central theme of this book is that merely deconstructing such moments can render a researcher immobilised, falling into what Alcoff (2009) refers to as a 'retreat' position, which is individualistic and politically untenable. It is here then that we wish to look forwards as well as backwards, considering the implications of Deb's responses for research relationships in this *ethically contentious moment* as well as what insights this offers for future research practices.

Deb's question – 'Can't they?' – was intended as a challenge to Jan's assertion that two boys cannot get married, a homophobic statement Deb felt she could not let pass as it might suggest that such beliefs or acts are tolerable – in effect, reproducing inequities. In this moment, however, Deb's comment was made *quietly*. This was an attempt to avoid having other educators in the close quarters of the communal eating room hear her intervention, which was important to Deb given Jan's precarious student status. Here, Deb was trying to balance the ethical responsibilities of her presence to each research participant as well as to her commitment to social justice. However, Deb's quiet interjection produced not only a *stutter* but a *cessation* of the intense carnivalesque moment. While it would have eventually stopped – as Grace and Tobin (1997) note such moments are ephemeral as their very appearance provokes that which destroys them, namely their regulation and rationalisation – we attribute the termination of the ribald moment *at that specific point* to a combination of factors resulting specifically from Deb's intervention. First, Deb's comment shifted the content of Zach and Jeremy's playful interactions from the transgressive to the 'normal' and 'allowable', at very least for one adult in the vicinity. As such, it no longer pressed at the boundaries of the setting's social order with the same force of protest.

Second, from a social justice perspective, Deb's comment made an important incision into the homophobia prevalent in early childhood settings (Robinson, 2002). Yet, in considering this moment we wonder if part of Deb's response was based on a misplaced heroism in trying to protect or 'save' the (child) participants (Alcoff, 2009). As Oswell (2009) argues, if political subjectivity is seen to be constituted solely by rational discussion and meaning-laden language, it becomes difficult to conceive of children, who use embodied and playful expression for example, as political actors. In this moment, Deb's comment ostensibly supported the boys playful exploration of a gay marriage; however, her intellectualised response – using an adult-associated form of discourse to make the intervention in a more recognisably political manner – may have had the effect of diminishing the boys' ways of challenging compulsory heterosexuality and rupturing the solidarity that the boys had established.

There was also an issue of how Jan interpreted Deb's question. Already feeling undermined by the boys' refusal to comply with her behavioural reproaches and perhaps nervous at being evaluated, did Jan feel that Deb's comments were a form of collusion with the boys' resistance? Although Deb's challenge was made gently, in this moment, Deb's position as a lecturer in relation to the student educator would lend anything Deb said an air of authority.

A final point is that although Deb's intention in making her comment *quietly* was to avoid subjecting Jan to more public scrutiny as a student, in looking back on the moment we wonder if there were an element for Deb of protecting her own position in the setting with access to observe and interview both children and adults in the setting. Intervening poses a risk in this regard, and by interjecting *quietly*, Deb was able to limit this risk among the educators solely to Jan. However, this left Jan's homophobic comment hanging in the public space of the church lunchroom.

We have engaged in this discussion to highlight the complex and interlocking factors involved in considering how researcher interventions, including silences, impact on research relationships. The concerns that we have raised, however, are in no way meant as arguments that social justice interventions, in research or otherwise, should not be made. The ethical questions of beneficence and maleficence, as well as political questions of equity and emancipation, are not resolved by avoidance; while Jan might have felt more comfortable if Deb had said nothing, the same cannot be said for others – both those present and more generally.

But it becomes important both ethically and politically to consider how social justice interventions can be made in ways that do not succumb to paternalism, assuming to 'know' better than participants what the political ramifications of particular practices are or how best to intervene just because of a researcher's status and intellectual attainments. It is to this discussion that we move next.

Conditions of risk and possibility: Acting with answerability

Negotiating research relationships is an uncertain endeavour. Any response a researcher makes, including silence, necessarily impacts on research relationships. Even in the most mundane and everyday of situations, relationships involve a certain amount of risk; however, we have been arguing that riskiness is exacerbated in *ethically contentious moments* that bring researcher practices in conflict with narratives of the 'good' educator and researcher, drawing out some of these implications in the specific examples just examined. From the perspective of the researcher, a risk in negotiating relationships is that access to people or settings can be compromised for the current or future research, a potential result if participants are alienated by researcher interventions. Risk is involved at the point of representation: making analytic claims, which involves intervening in participants' understandings of their own lives, necessarily opens up the researcher to critique, including that of ethnocentrism. But to evade such responsibility shifts the risk involved on to (often marginalised) participants. As we have noted, 'going with the flow' in *ethically contentious moments* – either as 'kewpie dolls' with open eyes and ears but closed mouth or 'nodding dogs' (Griffin, 1991) – is also risky in the sense that this can serve to condone and reproduce inequities.

These risky effects, we would argue, are the result of a number of factors that necessarily need to be taken into account when considering the political and ethical implications of researcher practices. First, these *ethically contentious moments* bring our ethical answerability towards others into contact and potentially conflict. How we answer one may not be how we would answer another. While Bakhtin (1993) presents answerability in a primarily dyadic fashion, in research and everyday life we have responsibilities to multiple others, both individuals and marginalised collectivities.

Adults and children experience different pressures and constraints to which they respond with various degrees of social agency. It is a result of these diverse positions and interests that researchers need to make difficult decisions, even in the most mundane of situations. In the first example discussed in this chapter, Rachel was answerable to various individual children and the educator; she was also answerable to both children and working-class educators as marginalised collectivities, including for the impact of her presence in the particular moment. In taking up the complexity of research where 'trouble' is expected, Griffin (1991) argues that researchers should consider 'talking back'. Here she emphasises making interventions against broader inequities rather than focusing on particular relationships with individual participants. However, this implies that individuals and our relationships with them can be easily separated from macro-level relations of power and inequities; as well, it implies that determination of inequality is clear cut. Dennis (2009) makes a similar assumption in her privileging of the interests, concerns, and needs of a particular group of research participants when engaging in social justice interventions: English-language learners. While we do not debate that these participants were discriminated against based on racist ideologies and the global hegemony of English, we do argue that – even with a commitment to social justice – research practice and analysis is rarely so clear cut. Inequities cut across generation, 'race', gender, sexuality, and class at both macro and micro levels.

Any researcher response is risky to a certain degree because it is embedded within power relations. Such relations mean that the *same* intervention can have *different* implications depending on when, where, and with whom it is enacted. To return to the earlier examples, would Rachel and the children have 'complied' with the educator's attempts to stop the 'hangings' had she been a higher-status member of staff (such as the head of the centre) with more power to control Rachel's access to the setting? Would Deb have intervened in the same manner if the educator had been a more established member of staff? Power relations not only affect *what* interventions researchers make but *how* such interventions are taken up. As we have noted already, even Rachel's tacit, embodied intervention (remaining quietly present despite the children's persistence in engaging in 'forbidden' activities) held sway because of the way that relations of 'race' and class were articulated in the setting.

Here we would also note our hesitance to overemphasise the deliberative decision-making involved in social justice interventions, arguing that it is the very limits of intentionality that, in part, constitute the risk in research relationships. Conceiving of researcher responses as *planned* or the result of *intentional actions* makes the mistake of construing answerability as a far more instrumentally rational process than we would suggest is possible. As Collier (1994) points out, even while accepting that reasoning is efficacious, there are limits to rationalism. For example, our acts may also be motivated by unconscious assumptions – as noted earlier in relation to physical risk, childhood, and vulnerability. We are not all-knowing actors: even with the best of intentions to act with answerability, our practices are also shaped by, for example, 'adult imaginaries' (Taylor, 2011) about children and childhood. This requires us to interrogate how conceptualisations inform our research relationships, the phenomena under study and, significantly here, our motivations for and effects of interventions.

Our acts may also be compelled by emotional concerns rather than deliberate decision-making. Deb, for example, responded in the moment to the educator's homophobic comment based primarily on emotions of concern and disquiet. We are not, however, suggesting that reasons and emotions are necessarily incompatible. While our actions are often 'emotional responses to the flow of experience', they are based on the continual ethical evaluations we make throughout the course of even the most mundane parts of our everyday lives (Sayer, 2011: 148). As Sayer (2011) further notes, emotions are generally a response to real situations and can prompt ethical reflection and reasoned action. We would caution, however, that these points do not negate the benefits of reflexivity and deliberation as these 'emotional responses' can become so practised that they are removed entirely from the actual 'once-occurrent' moment.

Further, rationalist views also minimise, or even ignore, the way unacknowledged conditions affect interventions, including the way our presence and actions are perceived by participants and how our research will be taken up by others – what Murphy and Dingwall (2007: 341) refer to as the 'indeterminacy of risk'. While we can, as Dennis (2009) points out, consider how people may respond to different types of interventions, we will certainly not be aware of *all* of the conditions that frame the way our interventions are perceived. It was not until reflecting on the 'gallows pole' example, *after the fact*, that Rachel realised that her attempts to be non-intrusive were likely interpreted as an embodied intervention given the raced and classed conditions of the social milieu. We can never predict *every* possible contingency either practically, because we are compelled to act on an ongoing basis, or ontologically and epistemologically, because of the multiple possible factors influencing the way our actions are taken up (Sayer, 2011).

Finally, rationalist explanations downplay the unintended consequences of an act. In intervening the way she did, Deb did not realise that she would halt the boys' carnivalesque engagements. Rachel did not realise that Kakali would experience guilt from Charlene's jump, which, while it was not caused by, was certainly not avoided by Rachel's tacit approval of the activity. We suggest, therefore, that accounts premised on notions of researcher intentionality will always only offer a partial insight in relation to the ethics and politics of intervention.

Research relationships are also fundamentally risky in the sense that they can challenge 'previous stabilities, convictions, or ways of being' (Skeggs, 2007: 437) for researchers, participants, and readers. It is this sense of risk, however, that is simultaneously a condition of *possibility*. Our acts in research relationships offer the possibility of gaining new insight into the research topic and oneself, forging new relationships, and even the possibility of transformation itself, a prospect we go on to explore later.

Given that there is a multitude of different ways to respond to *contentious ethical moments* – including remaining quiet; commenting (but to whom and when?); or addressing the situation in a playful or embodied manner – we will now elaborate a series of points we consider of importance when considering the ethical-political implications of our acts. First, ethical principles of beneficence, maleficence, and justice cannot merely be understood in terms of ethical obligations to *individual* participants – an interpretation rooted in Western liberal individualism (Murphy and Dingwall, 2007), but must also take into account ethical and political obligations to marginalised collectivities based on, we advocate, a social justice perspective. This requires careful consideration of intersecting inequities and answerability to *multiple* others, rather than an a priori aligning with one individual or group. In this sense then, ethics and politics are completely intertwined. Yet, while political issues of domination and exploitation generally cannot be resolved solely through ethical acts towards others, Sayer (2011) argues that it is ethics – what matters to people and why – that motivates us to care and act against such inequities.

This brings us to the question we have been circling around throughout this chapter: Which acts merely reproduce the status quo and which acts are socially transformative? This problem goes beyond the specific focus of this book and represents a major preoccupation of emancipatory social and political movements. In response, Žižek (2000) proposes that transformative acts are those that do not merely challenge, but 'redefine' the premises and 'remake' the borders of what is currently considered possible. By cutting through that which stabilises or protects, such acts clear space for the new. We offer an intervention Rachel made as a micro-level example. Matthew, one of the *primary* participants in Rachel's research, turned to the two girls involved in the play: 'You have to wait here. It's too scary for you.' Rachel, standing close by, turned to the two girls and said, 'Is it too scary for you? Why do you think he said that?' Matthew looked surprised by Rachel's intervention and acquiesced as Amal and Husna chose to accompany him in the mission to find a ferocious monster. We offer this not as a 'perfect' example by any means; however, it does contain some of the characteristics of Žižek's transformative act. First, it involved a dialogic challenge to the 'rules' of the game of hegemonic masculinity remaking possibilities for gendered participation in play. Second, Rachel opened herself up to risk by 'cutting loose' from Matthew, the 'precious object' that might have otherwise kept her 'in check' as she sought to protect the research relationships for the sake of her data (Žižek, 2000: 122). Finally, it opened up the possibility for dialogue as space was cleared for Amal and Husna to voice opinions and analysis.

The notion of dialogue leads to our next point. We suggest that answerability compels researchers to consider what analysis, intervention or challenge participants engage in during *ethically contentious moments*. This is important as a challenge to a view of an 'all-knowing' researcher intervening to save or protect powerless participants. Here we suggest that those interventions that involve people dialogically have the potential to be particularly transformative in that they can challenge patterns of inequity, including those between researcher and participant. Implied here is that the researcher and participants will be changed by the process, learning through dialogue with others. This is not to refute our earlier points about the necessity for researchers to take responsibility for their analysis and interpretation, but to recognise the fallibility of both participants' and researcher knowledge and understanding. Returning to our point about the intertwining of politics and ethics, we argue that this is not benign dialogue for dialogue's sake but a process of collaboratively considering questions of ethics, equity, and justice.

Finally, ethical and political research practices involve an ongoing process of reflective looking back–looking forward, united with our ongoing acts. *Looking back* allows us to consider some of the emotional or potentially unconscious motivations for our actions, as well as the way they were perceived and how they impacted on relationships and participants. *Looking forward* allows us to make use of these reflections to inform future research practices. Such a process is not about developing finalised solutions to ethical dilemmas but taking the risk to be a part of creating new transformative possibilities through our ethically answerable acts. It is this effort of *looking forward* that forms the basis of our next, and final, chapter, in which we consider how researchers can work in 'common cause' (Warming, 2005) with children to challenge inequitable power relations.

8
BUILDING COMMON CAUSE WITH CHILDREN

Reciprocity in the research process

In research, there has been a shift towards developing more reciprocal relationships between participants and researchers, in part gaining its impetus from researchers who are intent on challenging the unequal power relationship between themselves and those with whom they research. While this is not without its challenges, as we will demonstrate, these challenges are intensified in childhood research owing to inequities inherent in the generational and hierarchical ordering of adults in comparison to children (Mayall, 2008). An exploration of how adults can build common cause with children in research is therefore the central theme of this final chapter. Our use of the phrase 'common cause' stems from Warming's (2005: 61) work in which she uses the term to indicate her dedication to challenging ideas about children as unreliable, incomplete, and incompetent in comparison to adults, as well as her commitment to researching *with* children and *listening to them* as reliable commentators on their own lives.

Fundamental to the idea of building common cause with children, we suggest, is the idea that researchers embark on their research from the principle that children are accorded the *same* ethical considerations as adults, albeit noting that ethics are not transparent and given in either case, and that researchers start from a position of children's presumed competency. Moving forward to data generation in situ, it is necessary to respond in a far more nuanced way to the particularities of individual children and contexts (Christensen and Prout, 2002). As has been the case throughout this book, we have found the ideas of Bakhtin (1990; 1993) very helpful in this respect.

We will be examining the shift towards involving children more directly as participants in research, which has developed as a response to understandings of children as competent commentators on their own lives and has found expression in rights-based frameworks such as the United Nations Convention on the Rights of the Child (UNCRC). However, we are cautious of the methodological turn towards 'participatory methods' in the name of 'empowering children': Is it possible to 'give' power to another as this implies? What do such methods say about how children are conceptualised in relation to adults? And what do they enable or constrain in relation to developing research relationships with children?

We will be putting forward the idea that *being with* children rather than emphasising *tasks to do with them* supports a more reciprocal approach to research. In addition, we will consider how researchers might build common cause with children and other marginalised collectivities *beyond* their face-to-face interactions in the course of data generation. This prompts further questions: How can we build common cause with children in our work with students in higher education, with educators, and in our interactions with the wider research community? How might writing, and our reflections on it, help build common cause? In this sense, this chapter builds on the idea put forward in Chapter 7, that is important to *look back* on our research practices as well as *look forward* in order to inform our future research practices.

What do we mean by 'reciprocity' in research?

To summarise what is an extensive literature on the topic, the problematic of reciprocity in research is, we suggest, amplified for those engaged in *early childhood* research, as children aged 0–5 years are often viewed as especially vulnerable and dependent in comparison to older children and adults (Graue and Walsh, 1995). Moreover, as Johansson (2012) has noted, while generations are *interdependent* – as, at the most basic level, every society needs children for its continued survival – children (especially very young children) depend on adults to a great extent. Further, few adults are dependent on very young children to meet their basic survival needs, particularly in the 'First World/North' given the way generational relations are conceptualised and organised.

Assumptions about differentials in competency also skew adult–child relations. 'Early childhood' is a period that has been subjected to prolonged examination by those – notably Piaget – who have suggested that children move through qualitatively different stages, which has been criticised for confining children to a position of incompleteness (James et al., 1998) and for its implicit suggestion that adulthood is a 'fixed' or completed position (Lee, 2001). A further consequence of this way of conceptualising childhood is that young children's thinking is positioned as *less* able and *less* stable than that of adults prompting some to question the trustworthiness of data elicited from children (a point raised and critiqued by Dockett and Perry, 2007). And the corollary of such a positioning in research is reliance solely on *adult* interpretations of children's lives, denying the competency of children to understand the subject or the process of research (Robinson and Kellett, 2004).

We are not arguing that stability, rationality, and independence are prerequisites for reciprocity in research by any means, as this would imply that reciprocity is only possible with *certain* participants: those who conform to an Enlightenment notion of self that we are not certain is ever actually desirable or even possible to attain. However, if one's starting point for research with children is one based on a deficit model of childhood and, by extension, the flesh and blood children who participate in research, it is difficult to see how researchers can work in common cause with them. Thus, the principles on which one embarks when undertaking research are of vital consideration.

To elaborate, Christensen and Prout (2002: 478) usefully put forward a position in which ethical considerations start from a position of 'ethical symmetry' between all participants in research be they child or adult, which, we suggest, is worth exploring in more depth at this point. They argue that the starting point for research is one accordant with embarking from the principle that children are afforded the *same ethical considerations* as adults in research and that any differences in research with children, in comparison to adults, should emerge *from the situation in which this difference arises*. Further to this, children's 'difference', such as that based on notions of age-based competency, should not be *assumed* a priori thus enabling the researcher to respond as seems fit to individuals and groups of children. With these points in mind, Christensen and Prout (2002) make a distinction between 'research strategy' and 'research tactics'. The former relates to the underpinning principles behind the research – such as the 'equal moral worth' of participants (Malewski, 2005: 221) – and the latter relates to the more practical work of carrying out research in specific situations with particular people, which requires constant reflexivity. In writing this book, we too have put forward a number of 'principles' in relation to research beyond those noted by Christensen and Prout (2002); such as the need for embodied reflexivity (Chapters 3 and 4); the fallibility but necessity of interpretation and knowledge production (Chapter 6); and the centrality of political-ethical considerations in relation to both individuals and marginalised collectivities (Chapter 7 especially) – to name but a few.

Although not framed as such, we see a linkage between the idea of 'ethical symmetry' and Bakhtinian (1993) ideas of ethics that we have been exploring throughout this book. Thus, while ethical guidelines and codes certainly have their place, the universality they represent lacks the 'emotional-volitional tone' of 'once-occurrent' events characteristic of Bakhtinian (1993: 36) thinking. Bakhtin gives further sense of how the universal and particularistic come together by making reference to the idea of an object. We can all agree that something is a particular object such as a 'cup', but this object can be viewed from different places and positions and so 'its identicalness becomes overlaid with individualised and concrete features' (Bakhtin, 1993: 63). In outlining this viewpoint, there is a strong sense in Bakhtin's work that we need to try to study the object in some detail and that this takes time, thought, and care: indeed, indifference is a stranger to such a process. While we would not wish to describe children as 'objects', we think this is an important position in relation to building common cause with children. We need to hold principles about the position of children as a social group (Christensen and Prout, 2002) and to *care about them* as a social group. However, we also need to be able to respond to *real* children as individuals in *real* and *ongoing* situations, rather than to a non-existent hypothetical child who stands for 'all children'. This, we suggest, is an important point in relation to the standpoint of the researcher and one that is indispensable to developing reciprocity.

Beginning research from the point that children are social actors and participants in research accorded the same ethical considerations as adults marks a significant conceptual shift from viewing children as vulnerable, dependent, and incompetent – *only and in all circumstances* – to one in which their agency and competencies are acknowledged. Crucially, children and their views are not synonymised and subsumed within those of the adults in their families or the particular settings they attend (Christensen and Prout, 2002; Robinson and Kellett, 2004), albeit that these adults do offer important insights into children's lives (Clark and Moss, 2001) and that the lives of children are intertwined with the adults with whom they spend their time. This recognition of the child as 'participant' is formalised in the UNCRC and this new paradigm for thinking about children and research has demanded a process of 'de- and reconstruction' as 'it implies that we have to change our basic understanding' of children and childhood (Eide and Winger, 2005: 72). In research terms, this has prompted a growth in research aimed at 'listening' to children, which has at its starting point the idea of the child as competent commentator on matters that affect or are of interest to him/her. However, in seeing children as social actors, researching with children becomes more complex. As Christensen and Prout (2002: 482) have suggested: 'This does not merely *add* to the complexity of the field, but rather *multiplies* it.'

One such complication relates to the way reciprocity is rarely negotiated in a purely dyadic relationship. In this book, we have taken up this theme substantially to show how research with children is enmeshed within a web of relationships that includes – but is not limited to – other children, families/carers, and educators. In our research, for instance, we have demonstrated how educators were part of the contextual framing of our interactions with children and this involved complex negotiations, such as those discussed in Chapter 6, relating to whether and how to share observations with educators and those discussed in Chapter 7, in relation to challenging participants' homophobia. The marginal position of many early childhood educators, primarily working-class women, who are devalued in relation to other parts of the education sector is a salutary reminder that generation is not the only social category of inequality, and we have been at pains throughout this book to engage in critical reflection about practices in early childhood in a neoliberal context *without* recourse to pathologising individual educators. As a result, we argue that attention to developing reciprocity can never be limited to attempts to address power relations between adults and children, but must consider the way intersections of inequity inform power relations (Bilge, 2010).

A further dilemma, emblematic of the complexity of reciprocity, arises from the need to attend to individual differences and preferences among children in the context of research, rather than from an a priori assumption about children as a social group (Christensen and Prout, 2002). As with adults in research, we do not propose there is a universal voice that 'speaks' for all children, for all time, and recognise the plurality of children's experiences as well as the individual ways in which they experience the world (Greene and Hill, 2005). With this in mind, Warming (2005: 62) has indicated that different children will want and need different levels of information about a research project and, as a result, 'the most ethical practice might turn out to be unethical'.

Following Warming (2005), in both of our research projects we informed children about the research we were doing when they were gathered together as a *group*, but we attended to children's questions about our research *as and when they asked* with a view to responding on a more individual basis to children's needs and interests. Some children were fascinated by particular aspects of our studies and others were not, and this mirrored our experiences with educators and families/carers. It would be arrogance to assume that *all* participants have *equal* personal interest or investment in the research when compared to the researcher (Gordon, 2003). In her master's research, for example, Deb found that one child – Ian – became fascinated with the writing-up process to the extent of asking about how feedback from her supervisor was given and how she would deal with a word count that was too large. Deb's comment that her interest in the topic would never 'finish' on completion of her dissertation prompted discussion about whether writing closes off one's interest in a topic (Albon, 2005).

While we are putting forth the proposition here that all participants should be accorded the same ethical *consideration*, equitable treatment of research participants and the formation of 'quality' relationships cannot be based on assumptions that all participants need be accorded, in situ, the *same* amount of time, treatment and information (as we discussed in Chapter 5). We would add the caveat here, that in opening these possibilities for different responses to different participants, it is equally important that researchers concern themselves with considerations about which children approach them for further information and which do not. Here, relations of inequity become important: children's class, 'race', and language in relation to a researcher can affect their expectation of whether their questions will be treated with careful consideration. Rachel noted, for example, that it was generally the children who were more verbally articulate in English who approach her with questions about her status and activities in the setting. As a result, Rachel made efforts to position herself in close spatial proximity to children with different communication competencies, often engaging in similar activities as a way to open herself up to questions and, more broadly, the sensing practices of the diversity of children.

These dilemmas, which complicate reciprocity, are indicative of a thread that has run through this book: that there is a difference between *responsibility* and Bakhtinian (1990; 1993) notions of *answerability*. While researchers have a responsibility to adhere to agreed protocols of confidentiality and to inform participants of their research activities, resorting to a set of a priori and uniform principles alone is tantamount to relying on an 'alibi' and does not attend to difference. As we have argued throughout this book, in order to be *answerable*, researchers need to make decisions, however fallible, on the basis of the unique people and situations within which they are inextricably connected. And this can be likened to Christensen and Prout's (2002) 'tactics' in research, which work in *tandem* with universal principles or 'strategy'.

Participatory methods in early childhood research

The shift in the status of children, from 'objects' to 'social actors' and 'participants' in research (Woodhead and Faulkner, 2008), has prompted a trend towards developing a plethora of 'creative' methods (Veale, 2005) aimed at facilitating their greater participation in research (O'Kane, 2008). As Gallacher and Gallagher (2008: 501) observe, '"participation" has become both an *aim* and a *tool* in an ethical quest towards "empowering" children' as participatory methods are sometimes hailed as fostering a more *equal relationship* between adult-researchers and child-participants (Barker and Weller, 2003).

In part, the move away from the more 'traditional' methods of semi-structured interviewing and questionnaires reflects a recognition that adopting such approaches, especially with very young children, may reinforce what they cannot do rather than what they *can* do. Thus, for researchers such as Alderson (2004), reciprocity involves anticipating ways that will support children to participate in research in positive ways and will not relegate children, as a social group, to one deemed 'incompetent'. Our focus in examining participatory methods in this section, however, is not to interrogate the different tools that might be adopted (such as Clark and Moss, 2001; Hyder, 2002; O'Kane, 2008; Veale, 2005), but to explore their implications for research relationships between adult-researchers and child-participants.

Deb's experience of devising a participatory tool to use in research with children raises a number of significant issues in this regard. Encouraged as she was by her reading of participatory methods, Deb cut out the front of children's drinks' cartons and laminated these in order to make a game or 'visual prompt' (Albon, 2009: 144), which she thought would be an engaging way for children to talk about their snack times and about food/drink more generally. She wondered too whether she might generate data about children's knowledge of commercial products, an avenue in the research that she soon ignored as other areas became more prominent. She laid the labels on a table in the nursery inviting children nearby to look and talk about the laminated pictures using open-ended questions to prompt discussion. Her fieldnotes reflect her experience of employing such a tool:

> I spent a long time laminating the labels last night, excited at the possibilities of the activity I had planned. The educators seemed interested as it was the first occasion when I bought in an actual activity for the children to do.
>
> *Some* children were interested in this activity, but perceived it very differently to what I had envisioned. For them, the activity was about guessing who drank what drink or they seemed confused at the open-endedness of

the activity. Whilst it generated some useful data around friendships and identity in relation to food, I was left a bit despondent.

I think the children viewed the activity with suspicion – as yet another activity employed by an adult in the nursery and one that perhaps could be 'read' as done 'right' or 'wrong'. I tried to position the activity as part of the usual space in the nursery, and had been encouraged by the educators to use the writing table. I was reluctant to use this as I suspected it may have been off-putting for those children whose preference was to avoid activities overtly linked with literacy development.

On reflection, my initial research strategy of spending time with the children at play – sometimes with a food related theme – and during food events has generated far more interesting data. Moreover, I feel more comfortable that the children see that I am *genuinely interested in them*. Consequently, they invite me to join *them*.

(Deb Albon, Food events: Setting one)

While participatory methods aimed at 'listening' are often framed within a laudable commitment to children's participation in research as competent social actors (O'Kane, 2008), we suggest there is a problematic underpinning that is less articulated. First, in suggesting that children need 'special' techniques, *because they are children*, we are in danger of reinforcing the generational inequities that we are hoping to address. Second, in focusing on making methods 'fun', as Deb hoped to do, the implication is that there is something essential about the 'child' that requires a fun-loving, playful strategy that adults do not need. While we would argue that most adults would also prefer to have an enjoyable experience of research, we are reluctant to bind enjoyment to particular research tools, particularly those which are based on reductive links between children's dispositions, physically active engagements, and pleasure. Third, there is an assumption that in order to be 'empowered' to be agentic, children require the presence of *adults* (Gallacher and Gallagher, 2008). In contrast to Christensen and Prout's (2002) notion of 'ethical symmetry', we can see that children are considered a priori to require something *different* from adults.

In her excitement at planning such a participatory activity, Deb had thought little about how *any* adult-designed and led activity might be perceived by children in the context of a school-based nursery class. We suggest that in devising activities, however useful, researchers should always be mindful of the context in which they are presented. The 'writing table', although not the space Deb would have chosen within the room, is laden with ideas about 'work' and literacy and needs to be seen within a wider, national context that is currently putting a premium on raising the levels of boys' literacy in particular. Could the labels (with their inevitable 'environmental print'), situated on what was usually a 'writing table', have been perceived as yet another literacy task or 'work'? Several studies (e.g. Wing, 1995) have demonstrated that children make distinctions between activities associated with 'work' and those of 'play' and while we would want to challenge a bifurcation of activities as either being 'work' or 'play', we recognise that this as a dominant narrative in early childhood practice in the 'First World/North' (Grieshaber and McArdle, 2010). We suspect the activity was seen as akin to 'work' and that as Deb had not employed such a tool in her research to that point, it was viewed with suspicion as it conflicted with her usual presentation of self in the setting, one in which she adopted more reactive ways of being with the children. Some children with whom she had previously enjoyed many interactions did not come near the activity.

Furthermore, in replicating what seemed analogous to an adult-led classroom activity, Deb seemed to lose sight of the power dynamic that is associated with the educator–child relationship (cf. Waller and Bitou, 2011). Thus, what Gallacher and Gallagher (2008: 505–506) have described as the 'slippage between pedagogy and research' may well have taken advantage of 'children's "schooled docility" towards such activity' (see also Barker and Weller, 2003). In setting up a 'participatory' activity, there is, by implication, a prior and adult-centric sense of what 'participation' looks like, which is less than empowering (Gallacher and Gallagher, 2008).

A further criticism is that many participatory methods still employ *language* as the central driver of the data generation. For example, in research in which children are asked to draw pictures as a research strategy, it is often the *language* the child employs that accompanies the drawing that provides some window into the 'child's world' (Barker and Weller, 2003). In Deb's exemplar, she had thought that a visual strategy would be especially useful for children whose first language was not English, but she is now critical that she had thought this would somehow be a more 'participative' method when compared to gathering data from the real event of snack time – in other words, at a time when drinks were *really* being imbibed. She has since noted: 'It is almost as if, in my zeal to develop an exciting research strategy, I forgot my years of work as an educator, attempting to embed language in real and meaningful activities *with* children rather than within "gimmicky" tasks.' However, a valuable lesson was learnt from the activity. One of the children – Sarbjeet – linked the laminated drinks' labels to those who drank them, then picked some of the labels up, saying quietly 'my friends'. She cuddled them close to her chest, as if cuddling her friends (see Albon, 2009). Interpreting this now, some years after the event, Sarbjeet's actions spoke far more strongly than words could ever do; relationships, as we have argued at various points in this book (notably Chapter 3), are as much about *bodily connections* as they are about language.

While the use of participatory tools in the exemplar under discussion did not facilitate greater participation on the part of the children, or indeed result in 'better' quality data, we are keen that this should not be read as a dismissal of participatory methods per se but more as a 'cautionary tale'. The importance of the earlier mentioned critiques notwithstanding, the crucial point we want to stress here is that an *overemphasis* on the importance of developing innovative and 'participatory' tools displaces focus and attention from the fundamental importance of relationships. In her excitement at developing and engaging with a novel research method,

Deb may have momentarily lost sight of the centrality of relationships to the research process and instead focused her energy on more technical tasks, such as choosing and laminating labels to prepare the activity. Yet, we concur with Waller and Bitou (2011: 12) who have pointed out: 'The key message from the literature is that it is the research design and *relationships* that confer real participation and engagement' (emphasis added).

Towards methods in common cause with children: *Being with* children

To this point, we have argued that researchers should be mindful of foregrounding the inventiveness of their methods (as 'tasks') over the centrality of relationships developed with children, but researchers do – of course – need to generate data for their research projects. Yet, a focus on constantly 'doing' activities can sometimes overshadow the value of a *less driven* and *more flexible* strategy of 'hanging out' with children (Lahman, 2008: 296). We now want to propose that a way forward in research with children is one that acknowledges *being with* children through a process of 'sympathetic co-experiencing' (Bakhtin, 1990).

We have both found that 'hanging out' with children – or as we will describe it: *being with* children (following Suissa, 2006) in early childhood settings – generated detailed data and, crucially, seemed to offer greater possibility for being answerable to child-participants when compared to pre-planned, participatory strategies. This is not a comment about whether or not to use participatory strategies – to reiterate: we are not condemning such research tools to the dustbin – but the proposition of a particular *attitude* towards any of the activities we undertake in research. Furthermore, what we are putting forward here does not have its basis in essentialist notions of children's 'special' natures: while the focus for our discussion here is on *being with* children, we would also want to extend the position we are taking to educators or indeed other adult participants in research.

By '*being with*' children (or indeed adults), we mean taking the opportunity to respond to spontaneously occurring talk and potentially participating in the commonplace events in settings, a process of more informal relationship building (cf. Edmond, 2005; France, Bendelow, and Williams, 2000). As play is a dominant activity in early childhood settings in countries in the 'First World/North', *being with* children inevitably involved our playing with them. Edmiston (2005) – drawing on Bakhtinian theorising – contends that through play, children and adults can participate in research *together*, which is a position that can be contrasted with viewing children's play as something to be observed at a distance. In both our respective doctoral research projects, we aimed at 'sharing authority' (Edmiston, 2005, 2008) – as part of the 'least-educator' positioning we proposed in Chapter 3 – with the children in play, and in so doing we were able to raise and explore a range of issues that were important to us (as adult-researchers) and children. As Roberts (2008: 273) asserts: 'The time that they *(i.e. children)* devote to our research agendas is a gift, and one, which we should be prepared to reciprocate.' And this sense of reciprocity is reflected in Deb's (2010: 85–86) thesis:

> Sometimes I would be scribbling notes down frenetically as we pretended to make meals together, for instance, reflecting my own concerns as a researcher. At other times, I would be engaged in other kinds of play such as making rockets or playing with small cars, which reflected other aspects of the children's persistent concerns and interests and enabled me to further develop my relationships with individuals.

As well as 'sharing authority' with children, *being with* children also afforded opportunities to gain a sense of events from different children's perspectives. Bakhtin (1990) usefully outlines a position of 'sympathetic co-experiencing', which we suggest is helpful in conceptualising the value of *being with* children in terms of generating data in research. This should not be confused with pure empathy – as we have noted in earlier chapters, mere *coincidence* with another person or group of people would be to lose one's unique 'take' on an event and would relegate the researcher to a position of passivity (Bakhtin, 1990). Further, it is premised on a colonialist assumption that it is possible to 'know' another with certainty, an idea that we have critiqued throughout this book. While the term 'sympathy' can have similarly paternalistic connotations, Bakhtin's use of 'sympathetic co-experiencing' is quite distinct, with its emphasis on *uniqueness* and *mutual* transformation.

We have provided a number of exemplars in this book where we 'sympathetically co-experienced' with children such as: when Rachel made a stab at 'toilet humour' while playing with a group of children (in Chapter 3); when Deb played 'rockets' alongside Bhupinder (in Chapter 4); or when Deb co-experienced how dreadful cold potato tasted when being 'last' to get served at lunchtime (in Chapter 6). We do *not* suggest we experienced these events in the same way as the children did (Warming, 2005): rather, 'sympathetic co-experiencing' is about *trying* to appreciate where another is coming from, while recognising the fallibility of this knowledge. Here, our 'outside' positions as adult-researchers and child-participants actively engaged in those situations enabled us – adults and children – to generate *new* understandings of such events and therefore bring meaning to each other, through our 'excesses' of seeing. For us as researchers, this 'excess' might be derived from our personal and professional experiences of many other children and early childhood settings or our knowledge of early childhood research, policy, and practice (including issues of power in research). To treat such attributes as unimportant is, we suggest, a relinquishment of one's own unique position as well as one's professional skills: after all, in carrying out a research project with the weight of a university and/or funding body behind it, a researcher must have demonstrated *some* skills and knowledge in order to be granted permission to proceed.

We also wish to stress that this process of sympathetic co-experiencing is not unidirectional in terms of value and transformation, as we demonstrated in

Chapter 6 when Deb's note-taking prompted Avleen's increased interest in writing and Avleen's questioning prompted Deb's reflection on the observation process. Children may encounter different ways of being with adults or generate new ideas about a topic of shared interest through their acts of 'sympathetically co-experiencing' with researchers. And they may bring to an event their own 'excess of seeing', which might relate to their greater temporal experience of the setting (of which researchers are just a small part) or their greater knowledge of other child- or adult-participants in the research setting. But this 'outsideness', crucial to Bakhtinian notions of answerability, should not be confused with neutrality and indifference – a point we have noted at various points throughout this book. For Bakhtin (1990), one *cannot* co-experience with someone for whom one is 'unsympathetic', not least as co-experiencing involves an opening up of oneself to others.

So far we have outlined the value of sympathetic co-experiencing for research, but our aim now is to caution against viewing research relationships, such as generated through *being with* children, in purely instrumental terms. Rachel's fieldnotes are a useful entry point to this discussion:

> When I went in last week, Cecilia called me immediately over to the playdough table. Although I did not think this would prove to be a key place to generate research data, I did not want to spurn her invitation. Cecilia soon left the area, but I remained with Fatema and Gordon – two children I had rarely spent time with – working alongside each other as we rolled, stretched, squished, and ripped the playdough. We pretended to eat the cooked dough, laughing together as Gordon 'gobbled up' the entire playdough cake in one fell swoop.
>
> I didn't even reference the moment in my fieldnotes last week as it was so distant from my research focus, but it came back to me today as Fatema *approached me* for the first time. She took me outside and launched us into an imaginary world full of narratives, characters, and interactions permeated with themes which were highly relevant to my research. She had not previously joined such play but perhaps had observed me doing so with other children.
>
> I wasn't 'banking' on generating this rich research data with Fatema – which would have been a calculating view of the interactions we had had the previous week to say the least. Yet, I couldn't help but feel that the time we spent – engaged in *being together* in a pleasurable and non-goal oriented way – had made my acceptance in her more 'liminal' play possible and even desirable.
>
> (Rachel Rosen, Taboo play)

In demonstrating how the relationships we built with children by *being with* them were 'useful' in generating rich data, we are mindful of Stacey's (1988) powerful critique of ethnographic methods. In essence, she argues that the greater level of immersion in the field as well as emotional intensity and emphasis on developing deeper relationships with participants inherent in ethnography has the potential to be *more* exploitative than traditional methods. And we appreciate that there is tension in simultaneously wanting to generate rich data alongside rejecting the instrumentalism that this position seems to engender. An examination of Rachel's fieldnote will, we hope, further illuminate our position.

Crucially, the time Rachel spent in the playdough area with these children was not prompted by any calculating and instrumental intention that it would most likely result in some high-quality data at a later point in the research, akin to a 'cost–benefit analysis' of the situation. We could both have pointed to myriad occasions in our research when we enjoyed the pleasurable activity of purely *being with* children (and similarly with adults too), generating no data of 'use' to our respective research projects. In Rachel's fieldnote of earlier, there did appear – as far as one can tell – a later 'spin off' as Fatema later engaged in taboo play with Rachel in a way that they had not previously experienced together. But significantly, Rachel's actions stemmed from a position divorced from seeing her research purely in instrumental, utilitarian terms such as increased knowledge production, a focus on *outcomes* rather than the *process* of research (Edwards and Mauthner, 2002). While research relationships are inevitably bounded in time, and this too needs to be managed carefully, participants are human beings who exist beyond any research project. Consequently, answerability necessarily *transcends* the research process proper. And, as we have asserted throughout this book and developed in detail in Chapter 7, we are not purely answerable to individuals but also to marginalised collectivities such as children.

For Deb, having completed her PhD two years ago, it is interesting to reflect on this position further as she has continued to worry away at many of the seeming 'red herrings' of her data collection periods in the four settings. Research committees, in wanting to see 'progress', focus on 'topical' data; thus, the pleasurable and regularly occurring meanderings she had while *being with* children remained hidden from view and yet were integral to the experience of the research for Deb, the children, and the educators in the four settings. On days when Deb came home with few or no fieldnotes about her topic, there was a feeling of guilt that she had not been 'productive' with her time or had not moved 'forward' with her research. Deb realised she was keen to be seen as *doing something* as opposed to *being with* children, and this resonates with narratives of the 'good researcher' of neoliberalism – one who *produces* 'high-quality' data and research 'outputs' in a given time frame. In gathering no data on some days, this challenged such a positioning; after all, what could be shared with supervisors or research progress committees?

Of course, we are not against the idea of progressing along with one's research projects. At the time of writing this book, Rachel is finishing her doctoral research and this looms large as a project to complete! Our point is that *being with* children is fundamentally important if we are to research in ways that build common cause with children. But *being with* children in order to generate data takes time, and some of the activity of the researcher will not necessarily include generating data for the research. And here, we acknowledge that non-externally funded ethnographic research, such as outlined in this book, offers opportunities for researchers to *wallow* in areas of interest and develop relationships with participants unlike other forms of research, particularly when compared to research undertaken after a competitive tendering process, where data generation is more tightly linked to a tight schedule set out in a formal contract.

To what extent then – in the neoliberal context of the 'First World/North' – is a premium placed on 'value for money' over attention to negotiating relationships with participants, notably child-participants? Our concern here is that keeping costs down may be more likely to 'win' a bid over one's ethical stance in relation to spending time *being with* children, neglecting the importance of negotiating relationships with child-participants and devoting 'long periods of time with children on the children's terms' (Graue and Walsh, 1995: 146). We concur with Edwards and Mauthner (2002) who argue that researchers should not enter into contractual conditions if they feel ethical considerations are compromised, but there are no simple answers here.

In the university context in many 'First World/North' countries, there has been an intensification of neoliberal principles (Davies, 2005), and in the case of England, enormous changes to funding that mean that income generation, for example through competitive bidding for research contracts, is a necessity for sustainability. As Davies (2005: 6) stresses, neoliberalism: 'destroys social responsibility and critique . . . invites a mindless, consumer-oriented individualism to flourish, and kills off conscience' and, we would add, elevates cost reduction over relationships. Yet for Davies (2005), as, indeed, for us, the very survival of the institutions we work and study in are tied in with economic survival.

'Good' research in such a context may become coupled with easily measured impact and an exacerbation of technicist understandings of ethics; a fairly 'easy' process of ticking boxes and predicting likely 'risks' in the research (as if this can ever be predicted *in entirety*). This has *some* place, such as in the initial process of research design, but it does not reflect the many instances that can never be predicted a priori and how one responds to these. Bakhtin (1990), whose work we have drawn on extensively in putting forward the idea of a relational ethics, is adamant that it is not a good thing to be assured exactly what will happen in the future because this knowledge would contradict an *active* life in all its risk fraughtness and possibility.

Research in common cause: Beyond the here and now of data generation

In spite of the immense difficulties associated with *being with* children in the competitive and funding-driven neoliberal research environment, there are a number of things that researchers can do to build common cause with children, some of which go beyond the immediacy of data generation. We argue here that researchers can do *more* than purely attending to their interpersonal interactions, that is, those moments of *being with* children and being reflexive about these. As Burman (2006:

324) has persuasively pointed out, it is important to exercise some caution against reflexive wanderings, not least as 'talk has become the walk: the researcher's reflection on the action *is* the action.' A crucial question in seeking to work with reciprocity, therefore, must be: What *difference* can our research make to lives of marginalised collectivities – including the predominantly working-class and female early childhood workforce and the children in our research projects – during *and* beyond data generation?

One way in which we think it is possible to develop reciprocity beyond the research process proper is through dialoguing with students and the wider research community. As university lecturers working on an early childhood studies' programme, for example, we have sought to raise important issues in relation to destabilising inequitable relationships between adults and children as well as other marginalised social groups. With a large number of students who work concurrently as early childhood educators, this is an important opening through which it may be possible to effect change in settings and, for the purposes of this book, research carried out in them. While not directly interacting with children in this process, we argue that this is just as important a part of addressing inequitable relations in research as the micro-interactions that have formed the substantive focus of our discussion in this book.

To expand, while we have both struggled to teach in a way that does not reduce research practice to a technicist level, writing this book has made us think more deeply about the way in which we dialogue with students about research relationships and, crucially, about the importance of answerability. In particular, it has provoked us to question whether we are complicit in the way that ethics is often reduced to an instrumental practice. Previously, for example, we have both often provided students with a list of ethical 'concerns' – such as anonymity, data protection, and consent – to address in their research projects. As Rachel has noted: 'While I have often justified my previous efforts to make the research process – which often seems daunting and overwhelming for students – comprehensible, such simplifications are ultimately highly reductive.' And, as we have argued throughout this book, such an instrumental approach functions essentially as an 'alibi' for our political and ethical answerability to others.

In teaching a module on research methodology concurrently with writing this book, Rachel has made more explicit efforts to introduce questions and concepts the writing has provoked in her teaching. This has led to a series of dialogues with students in her class, for example, about the ways that the problematics of research observation, such as those we took up in Chapter 6, speak back to practice. One of the students noted that such issues were either rendered invisible or dismissed in her experience of early childhood practice. She commented that the entire way she thought about and approached observation, documentation, and dissemination of data about children in her practice was shifting as a result of the module. While we do not wish to collapse research into pedagogy, a point that has circled throughout this book, we concur with Eide and Winger (2005: 73) that 'the same basic sensibility and respect *(for children)* is demanded from pedagogues, teachers or researchers.' Moreover, we are conscious that this issue may have surfaced more for us as former early childhood educators compared to researchers who do not share this professional background.

Rachel has also tried to engage students in a process of rethinking how others, and children in particular, can be potential collaborators in research. This requires challenging dominant conceptions of childhood as a time of egocentrism and incompetence rendering children as mere 'objects' of research. In keeping with our attempts to think our way into the complexity of research relationships in this book, Rachel notes:

> In class, we discussed the tensions in building 'collaborative' relationships with children when research invariably emerges from student interests and university assessment criteria. In one discussion, we determined that collaboration does not have to mean that each person's input to research is the *same* but instead that collaboration implies a degree of openness and responsiveness to the input of others from anything ranging from the research topic to the withdrawal of participation.
>
> Unsurprisingly, these discussions have made the module less straightforward for students; many have commented to me about how difficult they have found the concepts we are engaging with. Ultimately, however, I hope the dialogues have introduced productive tensions which potentially encourage a more critical view of the research process and encourage students (as well as myself) to engage in a reflective process – rather than trying for the impossible of doing research 'correctly'.

It is the challenge to generational inequities and a view that research practice can be straightforward and transparent, simply a set of mandatory boxes to be ticked, in this last example, which we argue helps to build common cause beyond the here and now of data generation. For in encouraging students to consider the complexity of dilemmas they will face in research, we hope to generate a commitment to being politically and ethically answerable – ultimately making a difference to the lives of marginalised collectivities.

In addition to our direct work with students, we would argue that reflection, writing, and disseminating one's research are important activities that can also build common cause with children in ways which go beyond interpersonal interactions with them. Barbour (2010), for instance, argues that in writing one has an opportunity to debate and reconstruct the ethical journey one has taken in research. Christensen and Prout (2002) similarly advocate that researchers share their research stories as in sharing one's thinking with others, the research community can learn to 'do' research with children in more equitable and reciprocal ways. In essence, this has been central to the dialogic process we have engaged with in writing this book.

In writing this book, we have continued to 'dialogue' with our fieldnotes and the participants represented within them: the children and adults with whom we have encountered in our respective research projects, and in doing so we have 're-accentuated' (Bakhtin, 1981: 419–422) our former ideas. This, we would argue, is significant in terms of conceptualising 'relationships', as it extends the notion of the relationships a researcher has with participants *beyond* her face-to-face interactions with them; providing further weight to our assertion (following the ideas of Bakhtin, 1993) of the unfinalisability of relationships.

Over time, new ideas become prominent and challenge us to look afresh at what we once thought was 'ethical research practice' and to revisit, time and time again in some instances, critical moments from our research. And this is not merely an adult-centric process: children (as individuals and as groups) bring a new optic to our research endeavours and trigger new thinking in the action of our reflecting and writing about them. Once research has ended, we may or may not have a relationship with the individuals that involves seeing them face-to-face on a regular basis, but we do *continue to care* what happens to them as individuals and as a social group, including through how we represent them in the 'texts' that we produce as researchers (Gordon, 2003).

Towards a relational ethics

Relationships, as we have argued throughout this book, are *central* to research, but are never finalisable and 'achieved'. Instead, we have sought to provide insight into the ongoing and 'messy' interactions that occur in the research process, situated as they are within a context of generational and other inequities. As we have shown, the complexity of negotiating within a web of relationships in early childhood research, for our purposes early childhood settings in a neoliberal space/time, raises a number of complex dilemmas that cannot be reduced to 'abstract and formal' (Tronto, 1993: 27) rules that can be applied universally.

Inspired as we have been by the work of Bakhtin, we wish to reiterate what has been a central message in this book: while common ethical guidelines have an important place for researchers, and whilst we continue to argue for a politically engaged research practice starting from a commitment to social justice, these principles cannot and should not replace the political-ethical responsibilities that emerge in situ as research is undertaken. Being *answerable* to participants – be they children or adults – involves a complex mix of 'sensing practices', embodied reflexivity, reciprocity, and openness to being changed ourselves by way of examples; few of which can be predicted in advance of research in the field. Moreover, answerability goes *beyond* the face-to-face interactions researchers have with participants, necessarily involving a commitment to continued critical dialogue with the 'texts' generated through data collection.

In concluding this book, we wish to argue that reciprocity in research with children cannot be accomplished from a disinterested and uninvolved standpoint: to carry out research 'in common cause', it is necessary to be motivated to want to do research 'better' and to make a difference to the lives of marginalised groups, including children. And this means attending to the relationships we have with participants in the course of research, continuing to recognise our own fallibilities in the process. It also means engaging in radical and transformative dialogue motivated by concerns of justice and equity with others in the research community and beyond. By sharing some of our critical moments in this book – which we will *continue* to dialogue with – we hope we have added to this collective discussion.

REFERENCES

Abell, J., Locke, A., Condoer, S., Gibson, S., and Stevenson, C. (2006) 'Trying similarity, doing difference: The role of interviewer self-disclosure in interview talk with young people', *Qualitative Research*, 6 (2): 221–244.

Adler, P. A. and Adler, P. (1994) 'Observational techniques', in N. K. Denzin and Y. S. Lincoln (eds.) *Handbook of Qualitative Research* (pp. 377–392), Thousand Oaks, CA: Sage.

Ahmed, S. (2000) 'Who knows? Knowing strangers and strangerness', *Australian Feminist Studies*, 15 (31): 49–68.

Ailwood, J. (2003) 'Governing early childhood education through play', *Contemporary Issues in Early Childhood*, 4 (3): 286–299.

Ailwood, J. (2008) 'Mothers, teachers, maternalism and early childhood education and care: Some historical connections', *Contemporary Issues in Early Childhood*, 8 (2): 157–165.

Alanen, L. (2001) 'Explorations in generational analysis', in B. Mayall and L. Alanen (eds.) *Conceptualizing Child–Adult Relationships* (pp. 11–22), London: RoutledgeFalmer.

Alanen, L. and Mayall, B. (2001) *Conceptualizing Child–Adult Relations*, London: RoutledgeFalmer.

Albon, D. (2005) 'Writing up research involving child participants: Some observations of Ian aged 5 years'. Available at http://www.tactyc.org.uk/pdfs/albon.pdf (accessed 2 November 2012).

Albon, D. (2009) 'Challenges to the uptake of milk in a nursery class: A case study', *Health Education*, 109 (2): 140–154.

Albon, D. (2010) *An Ethnographic Study Examining Food and Drink Practices in Four Early Childhood Settings*, unpublished PhD thesis, London Metropolitan University.

Albon, D. (2011) 'A response to "Physical activity at daycare: Issues, challenges and perspectives" (Van Zandvoort et al., 2010)', *Early Years: An International Journal of Research and Development*, 31 (2): 193–200.

Alcoff, L. M. (2009) 'The problem of speaking for others', in A. Y. Jackson and L. A. Mazzei (eds.) *Voice in Qualitative Inquiry: Challenging conventional, interpretive, and critical conceptions in qualitative research* (pp. 117–135), London: Routledge.

Alderson, P. (1993) *Children's Consent to Surgery*, Maidenhead: Open University Press.

Alderson, P. (2004) 'Ethics', in S. Fraser, V. Lewis, S. Ding, M. Kellett, and C. Robinson (eds.) *Doing Research with Children and Young People* (pp. 97–112), London: Sage.

Alderson, P. (2005) 'Designing ethical research with children', in A. Farrell (ed.) *Ethical Research with Children* (pp. 27–36), Maidenhead: Open University Press.

Alldred, P. (1998) 'Ethnography and discourse analysis: Dilemmas in representing the voices of children', in J. Ribbens and R. Edwards (eds.) *Feminist Dilemmas in Qualitative Research: Public knowledge and private lives* (pp. 147–170), London: Sage.

Alldred, P., David, M., and Edwards, R. (2002) 'Minding the gap: Children and young people negotiating relations between home and school', in R. Edwards (ed.) *Children, Home and School: Regulation, autonomy or connection?* (pp. 121–137), London: Routledge.

Allen, G. (2011) *Early Intervention: Smart investment, massive savings. The second Independent Report to Her Majesty's Government*, London: Cabinet Office.

Alloway, N. (1997) 'Early childhood education encounters the postmodern: What do we know? What can we count as true?', *Australian Journal of Early Childhood*, 22 (2): 1–5.

Althusser, L. (1971) *'Lenin and Philosophy' and Other Essays*, New York: Monthly Review Press.

Angrosino, M. (2005) 'Recontextualizing observation: Ethnography, pedagogy, and the prospects for a progressive political agenda', in N. K. Denzin and Y. S. Lincoln (eds.) *The SAGE Handbook of Qualitative Research*, 3rd edn (pp. 729–745), London: Sage.

Anning, A., Cullen, J., and Fleer, M. (2004) *Early Childhood Education: Society and culture*, London: Sage.

Apple, M. W. (1999) *Power, Meaning and Identity: Essays in critical educational studies*, New York: Peter Lang.

Apple, M. W. (2006) 'Producing inequalities: Neo-liberalism, neo-conservatism, and the politics of educational reform (2001)', in H. Lauder, P. Brown, J.-A. Dillabough, and A. H. Halsey (eds.) *Education, Globalization and Social Change* (pp. 468–489), Oxford: Oxford University Press.

Archard, D. (2004) *Children: Rights and childhood*, 2nd edn, London: Routledge.

Bakhtin, M. M. (1981) *The Dialogic Imagination: Four essays*, Austin: University of Texas Press.

Bakhtin, M. M. (1984a) *Problems of Dostoevsky's Poetics*, Minneapolis: University of Minnesota Press.

Bakhtin, M. M. (1984b) *Rabelais and His World*, 1st Midland book edn, Bloomington: Indiana University Press.

Bakhtin, M. M. (1986) *Speech Genres and Other Late Essays*, 1st edn, Austin: University of Texas Press.

Bakhtin, M. M. (1990) *Art and Answerability: Early philosophical essays*, 1st edn, Austin: University of Texas Press.

Bakhtin, M. M. (1993) *Toward a Philosophy of the Act*, 1st edn, Austin: University of Texas Press.

Ball, S. J. (2003) 'The teacher's soul and the terrors of performativity', *Journal of Education Policy*, 18 (2): 215–228.

Ball, S. J. (2006) *Education Policy and Social Class: The selected works of Stephen J. Ball*, London: Routledge.

Ball, S. J. (2008) *The Education Debate: Policy and politics in the 21st century*, Bristol: The Policy Press.

Barbour, A. (2010) 'Exploring some ethical dilemmas and obligations of the ethnographer', *Ethnography and Education*, 5 (2): 159–173.

Barker, J. and Weller, S. (2003) '"Is it fun?" Developing children-centred research methods', *International Journal of Sociology and Social Policy*, 23 (1–2): 33–58.

Barro, R. J. and Lee, J. W. (2001) 'International data on educational attainment: Updates and implications', *Oxford Economic Papers*, 53 (3): 541–563.

Bash, L. and Coulby, D. (eds.) (1989) *The Education Reform Act: Competition and control*, London: Cassell.
Baxter, L. A. and Montgomery, B. M. (1996) *Relating: Dialogues and dialectics*, New York and London: Guilford Press.
Beach, J., Friendly, M., Ferns, C., Prabhu, N., and Forer, B. (2009) *Early Childhood Education and Care in Canada 2008*, 8th edn, Toronto: Childcare Resource and Research Unit.
Beck, U. (1992) *Risk Society: Towards a new modernity*, London: Sage.
Becker, G. S. (2006) 'The age of human capital', in H. Lauder, P. Brown, J.-A. Dillabough, and A. H. Halsey (eds.) *Education, Globalization and Social Change* (pp. 292–294), Oxford: Oxford University Press.
Ben-Ari, E. (1997) *Body Projects in Japanese Childcare: Culture, organization and emotions in a preschool*, Richmond, VA: Curzon Press.
Bender, C. (1998) 'Bakhtinian perspectives on "everyday life" sociology', in M. M. Bell and M. Gardiner (eds.) *Bakhtin and the Human Sciences* (pp. 181–195), London: Sage.
Bernard-Donals, M. (1998) 'Knowing the subaltern: Bakhtin, carnival and the other voice of the human sciences', in M. Mayerfeld Bell and M. Gardiner (eds.) *Bakhtin and the Human Sciences* (pp. 112–127), London: Sage.
Bernstein, B. (1975) 'Class and pedagogies: Visible and invisible', *Educational Studies*, 1 (1): 23–41.
Bernstein, B. (2000) *Pedagogy, Symbolic Control and Identity: Theory, research, critique*, rev. edn, Lanham, MD; Oxford: Rowman & Littlefield.
Bialostok, S. and Kamberelis, G. (2010) 'New capitalism, risk, and subjectification in an early childhood classroom', *Contemporary Issues in Early Childhood*, 11 (3). 299–312.
Bilge, S. (2010) 'Recent feminist outlooks on intersectionality', *Diogenes*, 57 (1): 58–72.
Bourdieu, P. (1977) *Outline of a Theory of Practice*, Cambridge: Cambridge University Press.
Bradbury, A. (2011) 'Rethinking assessment and inequality: The production of disparities in attainment in early years education', *Journal of Education Policy*, 26 (5): 655–676.
Britzman, D. P. (2007) 'Teacher education as uneven development: Toward a psychology of uncertainty', *International Journal of Leadership in Education*, 10 (1): 1–12.
Brooker, L. (2010) 'Learning to play, or playing to learn? Children's participation in the cultures of homes and settings', in L. Brooker and S. Edwards (eds.) *Engaging Play* (pp. 39–53), Maidenhead: Open University Press.
Brown, P. and Lauder, H. (2006) 'Globalisation, knowledge and the magnet economy', in H. Lauder, P. Brown, J.-A. Dillabough, and A. H. Halsey (eds.) *Education, Globalization and Social Change* (pp. 317–340), Oxford: Oxford University Press.
Brown, T. and Jones, L. (2001) *Action Research and Postmodernism: Congruence and critique*, Maidenhead: Open University Press.
Bruer, J. (1999) *The Myth of the First Three Years: A new understanding of early brain development and lifelong learning*, New York: Free Press.
Bruner, J. S., Jolly, A., and Sylva, K. (1976) *Play: Its role in development and evolution*, Harmondsworth: Penguin.
Buchbinder, M., Longhofer, J., Barrett, T., Lawson, P., and Floersch, J. (2006) 'Ethnographic approaches to child care research', *Journal of Early Childhood Research*, 4 (1): 45–63.
Burgess, R. G. (1989) 'Grey areas: Ethical dilemmas in educational ethnography', in R. G. Burgess (ed.) *The Ethics of Educational Research* (pp. 60–76), New York: Falmer Press.
Burman, E. (2001) 'Beyond the baby and the bathwater: Postdualist developmental psychologies for diverse childhoods', *European Early Childhood Education Research Journal*, 9 (1): 5–22.

Burman, E. (2006) 'Emotions and reflexivity in feminised action research', *Educational Action Research*, 14 (3): 315–332.
Butler, J. (1993) *Bodies that Matter: On the discursive limits of 'sex'*, New York and London: Routledge.
Cannella, G. S. and Viruru, R. (2004) *Childhood and Postcolonialism*, London: RoutledgeFalmer.
Caplan, P. (1997) 'Approaches to the study of food, health and identity', in P. Caplan (ed.) *Food, Health and Identity* (pp. 1–31), London: Routledge.
Castañeda, C. (2003) *Figurations: Child, bodies, worlds*, Durham, NC: Duke University Press.
Cederman, K. (2008) 'Not weaving but drowning? The Child.com in New Zealand and early childhood pedagogies', *International Journal of Early Childhood*, 40 (2): 119–130.
Center on the Developing Child Harvard University (2010) 'The foundations of lifelong health are built in early childhood', Harvard: Harvard University. Available at http://developingchild.harvard.edu/ (accessed 26 June 2012).
Chaput Waksler, F. (1991) 'Dancing when the music is over: A study of deviance in a kindergarten classroom', in F. Chaput Waksler (ed.) *Studying the Social Worlds of Children: Sociological readings* (pp. 95–112), London: RoutledgeFalmer.
Christensen, P. H. (2000) 'Childhood and the cultural constitution of vulnerable bodies', in A. Prout (ed.) *The Body, Childhood and Society* (pp. 38–59), Basingstoke: Macmillan Press.
Christensen, P. H. (2004) 'Children's participation in ethnographic research: Issues of power and representation', *Children & Society*, 18 (2): 165–176.
Christensen, P. H. and James, A. (eds.) (2008) *Research with Children: Perspectives and practices*, 2nd edn, New York and London: Routledge.
Christensen, P. H. and Prout, A. (2002) 'Working with ethical symmetry in social research with children', *Childhood*, 9 (4): 477–497.
Chung, S. and Walsh, D. J. (2000) 'Un-packing child-centredness: A history of meanings', *Journal of Curriculum Studies*, 32 (2): 215–234.
Clark, A. (2005) 'Listening to and involving young children: A review of research and practice', *Early Child Development and Care*, 175 (6): 489–505.
Clark, A. and Moss, P. (2001) *Listening to Young Children: The mosaic approach*, London: NCB/JRF.
Cocks, A. J. (2006) 'The ethical maze: Finding an inclusive path towards gaining children's agreement to research participation', *Childhood*, 13 (2): 247–266.
Coffey, A. (1999) *The Ethnographic Self: Fieldwork and the representation of identity*, London: Sage.
Coffey, A. (2002) 'Ethnography and self: Reflections and representations', in T. May (ed.) *Qualitative Research in Action* (pp. 313–331), London: Sage.
Coghlan, D. and Casey, M. (2001) 'Action research from the inside: Issues and challenges in doing action research in your own hospital', *Journal of Advanced Nursing*, 35 (5): 674–682.
Collier, A. (1994) *Critical Realism: An introduction to Roy Bhaskar's philosophy*, London: Verso.
Colley, H. (2006) 'Learning to labour with feeling: Class, gender and emotion in childcare education and training', *Contemporary Issues in Early Childhood*, 7 (1): 15–29.
Connell, R. (1987) *Gender and Power: Society, the person and sexual politics*, Cambridge: Polity Press in association with Blackwell.
Connolly, P. (2008) 'Race, gender and critical reflexivity in research with young children', in P. Christensen and A. James (eds.) *Research with Children: Perspectives and practices*, 2nd edn (pp. 173–188), London: Routledge.
Connor, S. (2005) 'Michael Serres' five senses', in D. Howes (ed.) *Empire of the Senses: The sensual culture reader* (pp. 318–334), Oxford: Berg Publishers.

Corsaro, W. (1985) *Friendship and Peer Culture in the Early Years*, Upper Saddle River, NJ: Ablex.
Corsaro, W. and Molinari, L. (2008) 'Entering and observing in children's worlds: A reflection on a longitudinal ethnography of early education in Italy', in P. Christensen and A. James (eds.) *Research with Children: Perspectives and practices*, 2nd edn (pp. 239–259), London: Routledge.
Dahlberg, G. and Moss, P. (2005) *Ethics and Politics in Early Childhood Education*, London: RoutledgeFalmer.
Dahlberg, G., Moss, P. and Pence, A. (2007) *Beyond Quality in Early Childhood Education and Care: Languages of evaluation*, 2nd edn, London: Routledge.
Daniel, P. and Ivatts, J. (1998) *Children and Social Policy*, Basingstoke: Macmillan Press.
Darling, J. (1982) 'Education as horticulture: Some growth theorists and their critics', *Journal of Philosophy of Education*, 16 (2): 173–185.
Davies, B. (2005) 'The (im)possibility of intellectual work in neoliberal regimes', *Discourse: Studies in the Cultural Politics of Education*, 26 (1): 1–14.
Davies, H. (2011) 'Affinities, seeing and feeling like family: Exploring why children value face-to-face contact', *Childhood*, 19 (1): 8–23.
Davin, A. (1996) *Growing Up Poor: Home, school and street in London 1870–1914*, London: Rivers Oram Press.
DCSF (2008) *Statutory Framework for the Early Years Foundation Stage*, Nottingham: Department for Children, Schools and Families.
Degotardi, S. and Pearson, E. (2009) 'Relationship theory in the nursery: Attachment and beyond', *Contemporary Issues in Early Childhood*, 10 (2): 144–155.
Delgado, R. and Stefancic, J. (2000) *Critical Race Theory: The cutting edge*, 2nd edn, Philadelphia, PA: Temple University Press.
Dennis, B. (2009) 'What does it mean when an ethnographer intervenes?', *Ethnography and Education*, 4 (2): 131–146.
DfE (2012) *Statutory Framework for the Early Years Foundation Stage*, Runcorn: Department for Education.
DfES (2007) *The Early Years Foundation Stage: Setting the standards for learning, development and care for children from birth to five*, Nottingham: Department for Education and Schools.
Dockett, S., Einarsdottir, J., and Perry, B. (2009) 'Researching with children: Ethical tensions', *Journal of Early Childhood Research*, 7 (3): 283–298.
Dockett, S. and Perry, B. (2007) 'Trusting children's accounts in research', *Journal of Early Childhood Research*, 5 (1): 47–63.
Douglas, M. and Nicod, M. (1974) 'Taking the biscuit: The structure of British meals', *New Society*, 30 (637): 744–747.
Dunn, J. (1988) *The Beginnings of Social Understanding*, Cambridge, MA: Harvard University Press.
Dunne, J. (2006) 'Childhood and citizenship: A conversation across modernity', *European Early Childhood Education Research Journal*, 14 (1): 5–19.
Edmiston, B. (2005) 'Coming home to research', in L. Diaz-Soto and B. B. Swadener (eds.) *Power and Voice in Research with Children* (pp. 55–76), New York: Peter Lang.
Edmiston, B. (2008) *Forming Ethical Identities in Early Childhood Play*, London: Routledge.
Edmond, R. (2005) 'Ethnographic research methods with children and young people', in S. Greene and D. Hogan (eds.) *Researching Children's Experience: Approaches and methods* (pp. 123–140), London: Sage.
Edwards, R. and Mauthner, M. (2002) 'Ethics in qualitative research: Theory and practice', in M. Mauthner, M. Birch, J. Jessop, and T. Miller (eds.) *Ethics in Qualitative Research* (pp. 14–31), London: Sage.

Eide, B. J. and Winger, N. (2005) 'From the child's point of view: Methodological and ethical challenges', in A. Clark, A. T. Kjorholt, and P. Moss (eds.) *Beyond Listening: Children's perspectives of early childhood services* (pp. 71–89), Bristol: The Policy Press.

Elfer, P., Goldschmeid, E., and Selleck, D. (2003) *Key Persons in the Nursery: Building relationships for quality provision*, London: David Fulton.

Elias, N. (1978) *The Civilizing Process*, Oxford: Blackwell.

Elias, N. (1994) *The Civilizing Process*, rev. edn, Oxford: Blackwell.

Elliot, E. (2007) *We're Not Robots: The voices of daycare providers*, Albany: State University of New York Press.

Ellis, C. (2007) 'Telling secrets, revealing lives: Relational ethics in research with intimate others', *Qualitative Inquiry*, 13 (1): 3–29.

Evans, J., Davies, B., and Rich, E. (2010) 'Schooling the body in a performative culture', in M. W. Apple, S. J. Ball, and L. A. Gandin (eds.) *The Routledge International Handbook of the Sociology of Education* (pp. 200–212), London: Routledge.

Feld, S. (2005) 'Places sensed, senses placed', in D. Howes (ed.), *Empire of the Senses: The sensual culture reader* (pp. 179–191), Oxford: Berg Publishers.

Fendler, L. (2001) 'Educating flexible souls: The construction of subjectivity through developmentality and interaction', in *Governing the Child in the New Millennium* (pp. 120–142), London: RoutledgeFalmer.

Fenech, M., Sumsion, J., and Shepherd, W. (2010) 'Promoting early childhood teacher professionalism in the Australian context: The place of resistance', *Contemporary Issues in Early Childhood*, 11 (1): 89–105.

Finnegan, R. (2002) *Communicating: The multiple modes of human interconnection*, London and New York: Routledge.

Fleer, M. (2002) 'Sociocultural assessment in early years education: Myth or reality?', *International Journal of Early Years Education*, 10 (2): 105–120.

Foucault, M. (1977) *Discipline and Punishment: The birth of the prison*, London: Penguin.

France, A., Bendelow, G., and Williams, S. (2000) 'A "risky" business: Researching the health beliefs of children and young people', in A. Lewis and G. Lindsay (eds.) *Researching Children's Perspectives* (pp. 150–162), Maidenhead: Open University Press.

Galbraith, J. (2007) *Multiple Perspectives on Superhero Play in an Early Childhood Classroom*, unpublished PhD thesis, Ohio State University.

Gallacher, L. A. and Gallagher, M. (2008) 'Methodological immaturity in childhood research? Thinking through "participatory methods"', *Childhood*, 15 (4): 499–516.

Gandini, L. and Edwards, C. P. (eds.) (2001) *Bambini: The Italian approach to infant/toddler care*, New York: Teachers College Press.

Gardiner, M. (2000) *Critiques of Everyday Life: An introduction*, New York and London: Routledge.

Gardiner, M. (2009) 'Schutzian phenomenology and the everyday lifeworld: A Baktinian critique', in J. Y. Park and H. Y. Jung (eds.) *Comparative Political Theory and Cross-Cultural Philosophy: Essays in honor of Hwa Yol Jung* (pp. 197–222), Plymouth, MA: Lexington Books.

Goffman, E. (1969) *The Presentation of Self in Everyday Life,* London: Allen Lane, Penguin.

Golden, D. (2005) 'Nourishing the nation: The uses of food in an Israeli kindergarten', *Food and Foodways*, 13 (3): 181–199.

Gordon, T. (2003) 'Intricacies of dissemination in ethnographic research', in C. Hughes (ed.) *Disseminating Qualitative Research in Educational Settings* (pp. 79–90), Maidenhead: Open University Press.

Grasseni, C. (2004) 'Video and ethnographic knowledge: Skilled vision in the practice of breeding', in S. Pink, L. Kurti, and A. I. Afonso (eds.) *Working Images: Visual research and representation in ethnography* (pp. 12–27), London and New York: Routledge.

Graue, M. E. and Walsh, D. J. (1995) 'Children in context: Interpreting the here and now of children's lives', in J. A. Hatch (ed.) *Qualitative Research in Early Childhood Settings* (pp. 135–154), Westport, CT: Praeger.

Greene, S. and Hill, M. (2005) 'Researching children's experience: Methods and methodological issues', in S. Greene and D. Hogan (eds.) *Researching Children's Experience: Approaches and methods* (pp. 1–21), London: Sage.

Gregory, E. and Ruby, M. (2011) 'The "insider/outsider" dilemma of ethnography: Working with young children and their families in cross-cultural contexts', *Journal of Early Childhood Research*, 9 (2): 162–174.

Grieshaber, S. (2004) *Rethinking Parent and Child Conflict*, London: RoutledgeFalmer.

Grieshaber, S. and McArdle, F. (2010) *The Trouble with Play*, Maidenhead: Open University Press.

Griffin, C. (1991) 'The researcher talks back: Dealing with power relations in studies of young people's entry into the job market', in W. B. Shaffir and R. A. Stebbins (eds.) *Experiencing Fieldwork: An inside view of qualitative research* (pp. 109–119), Newbury Park, CA: Sage.

Griffiths, M. (1998) *Educational Research for Social Justice: Getting off the fence*, Maidenhead: Open University Press.

Grosz, E. (1994) *Volatile Bodies: Toward a corporeal feminism*, Bloomington: Indiana University Press.

Guillemin, M. and Gillam, L. (2004) 'Ethics, reflexivity, and "ethically important moments" in research', *Qualitative Inquiry*, 10 (2): 261–280.

Gulløv, E. (2012) 'Kindergartens in Denmark: Reflections on continuity and change', in A. T. Kjørholt and J. Qvortrup (eds.) *The Modern Child and the Flexible Labour Market* (pp. 90–107), London: Palgrave Macmillan.

Gura, P. (ed.) (1992) *Exploring Learning: Young children and blockplay*, London: Paul Chapman.

Hammersley, M. and Atkinson, P. (2007) *Ethnography: Principles in practice*, 3rd edn, London: Routledge.

Hatch, J. A. (1995) 'Ethical conflicts in classroom research: Examples from a study of peer stigmatisation', in J. A. Hatch (ed.) *Qualitative Research in Early Childhood Settings* (pp. 213–222), Westport, CT: Praeger.

Haw, K. and Hadfield, M. (2011) *Video in Social Science Research: Functions and forms*, London: Routledge.

Hendrick, H. (1997a) *Children, Childhood and English Society 1880–1990*, Cambridge: Cambridge University Press.

Hendrick, H. (1997b) 'Constructions and reconstructions of British childhood: An interpretative survey 1800 to the present', in A. James and A. Prout (eds.) *Constructing and Reconstructing Childhood*, 2nd edn (pp. 34–62), London: RoutledgeFalmer.

Hoffman, D. M. (2009) 'How (not) to feel: Culture and the politics of emotion in the American parenting advice literature', *Discourse: Studies in the Cultural Politics of Education*, 30 (1): 15–31.

Holland, P. (2003) *We Don't Play with Guns Here: War, weapon and superhero play in the early years*, Maidenhead: Open University Press.

Holland, W. (2009) 'Promoting emotional security and positive behaviour', in P. Jarvis, G. Lane, and W. Holland (eds.) *The Early Years Professional's Complete Companion* (pp. 162–191), Harlow: Pearson Longman.

Holligan, C. (2000) 'Discipline and normalisation in the nursery: The Foucaultian gaze', in H. Penn (ed.) *Early Childhood Services: Theory, policy and practice* (pp. 134–146), Maidenhead: Open University Press.

Holloway, S. L. and Valentine, G. (2000) 'Spatiality and the new social studies of childhood', *Sociology*, 34 (4): 763–783.

Holquist, M. (1990) 'Introduction: The architectonics of answerability', in M. Holquist and V. Liapunov (eds.) *Art and Answerability: Early philosophical essays*, 1st edn (pp. ix–xlix), Austin: University of Texas Press.

Howes, D. (2003) *Sensual Relations: Engaging the senses in culture and social theory*, Ann Arbor: University of Michigan Press.

Howes, D. (ed.) (2005a) *Empire of the Senses: The sensual culture reader*, Oxford: Berg Publishers.

Howes, D. (2005b) 'Introduction: Empires of the senses', in D. Howes (ed.), *Empire of the Senses: The sensual culture reader* (pp. 1–17), Oxford: Berg Publishers.

Hyder, T. (2002) 'Making it happen – young children's rights in action: The work of Save the Children's Centre for Young Children's Rights', in B. Franklin (ed.) *The New Handbook of Children's Rights: Comparative policy and practice* (pp. 311–326), London: Routledge.

Jablon, J. and Dombro, A. (2001) 'Using what you learn from observation: A form of assessment'. Available at http://eclkc.ohs.acf.hhs.gov/hslc/tta-system/teaching/eecd/Assessment/Ongoing%20Assessment/edudev_art_00070_080505.html (accessed 11 September 2012).

Jackson, A. Y. and Mazzei, L. A. (eds.) (2009) *Voice in Qualitative Inquiry: Challenging conventional, interpretive, and critical conceptions in qualitative research*, London: Routledge.

James, A. (1993) *Childhood Identities: Self and social relationships in the experience of the child*, Edinburgh: Edinburgh University Press.

James, A. (2000) 'Embodied being(s)', in A. Prout (ed.) *The Body, Childhood and Society* (pp. 19–38), Basingstoke: Macmillan Press.

James, A. (2012) '"Child-centredness" and "the child": The cultural politics of nursery schooling in England', in A. T. Kjorholt and J. Quortrup (eds.) *The Modern Child and the Flexible Labour Market* (pp. 111–127), London: Palgrave Macmillan.

James, A., Jenks, C., and Prout, A. (1998) *Theorizing Childhood*, Cambridge: Polity Press.

Jenks, C. (1996) 'The postmodern child', in J. Brannen and M. O'Brien (eds.) *Children in Families: Research and policy* (pp. 13–25), London: Falmer Press.

Jipson, J. and Jipson, J. (2005) 'Confidence intervals: Doing research with young children', in L. Diaz Soto and B. B. Swadener (eds.) *Power and Voice in Research with Children* (pp. 35–44), New York: Peter Lang.

Johanssen, B. (2012) 'Doing adulthood in childhood research', *Childhood*, 19 (1): 101–114.

Johnson, B. and Christensen, L. B. (2008) *Educational Research: Quantitative, qualitative, and mixed approaches*, 3rd edn, Los Angeles and London: Sage.

Jones, L., Holmes, R., MacRae, C., and MacLure, M. (2010a) 'Critical politics of play', in G. S. Cannella and L. D. Soto (eds.) *Childhoods: A handbook* (pp. 291–305), New York: Peter Lang.

Jones, L., Holmes, R., MacRae, C., and MacLure, M. (2010b) 'Documenting classroom life: How can I write about what I am seeing?', *Qualitative Research*, 10 (4): 479–491.

Keddie, A. (2001) *Little Boys: The potency of peer culture in shaping masculinities*, unpublished PhD thesis, Deakin University, Melbourne.

Keenan, J. and Stapleton, H. (2009) 'It depends what you mean by feeding "on demand": Mothers' accounts of babies' agency in infant-feeding relationships', in A. James, A. T. Kjorholt, and V. Tingstad (eds.) *Children, Food and Identity in Everyday Life* (pp. 13–34), Basingstoke: Palgrave Macmillan.

Kernan, M. and Singer, E. (eds.) (2011) *Peer Relationships in Early Childhood Education and Care*, London: Routledge.

Kershaw, P. (2004) '"Choice" discourse in BC child care: Distancing policy from research', *Canadian Journal of Political Science*, 37 (4): 927–950.

Kincheloe, J. (2001) 'Describing the bricolage: Conceptualizing a new rigor in qualitative research', *Qualitative Inquiry*, 7 (6): 679–692.

Kjorholt, A. T. (2005) 'The competent child and "the right to be oneself"', in A. Clark, A. T. Kjorholt, and P. Moss (eds.) *Beyond Listening: Children's perspectives on early childhood services* (pp. 151–173), Bristol: The Policy Press.

Kjorholt, A. T. and Qvortrup, J. (2012) 'Childhood and social investments: Concluding thoughts', in A. T. Kjorholt and J. Quortrup (eds.) *The Modern Child and the Flexible Labour Market* (pp. 262–274), London: Palgrave Macmillan.

Kjorholt, A. T. and Seland, M. (2012) 'Kindergarten as a bazaar: Freedom of choice and new forms of regulation', in A. T. Kjorholt and J. Qvortrup (eds.) *The Modern Child and the Flexible Labour Market: Early childhood education and care* (pp. 168–185), Basingstoke: Palgrave Macmillan.

Lahman, M. K. E. (2008) 'Always othered: Ethical research with children', *Journal of Early Childhood Research*, 6 (3): 281–300.

Lather, P. (2007) 'Postmodernism, post-structuralism and post(critical) ethnography: Of ruins, aporias and angels', in P. Atkinson, A. Coffey, S. Delamont, J. Lofland, and L. Lofland (eds.) *Handbook of Ethnography* (pp. 477–492), London: Sage.

Lauder, H., Brown, P., Dillabough, J.-A., and Halsey, A. H. (2006) 'Introduction: The prospects for education: Individualisation, globalisation, and social change', in H. Lauder, P. Brown, J.-A. Dillabough, and A. H. Halsey (eds.) *Education, Globalization and Social Change* (pp. 1–70), Oxford: Oxford University Press.

Lawrence, E. (1952) *Friedrich Froebel and English Education*, London: University of London Press.

Leavitt, R. L. (1994) *Power and Emotion in Infant–Toddler Day Care*, Albany: State University of New York Press.

Leavitt, R. L. and Power, M. B. (1997) 'Civilizing bodies: Children in day care', in J. Tobin (ed.) *Making a Place for Pleasure in Early Childhood Education* (pp. 39–75), New Haven, CT, and London: Yale University Press.

Lee, N. (2001) *Childhood and Society: Growing up in an age of uncertainty*, Maidenhead: Open University Press.

Lenz-Taguchi, H. (2010) *Going Beyond the Theory/Practice Divide in Early Childhood Education: Introducing an intra-active pedagogy*, London: Routledge.

Lingard, B. (2009) 'Testing times: The need for new intelligent accountabilities for schooling', *QTU Professional Magazine*, 13–19 November. Available at http://www.qtu.asn.au/vo24_lingard.pdf (accessed 20 June 2012).

Löfdahl, A. and Hägglund, S. (2006) 'Spaces of participation in pre-school: Arenas for establishing power orders?', *Children & Society*, 21: 328–338.

Lupton, D. (1996) *Food, the Body and the Self*, London: Sage.

McGee-Brown, M. J. (1995) 'Multiple voices, contexts, and methods: Making choices in qualitative evaluation in early childhood settings', in J. A. Hatch (ed.) *Qualitative Research in Early Childhood Settings* (pp. 191–211), London: Praeger.

MacLure, M. (2009) 'Broken voices, dirty words: On the productive insufficiency of voice', in A. Y. Jackson and L. A. Mazzei (eds.) *Voice in Qualitative Inquiry: Challenging conventional, interpretive, and critical conceptions in qualitative research* (pp. 97–113), London: Routledge.

MacLure, M., Holmes, R., MacRae, C., and Jones, L. (2010) 'Animating classroom ethnography: Overcoming video fear', *International Journal of Qualitative Studies in Education*, 23 (5): 543–556.

MacNaughton, G. and Hughes, P. (2009) *Doing Action Research in Early Childhood Studies: A step-by-step guide*, Maidenhead: Open University Press.

MacNaughton, G. and Smith, K. (2005) 'Transforming research ethics: The choices and challenges of researching with children', in A. Farrell (ed.) *Ethical Research with Children* (pp. 112–123), Maidenhead: Open University Press.

Malewski, E. (2005) 'Epilogue: When children and youth talk back', in D. S. Soto and B. B. Swadener (eds.) *Power and Voice in Research with Children* (pp. 215–222), New York: Peter Lang.

Mandell, N. (1991) 'The least-adult role in studying children', in F. C. Waksler (ed.), *Studying the Social Worlds of Children: Sociological readings* (pp. 38–59), London: Falmer Press.

Manning, E. (2007) *Politics of Touch: Sense, movement, sovereignty*, Minneapolis and London: University of Minnesota Press.

Manning-Morton, J. and Thorp, M. (2003) *Key Times for Play*, Maidenhead: Open University Press.

Marmot, M., Atkinson, T., Bell, J., Black, C., Broadfoot, P., Cumberlege, J., et al. (2010) *Fair Society: Healthy lives: The strategic review of health inequalities in England post-2010*. Available at http://www.marmotreview.org/AssetLibrary/pdfs/Reports/FairSociety HealthyLives.pdf (accessed 12 July 2010).

Mason, J. (2002) *Qualitative Researching*, 2nd edn, London: Sage.

Mayall, B. (1994) 'Children in action at home and school', in B. Mayall (ed.), *Children's Childhoods Observed and Experienced* (pp. 114–127), London: Falmer Press.

Mayall, B. (2002) *Towards a Sociology for Childhood: Thinking from children's lives*, Maidenhead: Open University Press.

Mayall, B. (2008) 'Conversations with children: Working with generational issues', in P. Christensen and A. James (eds.) *Research with Children: Perspectives and practices* (pp. 120–135), London: Falmer Press.

Mead, M. (1930) *Growing Up in New Guinea*, Basingstoke: Penguin.

Millei, Z. J. (2005) 'The discourse of control: Disruption and Foucault in an early childhood classroom', *Contemporary Issues in Early Childhood*, 6 (2): 128–139.

Mills, R. (2000) 'Perspectives of childhood', in J. Mills and R. Mills (eds.) *Childhood Studies: A reader in perspectives of childhood* (pp. 7–38), London: Routledge.

Mohanty, C. T. (2003) '"Under Western Eyes" revisited: Feminist solidarity through anticapitalist struggles', *Signs: Journal of Women in Culture and Society*, 28 (2): 499–535.

Mol, A. and Law, J. (2004) 'Embodied action, enacted bodies: The example of hypoglycaemia', *Body & Society*, 10 (2–3): 43–62.

Moller, S. (2002) 'Supporting poor single mothers: Gender and race in the U.S. welfare state', *Gender and Society*, 16 (4): 465–484.

Morris, P. (1994) *The Bakhtin Reader: Selected writings of Bakhtin, Medvedev and Voloshinov*, London: Edward Arnold.

Morrow, V. (2005) 'Ethical issues in collaborative research with children', in A. Farrell (ed.) *Ethical Research with Children* (pp. 150–165), Maidenhead: Open University Press.

Morrow, V. (2010) 'Should the world really be free of "child labour"? Some reflections', *Childhood*, 17 (4): 435–440.

Morrow, V. and Richards, M. (1996) 'The ethics of social research with children (an overview)', *Children and Society*, 10 (2): 90–105.

Moss, P. (2012) 'Governed markets and democratic experimentalism: Two possibilities for early childhood education and care', in A. T. Kjorholt and J. Qvortrup (eds.) *The Modern Child and the Flexible Labour Market* (pp. 128–149), London: Palgrave Macmillan.

Mukherji, P. and Albon, D. (2010) *Research Methods in Early Childhood*, London: Sage.

Murphy, E. and Dingwall, R. (2007) 'The ethics of ethnography', in P. Atkinson, A. Coffey, S. Delamont, J. Lofland, and L. Lofland (eds.) *Handbook of Ethnography* (pp. 339–351), Los Angeles: Sage.

Mus, S. (2012) 'Craving for authenticity: Reconsidering the ethics of insider voices', paper presented at European Conference for Educational Research, Cadiz, Spain, September.

Namissan, G. B. and Ball, S. J. (2010) 'Advocacy networks, choice and private schooling of the poor in India', *Global Networks*, 10 (3): 324–343.

Nyberg, M. and Grinland, B. (2008) 'The influence of the room context in the meal experience: Examples from a hospital and a nursery', *Journal of Foodservice*, 19 (1): 35–43.

OECD Educational Directorate (2004) *Early Childhood Education and Care Policy Canada: Country note*, Paris: OECD.

O'Kane, C. (2008) 'The development of participatory techniques: Facilitating children's views about decisions which affect them', in P. Christensen and A. James (eds.) *Research with Children: Perspectives and practices*, 2nd edn (pp. 125–155), London: Routledge.

Okley, J. (1996) *Own or Other Culture*, London: Routledge.

Olssen, M. (1996) 'In defence of the welfare state and of publicly provided education: A New Zealand perspective', *Journal of Education Policy*, 11 (3): 337–362.

Opie, I. and Opie, P. (1959) *The Lore and Language of Schoolchildren*, Oxford: Oxford University Press.

Osgood, J. (2004) 'Time to get down to business? The responses of early years practitioners to entrepreneurial approaches to professionalism', *Journal of Early Childhood Research*, 2 (1): 5–24.

Osgood, J. (2010) 'Narrative methods in the nursery: (Re)-considering claims to give voice through processes of decision-making', *Reconceptualising Educational Research Methodology*, 1 (1): 14–28.

Osgood, J. (2012) *Narratives from the Nursery: Negotiating professional identities in early childhood*, London: Routledge.

Oswell, D. (2009) 'Yet to come? Globality and the sound of an infant politics?', *Radical Politics Today*, 1 (1): 1–18.

Paechter, C. (2003) 'Dissemination and identity – tales from the school gates', in C. Hughes (ed.) *Disseminating Qualitative Research in Educational Settings* (pp. 43–54), Maidenhead: Open University Press.

Penn, H. (2005) *Unequal Childhoods: Young children's lives in poor countries*, London: Routledge.

Penn, H. (2010) 'Shaping the future: How human capital arguments about investment in early childhood services are being (mis)used in poor countries', in N. Yelland (ed.) *Contemporary Perspectives on Early Childhood Education* (pp. 49–65), Maidenhead: Open University Press.

Penn, H. (2011a) 'Gambling on the market: The role of for-profit provision in early childhood education and care', *Journal of Early Childhood Research*, 9 (2): 150–161.

Penn, H. (2011b) *Quality in Early Childhood Services: An international perspective*, Maidenhead: Open University Press.

Penn, H. (2011c) 'Travelling policies and global buzzwords: How international non-governmental organizations and charities spread the word about early childhood in the global South', *Childhood*, 18 (1): 94–113.

Phelan, A. M. (1997) 'Classroom management and the erasure of teacher desire', in J. Tobin (ed.) *Making a Place for Pleasure in Early Childhood Education* (pp. 76–100), New Haven, CT, and London: Yale University Press.

Pilcher, J. (2007) 'Body work: Childhood, gender and school health education in England, 1870–1977', *Childhood*, 14 (2): 215–233.

Pink, S. (2007) *Doing Visual Ethnography: Images, media and representation in research*, 2nd edn, London: Sage.

Pink, S. (2009) *Doing Sensory Ethnography*, London: Sage.

Pole, C. (2007) 'Researching children and fashion: An embodied ethnography', *Childhood*, 14 (1): 67–84.
Prout, A. and James, A. (1997) 'A new paradigm for the sociology of childhood? Provenance, promise and problems', in A. James and A. Prout (eds.) *Constructing and Reconstructing Childhood*, 2nd edn (pp. 7–33), London: RoutledgeFalmer.
Qvortrup, J. (1985) 'Placing children in the division of labour', in P. Close and R. Collins (eds.) *Family and Economy in Modern Society* (pp. 129–145), Basingstoke: Macmillan Press.
Qvortrup, J. (1994) 'Childhood matters: An introduction', in J. Qvortrup, M. Bardy, G. Sgritta, and H. Wintersberger (eds.) *Childhood Matters: Social theory, practice and politics* (pp. 1–24), Farnham: Ashgate.
Qvortrup, J. (1999) *Childhood and Societal Macrostructures: Childhood exclusion by default*, Odense: Department of Contemporary Cultural Studies, Odense University.
Qvortrup, J. (2010) 'Diversity's temptation – and hazards', *Educação & Sociedade*, 31 (113): 1121–1136.
Readings, B. (1996) *The University in Ruins*, Cambridge, MA, and London: Harvard University Press.
Reay, D. (2005) 'Mothers' involvement in their children's schooling: Social reproduction in action?', in G. Crozier and D. Reay (eds.) *Activating Participation: Parents and teachers working towards partnership* (pp. 23–37), London: Trentham Books.
Reed, T. and Brown, M. (2000) 'The expression of care in the rough and tumble play of boys', *Journal of Research in Childhood Education*, 15 (1): 104–116.
Reinharz, S. (1997) 'Who am I? The need for a variety of selves in the field', in R. Hertz (ed.) *Reflexivity and Voice* (pp. 3–20), Thousand Oaks, CA: Sage.
Rikowski, G. (1997) 'Scorched earth: Prelude to rebuilding Marxist educational theory', *British Journal of Sociology of Education*, 18 (4): 551–574.
Roberts, H. (2008) 'Listening to children and hearing them', in P. Christensen and A. James (eds.) *Research with Children: Perspectives and practices*, 2nd edn (pp. 260–275), London: Routledge.
Robinson, C. and Kellett, M. (2004) 'Power', in S. Fraser, V. Lewis, S. Ding, M. Kellett, and C. Robinson (eds.) *Doing Research with Children and Young People* (pp. 81–96), London: Sage.
Robinson, K. (2002) 'Making the invisible visible: Gay and lesbian issues in early childhood education', *Contemporary Issues in Early Childhood*, 3 (3): 415–434.
Robinson, K. and Davies, C. (2010) 'Hatching babies and stork deliveries: Risk and regulation in the construction of children's sexual knowledge', *Contemporary Issues in Early Childhood*, 11 (3): 249.
Robson, C. (2002) *Real World Research: A resource for social scientists and practitioner-researchers*, 2nd edn, Oxford: Blackwell.
Rogers, S. (2010) 'Powerful pedagogies and playful resistance', in L. Brooker and S. Edwards (eds.) *Engaging Play* (pp. 152–165), Maidenhead: Open University Press.
Rosen, R. (2010) '"We got our heads together and came up with a plan": Young children's perceptions of curriculum development in one Canadian preschool', *Journal of Early Childhood Research*, 8 (1): 89–108.
Rosen, R. (2012) 'The scream: Examining multiple meanings in children's imaginative play', paper presented at Celebrating Childhood Diversity, Sheffield, July.
Salazar Perez, M. and Cannella, G. S. (2010) 'Disaster capitalism as neoliberal instrument for the construction of early childhood/care policy: Charter schools in post-Katrina New Orleans', in G. S. Cannella and L. Diaz Soto (eds.) *Childhoods: A handbook* (pp. 145–156), New York: Peter Lang.
Sayer, A. (2000) *Realism and Social Science*, Thousand Oaks, CA, and London: Sage.

Sayer, A. (2011) *Why Things Matter to People: Social science, values and ethical life*, Cambridge: Cambridge University Press.

Schafer, R. M. (1977) *The Tuning of the World*, Toronto: McClelland & Stewart.

Scheper-Hughes, N. (1992) *Death without Weeping: The violence of everyday life in Brazil*, Berkeley and Oxford: University of California Press.

Schlichter, A. (2011) 'Do voices matter? Vocality, materiality, gender performativity', *Body & Society*, 17 (1): 31–52.

Schmuck, R. A. (2006) *Practical Action Research for Change*, 2nd edn, Thousand Oaks, CA: Corwin Press.

Seigworth, G. and Gregg, M. (2010) 'An inventory of shimmers', in M. Gregg and G. Seigworth (eds.) *The Affect Theory Reader* (pp. 1–28), Durham, CT: Duke University Press.

Sevenhuijsen, S. (1998a) *Citizenship and the Ethics of Care: Feminist considerations on justice, morality, and politics*, London: Routledge.

Sevenhuijsen, S. (1998b) *Too Good to be True: Feminist considerations about trust and social cohesion*, Vienna: IWM Working Paper No. 3.

Shallwani, S. (2010) 'Racism and imperialism in child development discourse: Deconstructing "developmentally appropriate practice"', in G. S. Cannella and L. Diaz Soto (eds.) *Childhoods: A handbook* (pp. 231–244), New York: Peter Lang.

Shilling, C. (2003) *The Body and Social Theory*, 2nd edn, London: Sage.

Shilling, C. (2005) *The Body in Culture, Technology and Society*, London: Sage.

Shore, R. (1997) *Rethinking the Brain: New insights into early development*, New York: Families and Work Institute.

Shotter, J. and Billig, M. (1998) 'A Bakhtinian psychology: From out of the heads of individuals and into dialogues between them', in M. Mayerfeld Bell and M. Gardiner (eds.) *Bakhtin and the Human Sciences* (pp. 13–29), London: Sage.

Skånfors, L. (2009) 'Ethics in child research: Children's agency and researchers' "ethical radar"', *Childhoods Today*, 3 (1): 1–22.

Skeggs, B. (1994) 'Situating the production of feminist ethnography', in M. Maynard and J. Purvis (eds.) *Researching Women's Lives from a Feminist Perspective* (pp. 72–92), London: Taylor & Francis.

Skeggs, B. (2002) 'Techniques for telling the reflexive self', in T. May (ed.), *Qualitative Research in Action* (pp. 349–374), London: Sage.

Skeggs, B. (2004) *Class, Self, Culture*, London: Routledge.

Skeggs, B. (2007) 'Feminist ethnography', in P. Atkinson, A. Coffey, S. Delamont, J. Lofland, and L. Lofland (eds.) *Handbook of Ethnography* (pp. 426–442), London: Sage.

Smilansky, S. (1990) 'Socio-dramatic play: Its relevance to behavior and achievement in school', in E. Klugman and S. Smilansky (eds.) *Children's Play and Learning Perspectives and Policy Implications* (pp. 18–42), New York: Teachers College Press.

Spivak, G. C. (1988) 'Can the subaltern speak?', in C. Nelson and L. Grossberg (eds.) *Marxism and the Interpretation of Culture* (pp. 271–316), Urbana: University of Illinois Press.

Stacey, J. (1988) 'Can there be a feminist ethnography?', *Women's Studies International Forum*, 11 (1): 21–27.

Suissa, J. (2006) 'Untangling the mother knot: Some thoughts on parents, children and philosophers of education', *Ethics and Education*, 1 (1): 65–77.

Suissa, J. (2008) 'Lessons from a new science? On teaching happiness in schools', *Journal of Philosophy of Education*, 42 (3–4): 575–590.

Sutton-Smith, B. (1997) *The Ambiguity of Play*, Cambridge, MA: Harvard University Press.

Synnott, A. (1987) 'Shame and glory: A sociology of hair', *British Journal of Sociology*, 38 (3): 381–413.

Taylor, A. (2011) 'Reconceptualizing the "nature" of childhood', *Childhood*, 18 (4): 420–433.
Taylor, I. M., Ntoumanis, N., and Smith, B. (2009) 'The social context as a determinant of teacher motivational strategies in physical education', *Psychology of Sport and Exercise*, 10 (2): 235–243.
Thorne, B. (1993) *Gender Play: Girls and boys in school*, New Brunswick, NJ: Rutgers University Press.
Tizard, B. and Hughes, M. (2002) *Young Children Learning*, 2nd edn, Oxford: Blackwell.
Tobin, J. (1997a) 'Introduction: The missing discourse of pleasure and desire', in J. Tobin (ed.) *Making a Place for Pleasure in Early Childhood Education* (pp. 1–37), New Haven, CT: Yale University Press.
Tobin, J. (ed.) (1997b) *Making a Place for Pleasure in Early Childhood Education*, New Haven, CT: Yale University Press.
Tobin, J. (2004) 'The disappearance of the body in early childhood education', in L. Bresler (ed.) *Knowing Bodies, Moving Minds: Towards embodied teaching and learning* (pp. 111–125), Norwell, MA: Kluwer Academic Publishers.
Tobin, J. and Grace, D. J. (1997) 'Carnival in the classroom', in J. Tobin (ed.) *Making a Place for Pleasure in Early Childhood Education* (pp. 159–187), New Haven, CT: Yale University Press.
Tobin, J. and Kurban, F. (2009) '"They don't like us": Reflections of Turkish children in a German preschool', *Contemporary Issues in Early Childhood*, 10 (1): 24–34.
Todd, S. (2004) 'Teaching with ignorance: Questions of social justice, empathy, and responsible community', *Interchange*, 35 (13): 337–352.
Todorov, T. (1984) *Mikhail Bakhtin: The dialogical principle*, Minneapolis: University of Minnesota Press.
Tronto, J. (1989) 'Women and caring: What can feminists learn about morality from caring?', in A. M. Jaggar and S. R. Bordo (eds.) *Gender/Body/Knowledge* (pp. 172–187), London: Rutgers University Press.
Tronto, J. C. (1993) *Moral Boundaries: A political argument for an ethic of care*, New York and London: Routledge.
Tronto, J. (2002) 'The "nanny" question in feminism', *Hypatia*, 17 (2): 34–51.
Twigg, R. (1992) 'The performative dimension of surveillance: Jacob Riis. How the Other Half Lives', *Text and Performance Quarterly*, 12 (4): 305–328.
UNICEF (2008) *The Child Care Ttransition, Innocenti Report Card 8*, Florence: UNICEF Innocenti Research Centre.
Valentine, G. (2002) 'In-corporations: Food, bodies and organisations', *Body and Society*, 8 (2): 1–20.
Valentine, S. (2005) 'Where to next for food in schools? (Editorial)', *Nutrition Bulletin*, 30 (3): 209–210.
Vandenbroeck, M. and Bouverne-De Bie, M. (2006) 'Children's agency and educational norms', *Childhood*, 13 (1): 127–143.
Veale, A. (2005) 'Creative methodologies in participatory research with children', in S. Greene and D. Hogan (eds.) *Researching Children's Experience: Approaches and methods* (pp. 253–272), London: Sage.
Vincent, C. and Ball, S. (2005) 'The "childcare champion"? New Labour, social justice and the childcare market', *British Educational Research Journal*, 31 (5): 557–570.
Viruru, R. (2001) *Early Childhood Education: Postcolonial perspectives from India*, London: Sage.
Vološinov, V. N./Bakhtin, M. M. (1976) *Freudianism: A Marxist critique*, New York: Academic Press.

Walkerdine, V. (1990) *Schoolgirl Fictions*, London: Verso.
Waller, T. and Bitou, A. (2011) 'Research with children: Three challenges for participatory research in early childhood', *European Early Childhood Research Journal*, 19 (1): 5–20.
Warming, H. (2005) 'Participant observation: A way to learn about children's perspectives', in A. Clark, A. T. Kjorholt, and P. Moss (eds.) *Beyond Listening: Children's perspectives on early childhood services* (pp. 51–70), Bristol: The Policy Press.
Warming, H. (2011) 'Getting under their skins? Accessing young children's perspectives through ethnographic fieldwork', *Childhood*, 18 (1): 39–53.
Watson, C. (2009) 'The "impossible vanity": Uses and abuses of empathy in qualitative inquiry', *Qualitative Research*, 9 (1): 105–117.
Webb, J., Schirato, T. and Danaher, G. (2002) *Understanding Bourdieu*, London: Sage.
Whalley, M. (1992) 'Working as a team', in G. Pugh (ed.) *Contemporary Issues in the Early Years* (pp. 157–174), London: NCB.
Whalley, M. (2007) *Involving Parents in their Children's Learning*, 2nd edn, London: Paul Chapman.
White, L. and Jacobs, E. (1992) *Liberating our Children, Liberating our Nations: Report of the Aboriginal Committee, Community Panel, Family and Children's Services Legislation Review in British Columbia*, Victoria, BC: The Committee.
Whitehead, N. (1972) *The Evolution of the Nursery Infant School*, London: Routledge & Kegan Paul.
Wing, L. A. (1995) 'Play is not the work of the child: Young children's perceptions of work and play', *Early Childhood Education Research Quarterly*, 10 (2): 223–247.
Woodhead, M. and Faulkner, D. (2008) 'Subjects, objects or participants? Dilemmas of psychological research with children', in P. Christensen and A. James (eds.) *Research with Children: Perspectives and practices*, 2nd edn (pp. 10–39), London: Falmer Press.
Wyver, S., Little, H., Tranter, P., Bundy, A., Naughton, G., and Sandseter, E. B. H. (2010) 'Ten ways to restrict children's freedom to play: The problem of surplus safety', *Contemporary Issues in Early Childhood*, 11 (3): 263–277.
Youdell, D. C. (2006) *Impossible Bodies, Impossible Selves: Exclusions and student subjectivities*, Dordrecht: Springer.
Zeiher, H. (2003) 'Shaping daily life in urban environments', in P. Christensen and M. O'Brien (eds.) *Children in the City: Home neighbourhood and community* (pp. 66–81), London: RoutledgeFalmer.
Žižek, S. (2000) 'Class struggle or postmodernism? Yes, please!', in J. Butler, E. Laclau, and S. Žižek (eds.) *Contingency, Hegemony, Universality: Contemporary dialogues on the left* (pp. 90–135), London: Verso.

INDEX

access: in research practice 7–8, 35, 60, 108, 112–13; to children in research 42, 43; see also gatekeepers
adult–child relationships: power relations 5, 67, 73, 114, 117–18, 121; see also answerability; generationing; responsibility
agency 32, 81, 92, 113, 121
answerability 8, 14–15, 35, 55, 60,122; and adult–child relationships 80, 82, 99–100, 105, 113–14, 128–29; beyond data collection 129, 131, 133; and relational ethics 8, 15, 35, 55, 72, 99
authority: of adult-researcher 35, 47, 99; authorial 88, 94; challenge to 110–11, 112; institutional 2, 73, 95, 108; 'sharing authority' 38, 126–27
autonomy 96, 119

Bakhtin: Bakhtinian circle 8–9, 10, 13, 17n4, 86, 97; see also answerability; carnivalesque; chronotope; dialogic; 'non-alibi in Being'; 'once-occurrent event of Being'; outsideness; sympathetic co-experiencing
being with children 17, 79–80, 82, 119, 126–27, 128–29, 130
bodies: body rules 11, 39, 59, 61; 'civilising' 4, 11, 48, 54, 86–7, 107–9; emplacement 10, 41, 50; senses 8, 48–9, 96–7; unfinished 41, 119; see also sensing practices

capitalism 17n3, 27, 103
carnivalesque 8, 92; and body 35, 49; and resistance to rules 5, 110–11, 112, 115
childhood: becoming or being (Qvortrup) 11–12, 27; childhood innocence 13, 27–8, 46–7, 48, 96, 105; childhood irrationality 12, 48, 103, 119; childhood vulnerability 30, 65, 105–6, 107, 114; conceptions of 12–13, 30, 34, 39, 46–7, 132; in relation to adulthood 12, 21, 36–7, 38–9, 42, 46, 49, 105; malleability of children 4, 11, 31; see also 'civilising' children
children's participation 37, 70, 105, 116, 123–24, 125–26, 132; in educator research 74–5, 76, 78; evading 40; see also consent; participatory approaches to research
chronotope 18–19, 23–4, 33, 69
'civilising' children 48, 54, 109; see also bodies
communication 5, 75, 77, 88–9, 122
confidentiality 3–4, 73, 93–4, 122
consent: children's 3, 5, 74–5, 76; in educator-research 16, 68–9, 74–5, 77, 80, 82; filming and observation 84, 93;

informed consent 8, 74–5, 131; withdrawal of 78–9, 81
consumption *see* neoliberalism
critical moments 6–7, 15, 74, 80, 82, 133–34

data generation 4, 69, 97, 119, 125, 130–31; *see also* observation
developmental psychology 12, 86
dialogic 8–10, 16–17, 39, 116, 132
discourse: and discrimination 87, 110; and early childhood 19, 27, 65, 105; and maternalism 54, 62; 'teacherly' 59; technicist 58

early childhood education and care: *see* space; school readiness; neoliberalism
Early Years Foundation Stage 29–30, 56–7, 86
educator-researcher 68–9, 76–9, 81–2
English as an additional language 20, 114, 122, 125
ethics: in educator-research 80; ethical guidelines 81–2, 101, 120, 133; ethics and justice 15, 100, 115–16; ethics boards 8; relational ethics 8, 13–15, 18, 72, 97, 99, 130, 133; technicist approaches to 7–8, 18, 130–31; universalist ethics 8, 14; *see also* consent; intervention in research
ethnography 4, 35–6, 42, 89–90, 98, 128–29

'First World/North' 4, 6, 19, 21–2, 29, 38, 42, 52, 55, 64, 85, 96, 119, 125, 126, 130; definition of 17n3
'food event' 2, 4–5, 17n4, 19, 22, 87, 96

gatekeepers 51, 58, 74, 108
gaze: ethnographic 14–15, 89, 99; from children and educators 58, 60, 84, 90–1, 93, 95–6, 109; male 47
gender 26, 44, 47, 111, 114; and adult–child research relationships 12, 52, 59, 108, 116; gendering 13; *see also* gaze: male
generationing 2, 12–13, 21, 66
globalisation 6, 19, 26–7, 28, 85

habitus 39, 59, 88, 105
height 42, 46
higher education 7, 53, 72, 94, 106, 119
human capital 4, 26–28, 38
humour 49, 91, 111, 127

impression management 35, 42, 49
individualism *see* neoliberalism
inequities/inequalities 11, 26, 28, 86, 108–9, 111, 113–16, 133; economic 27; generational 4–5, 13, 36, 107, 118, 124, 132; in play 4
'insider' research 35, 58–9, 60, 67, 74, 78
instrumentality 7, 114, 128–29, 131
intentionality 58, 71, 114–15
interpretation 98–9, 116; fallibility of 36, 41, 100, 119; of observations 58, 87, 100; participants' interpretations 60, 75
intervention in research: and ethics 16, 102, 112–13, 114–15, 116; in risky situations 20, 104–5, 106–7, 108, 111–12, 116
intimacy 8, 10, 46–7

key person 56–7, 59, 69
knowledge: experiential 63; fallibility of 17, 87, 89, 9–100, 116, 120, 127; production of 5, 13–14, 16, 35–6, 47, 93, 99, 103, 107, 110, 123, 127–29

'least-educator' 16, 38–9, 40–1, 47, 59–60, 126
listening to children *see* participatory approaches to research

maternalism 62
mealtimes 53, 58, 87, 96, 109–10
motherhood 54, 61–2, 63

neoliberalism 7, 24; and consumerism 24–5; critique of 25–6, 27; and early childhood spaces 19, 29, 33, 52–3, 93, 97; and higher education 53, 72, 94, 129–30; individualism 7, 25; market logic 16, 24, 29, 33; *see also* human capital
'non-alibi in Being' 15, 82, 122, 131

observation: classification of children 29, 55, 86–7, 93–4; as part of pedagogy 12, 55–7, 69, 85–6, 89; as research method 57, 70, 80, 85, 87–9, 90–2, 100, 131
'once-occurrent event of Being' 13, 15, 18, 62, 82, 106, 115, 120
outsideness: in Bakhtinian sense 53, 60, 80, 82, 94, 128
'outsider' research 6, 16, 38, 59, 64; difference to 'insider' research 69–70, 71–2; problematising 'insider'/'outsider' dichotomy 51–2, 66; *see also* 'insider' research

participatory approaches to research: listening to children 85, 121; participatory methods 17, 119, 123–25
play: blockplay 67, 69, 70–1, 72, 74, 79–80; in early childhood education and care 13, 21–3, 25–6, 28–9, 53, 93, 105–7, 110, 116; imaginative 2, 4–5, 7, 35, 37, 47; as a research strategy 4–5, 31–3, 35, 39–40, 43, 45, 55–7, 59–61, 124–25; taboo 4, 38, 71, 89, 93, 129; and work 37; *see also being with* children
power relations *see* adult–child relationships
production 24, 26–7, 29
proximity: child–educator 32–3, 76; in research practice 33, 39, 41–4, 47, 59, 90, 97, 122

'race' 12, 26, 52, 108, 114–15, 122; and racism 22, 41, 108
reciprocity: researching in 'common cause' with children 119, 121–23, 127, 131, 133; and responsibility 3, 7
reflexivity 6–7, 98, 100, 115, 120; embodied reflexivity 16, 46, 50, 64, 120, 133; value of doubt 57–8
relationships: unfinalisability of relationships 10, 15, 17, 40, 50, 133; web of relationships 9, 16, 18, 50, 107, 121, 133; *see also* adult–child relationships; intimacy
relativism 8, 100
representation 73–4, 88–9, 94–5, 113
research ethics boards 8
responsibility 7, 14–15, 23; collective responsibility 27–8; of educators 32, 57, 69, 71; given to children 23, 73; and neoliberalism 25–6, 27; and representation and analysis 113, 116; in research practice 39, 55, 72, 82, 98–9, 122; *see also* risk
risk: and bodily contact 80; emotional 106; health and safety 31, 54, 57, 87, 101; minimising harm in research 8, 130; physical risk and risk-taking 16, 102–8, 114; risk and discursive gap/new possibilities 3, 14–15, 113–17, 130; risk society 103

school readiness 23, 31, 85
sensing practices 16, 95–7, 99–100, 122, 133
sexuality 46–8, 109–12, 114
size 21, 23, 35, 41–3, 52
social justice 8; commitment to 15, 18, 102, 111–15, 133; *see also* critique of neoliberalism
space: early childhood spaces 19, 21, 25, 33–4, 71, 88; geography of early childhood settings 31–2, 33–4, 42–3, 47; in research practice 47, 72, 79, 95, 122, 124; 'islands of dislocation' 2; outside space 61, 95; spatial disciplining 23, 57; *see also* chronotope
surveillance: of children 4, 31–2, 86–7, 93; of educators 38, 52
sympathetic co-experiencing 14, 126–28

technicism 7–8, 15, 18, 58, 71, 130–31
temporality 4, 111; *see also* chronotope
'Third World/South' 19, 85; definition of 17n3

touch 23, 43–4, 46–7, 88, 96–7, 110
trust 7, 56, 59–60, 107, 119

UN Convention on the Rights of the Child 118

video 4, 84, 88–90, 98, 104
'voice': children's 'voices' 85; critiques of idea 82, 85, 100, 121; 'double-voiced' 46, 86, 95, 97

weight 42–3, 63–4